ASIAN STUDIES ASSOCIA'

Southeast Asia Publications Series

KAMPUNG, ISLAM AND STATE IN URBAN JAVA

KAMPUNG, ISLAM AND STATE IN URBAN JAVA

Patrick Guinness

Asian Studies Association of Australia
in association with
UNIVERSITY OF HAWAI'I PRESS
HONOLULU

First published by:

NUS Press
National University of Singapore
AS3-01-02, 3 Arts Link
Singapore 117569

Published in North America by:

University of Hawai`i Press
2840 Kolowalu Street
Honolulu, HI 96822
www.uhpress.hawaii.edu

Library of Congress Cataloging-in-Publication Data

Guinness, Patrick.
  Kampung, Islam and State in urban Java / Patrick Guinness.
    p. cm. – (Southeast Asia publication series, Asian Studies Association of
Australia)
  Includes bibliographical references and index.
  ISBN 978-0-8248-3360-2 (pbk.: alk. paper)

  1. Yogyakarta (Indonesia) – Social conditions. 2. Community life – Indonesia –
Yogyakarta. I. Title.

  HN710.Y6G85 2009
  306.09598'27 — dc22
                           2008038367

Cover: RT leader Sugi chats to neighbours. All photographs by author.

Printed in Singapore

For Daniel and Harry
In memory of Mas Sugiharjo

Contents

List of Figures

Preface

This book sheds light on the nature of community within urban off-street neighbourhoods (*kampung*) in Java, examining the concept of community in the light of state programs of administration and control, religious reform movements, and local residents' responses to these and to conditions during both the New Order and Reformasi period after 1998. Much of the material in the book focuses on one such kampung that I call Ledok, where I have conducted research since 1975. An earlier book (Guinness, 1986) presented my research findings on the nature of economic activities and social relations that I observed in Ledok over the period 1975 to 1980. Later writings have added to those interpretations. In this book I review the literature and research on kampung in Java over the last 30 years and bring the whole account up to recent times with an interpretation of developments since the end of the New Order in 1998. In addition I aim to address two central issues that have arisen in the literature about urban low-income neighbourhoods. The first is the extent to which low-income neighbourhoods can still be seen as autonomous communities after the attempts of successive governments to construct them as 'communities' to do the state's bidding. This is an especially relevant question in the light of current enthusiasms for participatory development. The second issue concerns the character of change in low-income neighbourhoods and the proposition that much of the change in such settlements reflects the initiative and energies of individuals and groups within the kampung rather than the planning and expenditure of state authorities and outside agents.

The urban settlements labelled kampung in Java have varied origins and reflect different characters. In Yogyakarta the earliest kampung formed the quarters or official compounds of princes and nobles, or of traders and other occupation groups engaged in the city, or of distinct ethnic groups from outside Java. As time passed and rural people flocked to the city, kampung became 'vulgarized' (Sullivan, 1992: 22–5), no longer the revered quarters of the city's functionaries but the residential quarters of the urban *wong cilik* or 'little people', many of whom were migrants to the city from outlying villages. Over half the population in many of Java's cities live in such kampung. Today the urban communities of the kampung may not be able to lay claim to long-held traditions such as those in rural communities, yet contemporary residents in many urban neighbourhoods do lay claim to a shared corpus of interests and do construct much of their lives in terms of the symbols of community. Such claims to community run counter to recent assertions by scholars, particularly in discussions on the strategies of the New Order militaristic state, that kampung communities were little more than the construct of a state focused on channelling the 'masses' to conform to the directions of the state elite. This is the essence of the debate that I address, reviewing in the first chapter the main lines of argument in this debate, then in subsequent chapters detailing ethnographically the evidence that both supports and questions the existence of relatively autonomous communities in urban kampung.

The examination of community within urban neighbourhoods has to be set both within a historical context and the economic and political context of the wider city and nation. At certain periods of the Dutch colonial regime, the Japanese war administration and the Old Order and New Order regimes, kampung were structured and restructured to facilitate government administration, often undermining local expressions of community. The present period of reform since 1998 has introduced yet another perspective to this relationship between common people (*rakyat*) and the state, accentuating the importance of diachronic change to the construction of kampung relations. With the expansion of industry, commerce, government and tourism within the city of Yogyakarta, kampung have become less marginal to city planning and administration. Kampung residents form a vital part of the city workforce, both in formal and informal sectors. The value of kampung land has escalated, prompting government efforts to determine title over what was previously often untitled land. Kampung populations have also been included in city visions to beautify and make more secure urban neighbourhoods through local infrastructure such as roads, rubbish outlets, flood walls, and public lighting.

The aim of this book is to examine urban societies in Java, focusing on low-income settlements as alternative modernities in the context of contemporary urban political economies.

Acknowledgements

This book is based on some 30 years' acquaintance with the city of Yogyakarta in central Java, and with one particular urban settlement or kampung I call Ledok. From my first arrival in that woody, riverside, sparsely settled neighbourhood in 1975 to my most recent stay in 2004 in what has become a densely populated, built-up settlement, I have benefited from the assistance, advice and friendship of numerous people. Firstly to my friends in Ledok itself, too many to mention by name and scattered throughout the kampung, and particularly to my hosts, almarhum Fx. Sugiharjo and Bu In and their RT neighbours, I owe enormous gratitude for their patience and tolerance in repeatedly welcoming me back to spend time with them and to ply them with all those questions. They have welcomed me to their rituals, shared with me their ideas, put up with my faulty use of the Indonesian and Javanese languages, and patiently explained the most obvious details of their lives. I hope this book does them no disservice.

My colleagues at the Gadjah Mada University provided me with the support to continue this study over all these years. The late Professor Dr Masri Singarimbun first brought me to Yogyakarta to work with him in the Population Studies Institute and encouraged me to write on urban kampung. He and his wife, Ibu Irawati, were an inspiration and an example in their enthusiastic devotion to scholarship and to ethnographic research. I enjoyed warm friendships and intellectual support from all in the Institute in those first years in Yogyakarta. Staff within the Anthropology Department of the Gadjah Mada University have remained friends and colleagues over the years, encouraging me to write, teach and discuss my findings, and sharing generously from their own scholarship and personal experiences.

I am immensely grateful to my colleagues at the Australian National University. Again there are too many to name, first in the Department of Anthropology of the Research School of Pacific and Asian Studies where I was located as a research scholar (1978–82) and research fellow (1985–89), second in the School of Archaeology and Anthropology where I have been teaching since 1994, and third across the campus-wide association of Indonesian and Southeast Asian scholars. Without the rich intellectual life of ANU in seminars, workshops and everyday informal discussions, this research could not have achieved the form it has.

It is a privilege to carry out research in another country and be accorded access to the public services of that country, and I am grateful to the many Indonesian Government officials who made that possible. I acknowledge the good services of the officers of the Government of Indonesia, both within Lembaga Ilmu Pengetahuan Indonesia (Indonesian Institute of Sciences) and within the Provincial government of Yogyakarta.

Finally, to those who have patiently read and edited this manuscript in its many forms and helped me to sharpen its focus and expression, I thank you. Particularly I thank Professor Howard Dick, Editor of the Southeast Asian Publication series, for his extraordinarily detailed comments and editing of the manuscript, and his reviewers for their incisive comments. Cathy Hales provided support and painstakingly commented on early versions of the manuscript.

1

Introduction

RESEARCHING THE URBAN COMMUNITY

In September 2006 my friend, host and main informant Sugi was killed in a motorcycle accident while plying his trade as a clothes salesman among the mountain villages outside Yogyakarta. I had first gone in search of Sugi in 1975. Friends had suggested that he might be able to provide me with accommodation in his home beside the Code river in the middle of the city. I immediately warmed to the riverside location with its fruit trees and bamboo and open spaces, and to Sugi and his wife In, so we arranged that I stay with them, only a short distance from my place of work as lecturer and researcher at the Gadjah Mada University. At the time I had no intention of researching the neighbourhood community that Sugi and In called home, but I soon found myself engrossed in their community. In those first three years of my residence I wrote an article about five families of sand-diggers who were my immediate neighbours (1977) but my main research was focused elsewhere in Indonesia. Any further research on the Yogyakarta riverside settlement began with my return as a PhD scholar in 1979. For the next 26 years I have returned regularly, every few years, to enquire after my friends and the neighbourhood life they constantly construct within a changing nation and city.

On every return visit I have been apprehensive, given the diffi-culty of remaining in contact with them once I returned to Australia. Will I find my friends and hosts alive and well? Will their economic situation have improved or faltered? Will they still welcome a *londo* ('white man', originally Dutch colonial) to stay for a while in the community? Was I observant enough to read the subtle ways in which these Javanese neighbours express their like or dislike of each other, and of me? Each time I was reassured for they welcomed me — and after 1979 my wife — back into their midst, spending hours bringing me up to date with affairs in the low-income, off-street settlement (kampung). We participated as much as possible in all the events of the kampung, attending ceremonies and religious rituals, playing sport, joining recreational trips, contributing both finance and labour to development projects, labouring on construction projects, discussing ways of improving their lives or negotiating with outside elites, and dropping into those endless conversations in the narrow alleyways that forge neighbourhood. Central to our participation in all those events was our association with our hosts Sugi and In, who over those 30 years played key roles in the life of the immediate neighbourhood and that of the Catholic deaconate. Both of them showed great patience in explaining the dynamics of kampung life and in making sure we were informed of ongoing events. Sugi's death is therefore a huge loss to me personally.

Returning to the same research site over such a long period of time has tremendous advantages. People know me and are keen to bring me up to date with their lives. During the 12 months of my doctoral research I tried to familiarise myself with all households in this population of about 5,000 and came to know every pocket of this rugged terrain adjoining the river. On my return visits I was able to revisit all these corners of the kampung and be guaranteed that someone would remember me and call me over for a chat, despite the population changes through generation succession and migration. Another important benefit of such a long acquaintance with this community is that I have been able to observe changes and engage my friends in discussing these, including many aspects of which a newcomer would never be informed. Whereas some outsiders (to whom I refer later) have condemned kampung residents as resisting change, my longer-term observations alerted me to a myriad of ways in which these residents had embraced a great deal of change. I am therefore able in this book, in some sense a retrospect of these 30 years, to focus on change — in density of population, in occupations, in household structures, indeed in the nature of community itself. In addition, although I have spoken and written about the kampung extensively during these years, in the last ten years my understanding has been richly augmented through my association with members of Yayasan Pondok Rakyat (YPR — People's Shelter Foundation), who have shared with me their knowledge of a number of other kampung in Yogyakarta. I discuss YPR in more detail in a later chapter.

My research in this urban kampung was not dissimilar to research I have done in rural communities. I participated in community events, engaged groups in conversation, met with key informants and gathered what there was of official statistics. On several occasions I collected household data through surveys. My main strategy was through convincing those with whom I lived of my credibility as friend and researcher. I constantly assured them that I was eager to tell those in Indonesia or abroad who had never experienced kampung life what it was like. I shared the sentiments and commitment of my YPR friends that kampung lifestyles were marked by dignity, initiative and courage. However, in an important way this research location was very different from those rural researches, in that in most cases I became familiar only with kampung residents' lives when they were home in the settlement. Except in rare cases, I did not follow my informants into the wider city, although I recorded much of their tales of such daily ventures. My analysis, therefore, is concentrated on what happens at home rather than in the wider city.

Because of the large number and diversity of occupations of these neighbours, I could not hope to know them all in depth. In the main, my knowledge of residents was deepest among those who shared an alleyway with me, or were fellow-members of the same RT (*Rukun Tetangga*) neighbourhood group, but I added to this by developing a very wide network of kampung friends, whom I was able to visit regularly during my research trips. These informants were open in describing life in their particular alleyways and neighbourhoods, and in making their own often sharp comparison with the neighbourhood and alleyway with which they primarily associate me. I therefore came to feel I had good knowledge of life throughout what is in some particulars a very diverse society and culture.

Exploring the changes I have observed over these 30 years allows some reflection on the nature of change and the significance of 'development'. In Indonesia *pembangunan* (development) became the hallmark of the Suharto New Order government, whose cabinet was referred to as the *Kabinet Pembangunan*. This was reflected at the local level with a *Seksi Pembangunan* in every neighbourhood. Yet improvements in the human condition were not necessarily of the type identified by the State as pembangunan, nor were all changes at the behest of government. This book will therefore explore the nature of change and development from this local perspective. It will examine urban societies in Java, and more generally in Southeast Asia, as exemplifying alternative modernities, focusing on low-income settlements as representing 'communities' of different degrees of sociality, not as the remnants of some past 'traditional' ties or as marginals to national and urban development, but as alternative modernities in the context of contemporary urban political economies.

COMMUNITY AS AN ANTHROPOLOGICAL CONSTRUCTION

Yok-Shiu Lee (1998: 994), who worked in urban slums in Bangkok, defines the community as "a group of people with face-to-face contact, a sense of belonging together, and shared interests and similar values" and suggests that within an urban low-income settlement, community can be said to exist when residents identify with the area and share an interest in its betterment. As Emma Grant (2001: 978) points out, such a community can provide mutual aid and defence and, conversely, can be used by dominant parties to take advantage of poorer neighbours. Reviewing the commonly accepted idea of community in the sociological literature, Rosemary Wearing suggests that community is seen as incorporating "solidarity, cohesion, conformity, social control, traditions, discipline, and 'belongingness'" (Wearing, 1996: 130). She identifies both a sense that individuals participating in community find in it a freedom to be themselves and a warning to them that their obligations in community will curb their freedom. They may struggle against the curbs on their activities that living in community entails and yet be strong in their support of community obligations. Communities thus have the potential to both enhance and restrict residents' lives.

Some social scientists, and especially anthropologists, have long been identified with the search for and study of communities, finding rich skeins of social relations where other observers may see only disorganisation and chaos. They have often represented those communities as harmonious, timeless worlds, a view that reflected the former structural-functionalist perspectives of anthropology. Such a political evaluation of the purity or worth of such communities in a changing world is increasingly challenged as an ethnographic reality and as a theoretical perspective. In some cases the ethnographic presentation of community as harmonious may reflect an elite view within the local community where people of unequal standing negotiate shared meaning and common action in the name of 'community' goals. More powerful members of society may appeal to community to gain the acquiescence of others to their plans while the poor and powerless may also appeal to 'community' to stress the obligations of the rich towards their poorer neighbours (Scott, 1985).

This has become true of urban 'communities' as well. However, as Chris Eipper points out, social observers are inclined to be sceptical about the quality of community, especially that found in the cities.

> If authentic community is the elusive ideal, then actual communities nevertheless constitute some all-too-human approximation of it — flawed, fragile, contested and compromised as they inevitably are. Whatever city folk may mean by this word community... the notion is symbolically significant in terms of what they share with those among whom they belong and of what distinguishes them from others (Eipper, 1996: 88).

This intellectual scepticism towards community as practice, not just symbol, assumes the primacy of individual autonomy and freedom. Community is seen as a curb on individuals' freedom and only likely to be accepted by them if it is to their individual advantage or tolerated if it is imposed by authorities. Whether or not the practice of community curbs that freedom, Eipper's point is that community may remain a powerful symbol of what urban residents ideally share with others and that ideal will influence the daily negotiation of neighbourhood practices. Arjun Appadurai wrote of the misrecognition by ethnographers of locality as the ground, not the figure, of their investigations and calls for a fresh approach to locality, "neither recognising its fragility nor its ethos as a property of social life" (Appadurai, 1996: 182). He thereby calls for attention to the production of locality, including the roles played by "organic intellectuals, administrators, linguists, missionaries and ethnologists" in that production.

In her recent book, *The Trouble with Community*, Vered Amit suggests that anthropologists are "encumbered with the baggage of a disciplinary tradition that has privileged collectivities as the primary locales and agents of sociality" (Amit and Rapport, 2002: 14). "Anthropologists whose fieldwork methods have privileged face-to-face relations now rely on an idea of community increasingly devoid of social content as a means of locating their own practices and gaze" (Amit and Rapport, 2002: 4). In the complex contexts of modernity, it is less and less plausible to limit anthropological investigations to the local community, Amit claims, yet it represents a fallback position for anthropologists who otherwise are attempting, particularly in analysing urban contexts, to portray the complexity of individual agents "jostling for position and denotation" (Amit and Rapport, 2002: 16). Her point is that community cannot be assumed, particularly in an urban and highly mobile world, nor should we "minimize the considerable difficulties of structure, logistics, persuasion, ideology and opportunity involved in constructing actual as opposed to imagined communities" (Amit and Rapport, 2002: 24).

Discussions of modernity frequently point to increasing seculari-zation, individualism and individual self-fulfilment as a hallmark of progress. As a necessary consequence, community and collective identi-ties are portrayed as being in retreat and social alienation on the increase. Modernity, says Dilip Gaonkar (2002: 5), "in its multiple forms seems to rely on a special form of social imaginary that is based on relations among strangers". Charles Taylor suggests that in this dominant modern social imaginary, people assume "the rise of 'individualism' (comes) at the expense of 'community' .... We read the displacement of older forms of complementarity as the erosion of community as such" (Taylor, 2002: 99). Taylor, however, does not accept such a view, insisting that modernity brings also the rise of new principles of sociality, new forms of social imaginary conceived as a world of independent associations, a civil society for the mutual benefit of equal participants and the mutual defence of individual rights. Taylor recognises that there has been an assumption in development practice that other societies will come to resemble Western society in its modern social imaginaries, but he insists on recognising alternative modernities as they emerge across the world.

Anthony Cohen refutes those who conclude the end of commu-nity within the city. Community, he suggests, is best understood as an experience, and the task of the social observer is to identify the nature and scope of people's conceived community and to analyse how they construct it symbolically and attach meanings to it. People in the city choose to make community by putting out social markers symbolically. They "map out their social identities and find their social orientations among the relationships which are symbolically close to them, rather than in relation to an abstracted sense of society" (Cohen, 1985: 27). This is a notion of community based on a perception of a commonality of ways of behaving that ignores or minimises the divergent meanings that members may impute to this behaviour. For him community is based on people's feelings of belonging, feelings often symbolised in people's constructions of distinctive myths, expressions, and traditions, and their sense of ownership of certain distinguishing rituals and ways of behaving. Contrary to Durkheim, who stressed in community the integration of different functions into a solidarity, Cohen suggests that community is an aggregating device built on symbolic coherence. 'Neighbourhood' may thus be examined not just as a solidarity of programmed activities but also as a symbol of what is important to people in constructing their urban identity.

This literature shows the importance in the contemporary world of problematising the occurrence of community and of looking clearly at its construction and constant reconstruction. This is of particular significance in urban society, where social commentators have long contested the existence of any significant expression of community.

'COMMUNITY' IN THE DEVELOPMENT DISCOURSE OF THE STATE

At the policy level, donor agencies and NGOs in recent decades have increasingly employed the concept of community to link 'sustainable development' or 'community-based' and 'participatory' approaches in development to representations of community that stress harmony, equality and tradition (Li, 1996: 502). 'Community' in these cases becomes part of a political rhetoric that rejects all the arguments about the tragedy of the commons, peasant ignorance, the pre-eminence of private property and individual acquisitiveness, or the managerial wisdom and effectiveness of the state, to suggest that communities are still the best option for achieving development and managing resources. Community-based natural resource management, for example, has even been adopted by such powerful bodies as the World Bank in their approach to assisting developing countries or 'indigenous communities' or the poor.

'Community' has thus become part of a convincing discourse mounted by development planners, both state and non-state, that identifies it as a fundamental element in the most progressive development policies and plans. In the 'developed' world the community has become part of state planning in regard to the city. In England the Hampshire County Council Structure Plan of 1994 mentioned the need to defend "community identity, a sense of place and belonging" against larger economic and political patterns that brought with them a loss of sense of space and place (Healey, 2000: 524). Since 1997 New Labour policies in the UK refer to community in local social spaces as sites for policy intervention. The politics of community "seeks to address the effects of inequality through the distribution of public goods, and the public redistribution of private goods" (Tonkiss, 2000: 596). Patrick Troy remarks that in post-Second World War Australia the neighbourhood was the basic building block of city planning and that this population's activities, focused on the local government-funded primary school and local shopping centre, "would provide the yeast for the development of a sense of engagement and commitment" (Troy, 2000: 549).

The term 'community' is used in many different ways. Its meaning and weight is constantly under negotiation, whether among international agencies, state governments or local actors. Tania Li (2002) makes the point about Indonesia that community and state have over decades engaged in a dialogue in which communities represent or constitute the state at the local level — and in that process are formed and reformed by the state — yet often simultaneously express identities in opposition to, or distinct from, the state.

It therefore is no longer possible, if it ever was, to separate communities from the impact of the state. The nature of this dialogue is as central to the continuity and livelihood of all such communities as it is to the survival of the state itself. The Indonesian state cannot afford to ignore the 'floating mass' of the urban population who identify themselves with local communities. The *rakyat* or 'common people' provide a certain legitimacy to the state as targets and recipients of its program of development and take to the streets to give life to its election campaigns. Yet as this book will explore, these local communities also have a life and an identity distinct from the state. Li (2002: 510) quotes from Robert Hefner (1990: 2) that "economic change is never just a matter of technological diffusion, market rationalisation or 'capitalist penetration'. Deep down, it is also a matter of community, morality and power". The same might be said of the penetration by state mechanisms of administration and control, that beyond and within those the community exists in all the complexities of people's negotiations of power and morality.

Eric Wolf (2001) shows how the closed corporate peasant communities found in central Java were a specific social form representing an attempt by rural residents to cope with the restraints imposed on them by the colonial regime, which limited access to land, water, trading opportunities and employment and insisted on communal taxes in preference to individual tax. Commenting on this, Andrew Walker suggests that 'community' has appeal for those looking for alternatives to state systems of management and moral authority and for those keen to explore non-commercial economic pursuits. However, cautioning against uncritical acceptance of such assertions of idealised community at face value, he argues that "community simplifications tend to gloss over the micro-political economies of conflict, coercion and differential access to resources, as well as the macro-political economies of articulation with state formation and economic transformation" (Walker, 2001: 6). In his critique of James Scott's *Seeing like a State* (1998), Walker argues that Scott has simplified notions of community and state to ignore the ambivalence of both terms. Scott's categorisation allows him to contrast the "thin formulaic simplifications imposed by the agency of state power" (Scott, 1998: 309) with the rich practical knowledge of homogeneous communities. Walker criticises not only the supposition that village communities are homogeneous but also the suggestion of a fundamental distinction between state and community because historical accounts of communities amply document the role of the state in creating the institutional foundations of many communities. Walker points out that there is no basis for assuming that those occupying a common territory naturally or inevitably share common ties. Village 'communities', he says, are a construction of colonial and post-colonial nation-building and economic development. Their viability as social entities in their own right must be critically examined.

Flip Vanhelden (2001: 23) makes the point that communities are conflated simplistically with the people who live in proximity, ignoring the differences in religion, class, kinship, ethnicity and occupation that frequently distinguish fellow residents. Project planners and policy-makers, Vanhelden says, have an interest in viewing communities as clearly bounded, internally homogenous and single-voiced entities with whom cooperative arrangements may be developed. In the case of urban 'communities', co-residence is assumed by such interests to paper over all sorts of differences among people who may come from diverse rural and urban origins, pursue diverse occupations and recognise few kinship links.

On the other hand, Walker (2001: 9) argues that community might be better understood as an alternative source of moral authority "in response to an expansive capitalist and bureaucratic system". He thereby recognises that community may represent either a construction of the nation-state in its bid to control and 'develop' its populace, or a construction of the local populace in dealing with state and market demands on them. Either way, he suggests, we are in danger of romanticising and essentialising local togetherness and creating a false standard. "Seeing like a moral economist seems to deploy the technique of simplification whereby the concept of community has come to encapsulate normative images of unity, relative homogeneity, environmental sustainability and non-commercial economy" (Walker, 2001: 14). Walker's solution is to "focus less on community itself than on the fluid and contested processes of community formation.... There is a need to focus on if, when and how people come to have a sense of shared belonging that may amount to 'community'" (Walker, 2001: 15). That depends on good ethnography, "uncomfortably intimate accounts of the problematic and idiosyncratic processes of community formation" (Walker, 2001: 17). The implications of such an approach are that there may be differences in the importance members of residential populations give to community, as well as the circumstances in which community assumes importance in one population and not in another.

KAMPUNG AS LOCATIONS OF THE URBAN POOR AND MARGINALIZED

The physical conditions in many poor kampung throughout Indonesia's cities contrast sharply with the wealthy lifestyles found on 'streetsides' elsewhere in the city. Alison Murray, for example, notes that in Jakarta the distinction between the rundown kampung and the modern elite houses concealing them is an "inescapable feature of Jakarta". Kampung people construct their lifestyles "in opposition to the metropolitan superculture and its structures of power and policy" (1991: 15). Howard Dick (2002: 397) describes real estate developments in Surabaya where luxury housing has been established behind security walls to provide a "safe and secure environment well away from the pressures and threats of the crowded kampung and city streets". There is a clear distinction made in Indonesian society between the urban middle class, who privatize the enjoyment of consumer durables behind raised fences and locked doors, and the rakyat 'masses' of the kampung, among whom consumer durables are shared (Dick, 1990; Mahasin, 1990).

   The contrast between the poor kampung and the expanding luxury housing in Indonesia's cities was taken up in the national press in 2000, when a workshop in Jakarta focussed on issues of housing and locality in Jakarta. Sardjono Jatiman, professor of sociology at the

University of Indonesia was reported as saying that in the past there were no conflicts among 'citizens' (*warga*, denoting a formal/legal membership of a society or nation) because there was still public space and open spaces like markets, where people could interact. What has happened, he added, is that now the houses of the wealthy are separated from the kampung of the poor because the wealthy are clustered in their own exclusive housing estates and there is no interaction at all between rich and poor (*Kompas*, 18/10/2000). The distinction between the urban poor in their settlements and an increasing number of elite and middle class in housing estates is therefore not just one of location but of social distinction and distancing. An Indonesian student of Urbanism and Architecture at the University of California, Ridwan Kamil, wrote in *Kompas* (29 October 2000) that gated communities, exclusive housing estates surrounded by impregnable fences, were appearing in Jakarta and that these reflected an architecture of fear, in Robert Bellah's words, "hyper-individualism syndrome", or in the thinking of Italian geographer Giuseppe Sacco, "medievalisation". Ridwan Kamil concluded that what was needed was a revitalisation of "communitarianism", which he saw as missing from such estates, otherwise Indonesia would lose its cherished "family values" and "social sensitivity". More cynically, he added, "perhaps we should just sit by and watch it (hyper-individualism) happen because this family culture of ours is just a huge illusion". He thus alludes to a growing debate among observers of urban society in Indonesia as to whether proper residential communities exist in the nation's cities, or whether they are constituted primarily by a government discourse that aims to control and subvert the public masses.

YOGYAKARTA KAMPUNG AS COMMUNITIES

In 1992 John Sullivan published *Local Government and Community in Java* as the result of his and his wife Norma's association over 15 years with a kampung neighbourhood in inner-city Yogyakarta. In that book he traced how the state is "tightening central control of local government as rapidly as it can", matching a supportive-constrictive administrative unit to each kampung-communal unit (Sullivan, 1992: 229). Within all urban residential areas the state imposes centrally defined administrative divisions as the true organs of stable, cohesive community. Sullivan considers the public harmony depicted by such urban neighbourhoods to be largely a construction of these state programs rather than locally generated cooperation and solidarity.

At issue here are the neighbourhood divisions of *rukun tetangga* (RT), *rukun warga* (RW) and *rukun kampung* (RK). These divisions originated under the Japanese wartime administration and were adopted under post-Independence governments as an effective way of governing urban populations. Each of these administrative units include a number of local office-holders, working with an RT, RW or RK head, all of whom are elected locally and none of whom is salaried. Ideally RT comprise no more than 30 households and RW three to seven RT. Rukun kampung (which were phased out in 1988–89 in favour of the smaller RW) designated a geographically defined and bounded urban area averaging nine hectares, with populations in 1987 ranging from 500 to well over 6,000 (Sullivan, 1992: 159). RK were "authorized to assemble tax monies, register and monitor residents and visitors, collect demographic and economic data, disseminate state directives, promote government plans and policies, extend local infrastructure, administer social welfare services and generally help to advance national development" (Sullivan, 1992: 37). RT and RW office-holders had similar roles for their respectively smaller populations. It is clear from this description that these formal bodies were created by the government for the administration of government business, though their officers were and are not civil servants but residents elected and appointed by the local RT, RW and RK populations. As Sullivan points out, it is a cost-effective way to implement state programs and maintain order.

> But the *rukun warga* is, none the less, a state creation designed and directed to achieve state aims; its functionaries are state-approved and its major functions are specified and constantly regulated by higher authorities. Like its forebears in Java, Japan and China, it is an instrument of social control. Its most basic task is to maintain civil order in areas where the mass of the people reside (Sullivan, 1992: 162).

Sullivan asserts that genuine community structures exist only at the level of the neighbourly cell, while larger 'communities' exist largely at the behest of the state. He identifies cells as clusters of families living in close proximity and in constant cooperation, focused on a leading family. Cells are sustained predominately by women and the central organiser is always a married woman (Sullivan, 1992: 46–7).

> The relations between households within clusters seemed the closest, most spontaneous and most neighbourly in the kampung. Only in

relations between cell fellows did it seem one would find anything approaching the positive aspects of egalitarianism, generosity, and considerateness so warmly identified as essential *gotong royong* traits (Sullivan, 1992: 98).

He adds: "Thus, the *rukun tetangga* extends the support offered by the cell association and tends to be overacclaimed for its services as it basks in public homage which should go to the humble unacknowledged cell" (Sullivan, 1992: 147). Also in Yogyakarta, H. Bremm identified this pattern of networks "localized among those whose doors face onto the same walkway and thus have regular face-to-face contacts" (Bremm, 1988: quoted in Evers and Korff, 2000). In exploring what might be considered to be genuine community cooperation, Sullivan thus refers to the Javanese term *gotong royong*, identified by Koentjaraningrat (1961) in villages near to Yogyakarta as referring to practices of neighbourly cooperation around bereavement, community work projects, *slametan* 'ritual feasts', house repairs, and agricultural production. Community cooperation in the kampung also revolved around bereavement, community work projects, slametan and neighbours' mutual cooperation in matters such as house repairs.

In the kampung, "the community is formed and sustained by the *gotong royong* cooperation of its member cells, and to maintain kampung membership, individual cells and families must participate adequately in *gotong royong* activities" (Sullivan, 1992: 130). He denigrates development efforts at levels higher than the cell as "misrecognitions" or self-deception by residents of what are essentially state impositions of 'community' cooperation. In a similar vein, John Bowen writes that the term gotong royong "corresponds to genuinely indigenized notions of moral obligation and generalized reciprocity, but it has been reworked by the state to become a cultural-ideological instrument for the mobilization of village labor" (Bowen, 1986: 546). Bowen thus suggests that there is a government reconstruction of the concept of gotong royong as development practice that exists in conflict with indigenous ideologies and practices.

Sullivan defines his own position in contrast to that adopted by Theodore Bestor (1989), who repudiates the argument that the identity of local communities is largely based on the imposition of administrative institutions in his account of 'neighbourhood Tokyo'. "He (Bestor) feels that such claims deny the social relationships, values, and diverse labours of community members themselves, an entirely reasonable reservation yet, as will be explained, in the Javanese case, administrative institutions do take a leading role in the construction and maintenance of community in both rural and urban areas" (Sullivan, 1992: 4–5). Sullivan goes on to explain the nuances of the position he is adopting:

> While it is true the ideology (of community) at issue is firmly endorsed and constantly activated by state authorities, it is also an ideology of the community itself, in a very literal sense, the community ideology. The community is not a passive object of state operations in this arena; it helped construct this discourse, continuously renews and vitalizes it, and though it is not really relevant to issues of complicity and control, it benefits directly from its everyday functioning (Sullivan, 1992: 11).

Nevertheless, he suggests that communal events and groupings will not be recognised by the local population as authentic neighbourly cooperation unless they have official recognition by RT/RW office-holders: "which is to say in respect of kampung groups and associations, those classified as genuinely communal are precisely and solely local government organs" (Sullivan, 1992: 101).

Sullivan appears to undermine his own argument when he discusses the contribution of RW leaders to community life. They are, he says, "of the community and ready to defend it" against the demands of the state. Suggestions and instructions from above are ignored or reinterpreted, such as action against gambling, prostitution, drunkenness and illegal liquor stalls, or accurate assessment of tax (Sullivan, 1992: 166). However, he asserts that these are minor gestures within their largely subservient role in state hierarchies. "The state now supplies, controls, or structures all major occasions and opportunities for the celebration and reaffirmation of kampung community" (Sullivan, 1992: 211). He portrays the dilemma thus:

> The difference between a primarily communal leader serving an implacable state and a primarily state-political functionary serving a local community is exceedingly subtle. Yet there is a difference and it is important. The former view — the community view — tends to make kampung members accomplices in their own oppression. Believing the *rukun warga*, its offices, and officials are theirs, they readily assist the state to cramp their movements, to limit their employment opportunities, to constrain their incomes. In troubled times they perceive the kampung as a haven, its functionaries as

protectors, when it might be safer to view the former as a trap, the latter as a threat. Through their willing cooperative efforts, they free state funds to advance the interests of the already rich and powerful (Sullivan, 1992: 170–1).

In contrasting his approach to analyses by a range of anthro-pologists[1] whom he sees as mirroring Javanese views of local worlds Sullivan suggests that the political analyst looks beyond kampung interpretations to the political reality of the manipulation of kampung by the state. 'Social harmony', 'communal calm', and 'absence of overt conflict' are synonyms for civil order, especially the brand favoured by rulers whose systems of local government rest on relatively uncoerced tranquillity of myriad small communities' (Sullivan, 1992: 107).

These views of Sullivan provide a useful start to my examination of the nature of kampung community in Java and their relations with the state over the periods of the New Order and the subsequent Reformasi government. As Sullivan acknowledges, it is none too easy to assess whether people believe in and act out community because it primarily benefits themselves or because it has been imposed on them by the state. Similarly there are issues raised by Sullivan's suggestion that anthropologists reflect too closely their informants' views, while political scientists are able to identify when a political ideology has coerced a subordinate people into misrecognition of their actions. Later chapters will reveal my own view on this. This chapter reviews the published findings of observers of urban low-income neighbourhoods from a diversity of academic disciplines. If Sullivan is right, we would have to take into account their disciplinary background when assessing their findings. I suggest that disparity in their findings reflects the diversity among settlements as much as the kind of data they collected. In both cases, it does not come down to a simple dichotomy between the political scientist and the anthropologist.

COMPARISON OF LOW-INCOME URBAN SETTLEMENTS THROUGHOUT SOUTHEAST ASIA

Clifford Geertz (1973) and James Peacock (1968) provide some support for Sullivan's interpretation in their accounts of urban kampung in East Java under the pre-1965 Soekarno government. They identified the imminent demise of community and communal values of social harmony (*rukun*) in the face of modern preoccupations with reformist

Islam, competing political parties and government promotion of progress (*kemajuan*). Geertz described how a boy's funeral ritual was against all tradition torn apart by the tension in the urban settlement between supporters of a secular political party and supporters of a reformist Muslim party. He concluded from that incident that the changes of modernisation were undermining traditions of neighbourhood solidarity. Based on research conducted in a Jakarta kampung in the early 1970s, the political scientist Dennis Cohen concluded that "local development projects tend to be implemented by local officials in a more authoritarian manner. There is little participation in most low income areas of the city…. They are simply given instructions by the local leaders and so must depend on these leaders for the impetus to get things done" (Cohen, 1988). One of the ways he saw this happening was through the formalisation of gotong royong as the means to implement development, a cooperation instituted from the top down rather than owned by the community.

Nevertheless, in reviewing some of this literature, Mary Hawkins (1996) emphasised the continuing importance of the Javanese notion of rukun (social harmony) in both urban and rural community ideology. Rukun, she wrote, was a constant referral point in kampung residents' discussion of their social relations, at community, household and marital levels. Hildred Geertz (1961: 147), in her study of pre–New Order East Javanese society, described the moral imperative denoted by rukun to control one's impulses so as not to set up emotional responses in others. Jay, who emphasised the key role of close residence in villagers' construction of networks of cooperation and trust, suggested that rukun was a "state in which all parties are at least overtly at social peace with one another. As a mode of action it requires the individual to subordinate, perhaps even sacrifice, his personal interests" to achieve a state of communal health and sharing through collective action (Jay, 1969: 66). The harmony thus achieved in public performance might, therefore, conceal a level of disharmony or disjuncture between coexisting parties.

While Jay and Geertz were writing about rural Java, the concept of rukun as communal health held sway in many urban kampung, as an ideal around which urban residents organised their affairs (Guinness, 1986). Hawkins noted that some may interpret rukun as a "strategic device which the wealthy only profess to uphold" for their own financial or political benefit, but that this view did not reflect the bulk of Javanese views on the matter (1996: 226). As she pointed out in relation to Javanese living in South Kalimantan, rukun is an ideology of social relations at the neighbourhood level by which people express and justify their actions (Hawkins, 1996: 231). She was thus identifying an ideology and its associated activities that exist primarily as a local construct rather than a state imposition. In reference to Javanese in Jakarta's kampung, Somantri concluded that community values remained strong:

> According to Javanese values, the opinions and feelings of one's neighbours must be considered. When they conduct *slametan* or *kenduri (kendhuren)*[2] they have to invite the nearest neighbours first. When a neighbour is ill, he should be visited. When neighbours suffer a calamity, a good Javanese should make a visit of condolence (Somantri, 1995: quoted in Evers and Korff, 2000: 231).

Similarly, in her study of a peri-urban Yogyakarta kampung, Barbara Hatley emphasised how *ludruk* theatre, and even National Day celebrations, expressed and reinforced neighbourhood pride and solidarity. Membership in a kampung involved "participation in the mutual-aid networks of the kampung, self-identification with the local community, and being identified by one's neighbours as being of, rather than merely in, the kampung" (Hatley, 1982: 57).

Erhard Berner and Rudiger Korff (1995), sociologists who studied the urban slums in Manila and Bangkok respectively, reviewed comparatively the various studies of Javanese urban kampung. Reflecting on the research of Sullivan and others, they suggested that Suharto's authoritarian New Order government prohibited the emergence of organisations outside state-sponsored and state-supervised cooperatives, unlike in Manila and Bangkok where a competitive political environment allowed local resistance. They described the emergence of loyalty, trust and solidarity in slum neighbourhoods, including the organisation of associations in Bangkok that successfully resisted the eviction ordered by government and arranged the rebuilding of houses after a big fire. J. Ockey (1997) described the growth of an almost siege mentality in the Bankhrua slum in Bangkok as its residents faced threats of eviction and arson. Residents organised a 24-hour patrol, mainly to prevent fires and, with the support of development agencies, local committees, including local Muslim leaders in this Cham settlement, constituted a level of leadership not experienced before. Lee (1998: 997) noted that slum dwellers' organisations in Bangkok mostly emerged during struggles against eviction. Discussing Southeast Asia generally, Korff considers that:

> The political framework is an important consideration for the success
> or failure of local organizations, and it also dictates the nature or
> character of local associations through which local interests are
> articulated. With liberalization and democratization of the political
> process and the diversification of elite groups, more opportunities
> for the rise of local movements are provided (Korff, 1996: 296).

In respect of Manila squatter areas, he cites Erhard Berner that the
local organizations that emerge among squatters have the objective to
define a specific territory and its members and to "serve as platforms
for the articulation of collective interests, improvement of communal
infrastructure, or organization of resistance against eviction" (Korff,
1996: 301). In Bangkok's Klong Thoey slum, it was some younger
residents with better education who initiated projects and acted as
intermediaries between administration and slum dwellers, gradually
replacing a committee of older slum leaders and providing a more
effective counter to state pressures.

Recognising the more hierarchical and formalised nature of relations in Indonesian kampung, Korff (1996: 303) notes: "Although most
studies of the kampung in Indonesia mention communal projects, it is
not at all clear whether these emerge from within as a result of social
integration and cooperation among neighbours, or from administrative
orders." Although Korff here admits to some equivocation regarding
the origin of urban communities, Alison Murray, whom he quotes,
appears to be unequivocal about the state construction of communities
in Jakarta:

> Kampung has been idealised in terms of social harmony (*rukun*)
> and supposedly traditional mutual help. The ideology of *rukun*
> and the patron-client model of society is institutionalised in the
> urban administrative structure as a means of imposing order, and
> the meaning of *rukun* — social harmony as a state of being — is
> interpreted as a desirable attitude of fatalism.... *Gotong royong*
> has been taken up as a national political symbol and is formally
> imposed on the kampung to achieve development goals (Murray,
> 1991: 64).

Jakarta, Murray reports, was divided in 1982 into 2,098 RW and
24,954 RT. "Order is imposed through institutionalizing the ideology
of harmony and mutual help in the administrative structure" (Murray,
1991: 23). "Locally elected heads of RW and RT are usually some
kinds of civil servants, and RW heads ... often live on the streetside

and are not directly involved in community life" (Murray, 1991: 33). However, despite this imposition of state structure, Murray notes a strong element of self-initiated community among this population that appears to qualify her otherwise unequivocal remarks. "The kampung is ... a community of individuals adapting to their urban situation and the arrival of more and more people with a balance of co-operation and competition, which is to some extent non-capitalist in that ideas of community membership supersede those of profit" (Murray, 1991: 61). She thus distinguishes the formal structures built around civil servants sustaining local level community organisation from informal expressions of neighbourly cooperation.

Like Norma and John Sullivan in their research in Yogyakarta, Murray identified women-centred networks as defining kampung community membership in Jakarta. Women gather for Koran-reading sessions and rotating credit societies, but "they do not seem to involve the same social implication and obligations (as in Yogyakarta where such cells organise ceremonial feasts), partly because the population is too heterogeneous and fluctuating" (Murray, 1991: 80). A declining population due to government sanctions on the informal sector meant that celebrations of births and weddings were infrequent. However, she mentioned the annual Independence Day celebration when the whole kampung turned out to take part in comedy skits and local *dangdut* music was performed by local residents. Murray saw the kampung as anarchic, in the sense of being "self-regulated, without recourse to the central government" (Murray, 1991: 84). RT leaders, for example, assisted neighbours in concealing trishaws from government raids. The sense of familiarity and cooperation within the community enabled them to resist the pressures of the state. Murray's conclusion, however, is that although a sense of community was still important in daily survival, the younger generation was "increasingly disaffected with communitarian anarchy as a way of life. The creation of aspiration to own possessions constitutes a process of individuation which contra-dicts alleyside co-operation" (Murray, 1991: 140). Murray's account, therefore, appears equivocal, emphasising the state construction of com-munity, on the one hand, yet recognising the autochthonous character of much of the community cooperation she identified there.

Lea Jellinek, who studied a kampung in Jakarta through the 1970s and 1980s, concluded that neighbourhood communities in Jakarta kampung did not have the strength to provide much support to residents (Jellinek, 1991). Her account focuses on the kampung of Kebun Kacang which was demolished by the city government in 1981. She recounts how residents faced with eviction from the kampung, after an initial period of hesitancy began to organise through the three prayer houses in the area. Some of the better-educated residents protested against the demolition through the media and a legal NGO and gained some concessions from the government. However, their fragile unity collapsed when some negotiated surreptitiously with government. Compensation funds were more attractive to these individuals than the preservation of their communities (see also Somantri, 1995). The construction of office and commercial buildings threatened densely populated kampung in central Jakarta and put huge economic pressure on the petty entre-preneurs in the kampung. Jellinek summed up the post-1978 situation in the kampung by saying that families began to be secretive about their possessions as they became more acquisitive and distanced themselves from one another. "The loosening of ties between households that had once shared so much was one factor that led kampung dwellers to question the moral basis of their society", referring to it as *zaman kurang ajar* (times of declining morality) (Jellinek, 1991: 21). Jellinek described the loosening of marital ties and the increasing fluidity of household membership in kampung neighbourhoods and contrasted these with the social solidarity of those who lived in communal lodging-houses (*pondok*), mostly migrants who originated from the same village and helped ease each other into income-earning activities in the city.

However, Jellinek's previous description suggested a much greater degree of communal cooperation. In her portrayal of the neighbourhood community of 77 households where she did most of her research, Jellinek suggested that:

> households were bound together in a mesh of complex, intersecting and ever-changing relationships which together defined the com-munity ... The essence of all these relationships was the reciprocal exchange of information, goods and services between individual members of different households. The strength of these relationships was indicated by the frequency and continuity of these exchanges (Jellinek, 1991: 27).

Neighbours had credit relationships with each other, shared medical expenses, bought and sold goods and services to each other, chatted, provided accommodation to each other's visitors, joined together to listen to the radio or watch television, borrowed cups, plates and chairs from each other for family celebrations, shared food and advised each other on how to trade or cope with disobedient children or unfaithful husbands (Jellinek, 1991: 35). Rotating credit societies sprang up among neighbours, in most cases organised by one of the women. Marriages, deaths and circumcisions brought neighbours together to share food and monetary assistance. Better-off neighbours who distanced themselves from such social relationships were no longer regarded as members of the neighbourhood community. Islamic prayer houses provided the main focus for more formal social organisation, the entire neighbourhood coming together to rebuild one prayer house in the 1970s. Men's and women's prayer groups met regularly and the prayer house organised the distribution of rice at Lebaran and meat on the Idul Adha holy days.

Despite these neighbourhood ties, Jellinek insisted that community-wide cooperation was almost non-existent and that residents were convinced that social ties were breaking down as affluence increased. "There was constant tension between the need to accumulate wealth for oneself and one's own family and the tradition of sharing and exchanging with neighbours and kinsfolk" (Jellinek, 1991: 54). Government administration of RT/RW according to Jellinek was "spottily organized and little utilized" (Jellinek, 1991: 109). Registration of residents, for example, was not implemented, and family planning programs were ignored by 'local headmen'. It was only when threatened with demolition in 1981 that residents began to organise and gain a sense of belonging to the wider area of 16 neighbourhoods earmarked for demolition (Jellinek, 1991: 133). Sixteen headmen and 19 other more politically aware or educated members of the area were chosen to act as representatives of the community in its confrontation with the government. However, as negotiations took a long time and were often not reported back to residents, indecision, uncertainty and demoralization set in and many residents moved out. Headmen competed to obtain higher rates of compensation through illicit deals. Jellinek concluded that "they lacked the leadership and ability to organize to defend their own interests. But most of all they lacked trust in each other to work together for a common purpose" (Jellinek, 1991: 178).

Jellinek thus described a kampung settlement where RT/RW leadership was minimal and the population was so mobile that residents often did not know each other. On the other hand, she identified neighbourhood communities, often organised by leading women, where cooperation and sharing characterised the interaction of households and influenced the election of headmen. She noted that accounts by Sullivan and Guinness of poor kampung in Yogyakarta "emphasize the strength of social ties, in marked contrast" to her own findings. The distinction she draws, however, appears to be less between the kampung of Jakarta and Yogyakarta and more a reflection of the different perspectives of the observers. In characterising the kampung as lacking community, Jellinek appears to have in mind the organisation of the whole settlement and the breakdown of organised resistance across an area of all 16 neighbourhoods (3,000 people). This level of organisation would also be rare in Yogyakarta, although the equivalent RK unit of Ledok that I studied before 1989 provided some coordination and symbolic unity across such a population. Her case may well support the Sullivan argument that such community only exists where it is constructed by the state and the absence of state structures at an RK level in Kebun Kacang could be seen as its greatest weakness. Jellinek's account certainly gives little detail on RT/RW structures or on the more prosaic aspects of neighbourhood organisation, which may be the consequence of her greater interest in informal-sector economic activities and the history of slum clearance. However, it is also clear that a foundation of neighbourhood cooperation existed, albeit threatened by high population mobility. Murray echoed Jellinek's suggestion that increasing affluence and population fluidity mitigated against the consolidation of community in Jakarta kampung (Murray, 1991: 41). For both of them, communality was limited to small clusters of neighbours who cooperated with each other.

Despite the abundant evidence of local constructions of community, the accounts of kampung in Java have come to be dominated by a social science literature that characterises community as a state construction without strong foundations among urban residents. It is a view that sometimes threatens to dismiss local characterisations of communities as mere 'misrecognitions' or 'ideology'. Against such a view, it is desirable to review the evidence for community as an indigenous construction expressing an identity independent of the state.

In their broad study of Southeast Asian urban settlements, Evers and Korff were specifically interested in the conditions that allowed for mobilisation of residents of low-income settlements against outside threats to the community. In their studies in Manila and Bangkok, they suggested that the existence of denser social networks was particularly associated with new settlements, leading to stronger expressions of solidarity. "Initially close social relations emerge linked to spatial proximity, and are partly replaced in the course of time by relations covering a larger space" (Evers and Korff, 2000: 231). They quote the study of Manila by Jocano (1975) that relations with neighbours are an unavoidable outcome of the congestion and the need for mutual help and cooperation in the initial years of the settlement. According to Evers and Korff, overlapping horizontal ties based on friendship emerged in Bangkok neighbourhoods during the 1990s, while in Manila *compadrazgo* links provided a cultural framework on which local organisation could develop, leading to dense overlapping networks within squatter areas, allowing the rapid flow of information and potentially the mobilization of the people (Evers and Korff, 2000: 235). However, their conclusion from the Jakarta studies, particularly that of Jellinek, was that interdependencies revolved around income-generating opportunities and once these were disrupted the strength of the community dissipated. Kampung administrative officers provided another potential source of organisational strength but these office-holders could not be expected to act against wider state administration. A further possibility, they noted, was the prayer houses, but these were too weak to be effective alone (Evers and Korff, 2000: 237).

As a result, these authors were not convinced of the potential of kampung communities to defend their location or achieve their demands against state pressures. "Thus it seems that the urban poor do not organize themselves but they are organized by outsiders", that is, by student groups and NGOs (Evers and Korff, 2000: 237). In contrast, Evers and Korff, citing Berner, suggested that local organisations that are formed largely to resist eviction and organise land-sharing schemes are much stronger in Manila, centred on local leaders who have lived in the area for a long time and enjoy better incomes. In Bangkok also, the local organisation of Klong Thoey slum effectively resisted eviction and handled reconstruction after a fire. Evers and Korff suggested that, whereas in Indonesia NGOs tended to be intimidated by the authoritarian state and dealt only with low-level bureaucrats, in Bangkok and Manila NGOs defined themselves as the voice of development, a position that required their legitimation by the urban poor; "the possibilities to instrumentalize the 'poor' for their own ends are limited" (Evers and Korff, 2000: 239). Their point is that in these two cities wider local organisations sprang up when the situation demanded it, while in Indonesia organisations beyond the neighbourhood tended to be absent (Evers and Korff, 2000: 241). One reason they gave for this is that in Thailand and the Philippines the state administration was much less concerned with control down to the neighbourhood level, whereas in Indonesia the state had so infiltrated local organisation that it was difficult to disentangle Javanese traditional values and state ideologies. "In Jakarta the kampung dwellers are still mainly objects instrumentalized by different groups" (Evers and Korff, 2000: 242).

This book will present a very different picture of kampung dwellers in Yogyakarta, one which demonstrates strong local impulses to community, quite independent of state action. Rather than being mere objects of state constructions of control these residents have created a world for themselves with considerable autonomy from the state. To some degree this reflects the lack of assistance and direction provided by the state, in part it reflects residents' preference for alternate means of satisfying their needs. The kampung with its multiple lifestyles demonstrates the existence of a vital informal world, that is, a nexus of arrangements that guarantees a minimum of living conditions for all residents, independent of state strictures, even during the most authoritarian years of the New Order.

There is some evidence that even in Manila a community cannot unequivocally be characterised as confined to new settlements resisting demolition. Michael Pinches' research in Manila provides evidence of neighbourhood organisation in more established settlements. "Neighbourhood cooperation often extends not only to the mere physical production and maintenance of amenities, but to their production and maintenance in the face of state or private landlord repression. Indeed, Manila's squatters have frequently proved to be highly organised and politically effective in warding off depredations by the state and landowners" (Pinches, 1994: 23). Similarly in Kuala Lumpur, Malaysia squatter settlements, residentially segregated in ethnic communities of Malays, Chinese and Indian, were marked by a high level of social and political participation, independently of government pressure (Johnstone, 1981: 376). Sen reported that in the 1960s "mutual help and cooperation are widely practised even in activities that do not directly involve traditional or rural-based celebrations" (Sen, 1979: 193). The concept of community, once dismissed by Malaysian state elites as primitive social practices and values, was adopted by government as the antidote to the erosion of neighbourly cooperation that resulted from the pursuit of material progress. What the state identified and belatedly promoted was a community way of life that encouraged high moral values and fostered traits like "neighbourliness, co-operation, willingness to help, *gotong-royong* and courtesy" (Bunnell, 2002: 1695–6). This concept, clearly associated in Malaysia with village life, was subsequently deemed appropriate for a Malaysian-style urbanity (Kahn, 1992).

In post-1998 Indonesia, there has also been some political liberalisation, similar to that described for Manila or Bangkok, although former authoritarian habits die hard. NGOs have increased and kampung people talk openly of their rights in a new era of reform (Reformasi) characterised by the decentralisation of government functions and decision-making to provincial, district and village levels of government. The role of NGOs as partners of the urban poor is more apparent. However, such forms of resistance and local autonomy and community already existed in Jakarta kampung under the New Order, while in Surabaya under the Kampung Improvement Program communities were encouraged to organise themselves to exchange ideas, and to improve paths, lighting, garbage disposal and the natural environment (Silas, 1992: 38). In Kampung Penas Tanggul, a riverside kampung in East Jakarta, resistance to authoritarian and corrupt elite practices emerged prior to Reformasi. In 1986 an NGO came to assist the Penas community in health and schooling services. When in 1991 the settlement was served with an eviction notice, the Penas community with the support of the NGO demonstrated at the Governor's office and the People's Council. Some households were evicted but the community was allowed to remain. With new confidence they improved pathways, communal washing and toilet facilities and water pumps, and took turns to clean, repair or replace worn out parts, reflecting their cohesiveness as a community (Winayanti and Lang, 2004: 52). They continued to lobby the *kelurahan* office, the lowest level of salaried officials within the local administration, for RT status and in 2000 the NGO successfully lobbied the Minister of Human Settlements and Regional Development to obtain RT status for them. This allowed residents to become legal citizens and to access government programs such as micro-credit for small business under the Urban Poverty project. The relationship between the NGO and the local community became "a learning process for the community in organizing themselves, mobilizing their resources, and understanding their rights and obligations in the neighbourhood" (Winayanti and Lang, 2004: 57).

This case has been paralleled in Yogyakarta by the Code settlement associated with Romo Mangun and the NGO YPR (Yayasan Pondok Rakyat — People's Shelter Foundation) he established, where the successful consolidation of community and lobbying of government in the late 1980s and 1990s allowed these people to remain legally on the riverbank. A recent YPR newsletter termed it an "urban advocating movement" and began: "Eviction of the masses continues. It seems that our resistance through social movements has not yet been strong enough to win the right for common people to participate in determining their future. Our task in our social movements is to keep up the resistance and to propose alternative concepts, each in our own way" (my translation, *Yayasan Pondok Rakyat Newsletter*, 5/7/2004). A later chapter will examine the direction the YPR movement has taken in working alongside kampung residents in Yogyakarta.

As Anthony Cohen pointed out, consciousness of community is encapsulated in the perception of its boundaries, but those boundaries do not simply reflect state designations, nor are they to be accounted for simply as lines of resistance against the state. Community in the low-income settlements of Southeast Asia has as much to do with establishing networks of cooperation in often difficult economic and political and social conditions as it does with adopting government ideologies about norms of cooperation or being absorbed into the militaristic culture of the New Order. Clearly there is variation across these settlements in the strength and scale of community and the studies reviewed here have indicated a range of contributory factors — leadership, length of settlement, threats of eviction, religious organisation, generational change, mobility of residents and ethnic homogeneity. The question I explore in this book is to what extent community exists as an indigenous principle of organisation and identity independent of state constructions.

In the next chapter I explore the Ledok community from the view of a local entrepreneur and leader. The story of his and his household's life and role in Ledok illustrates many of the elements of community and the changing relations between kampung residents and the city administration, also between informal-sector workers and the formal city economy, which will be discussed in later chapters. The third chapter examines the way kampung residents interact with the wider administration and services provided by the city, focusing on the impact of the economic crisis that brought about the end of the New Order government of President Suharto. Chapter Four suggests that the informal strategies of the kampung represent an alternative to state programs and describes the diversity of such strategies. The fifth chapter examines Ledok in the light of perhaps the greatest threat to its continuity as a cohesive community — the threat posed by cohorts of male youth who at times have ignored the moral responsibilities of living in community for the perceived individualism of the wider consumerist society. Building on this account of kampung-state relations over several historical periods, the following three chapters explore the nature of community and the relevance of community in development in reference to three areas of social activity: the kendhuren/slametan ritual, the implementation of the 2004 elections, and the management of violence. The penultimate chapter examines the nature of the kampung community and its relations with the state and wider urban business interests from the point of the non-government organisation YPR, whose goals focus on people's empowerment and urban advocacy. The final chapter reviews the importance of community in responding to the state and in facilitating development.

2

Ledok and the Life of a Local Leader and Entrepreneur

Ledok is an off-street settlement close to the centre of the city of Yogyakarta. The area it occupies was considered so unattractive in colonial times that little of its land was registered. The land shelves sharply to the river, which from time to time used to flood a riverflat 50 metres wide. The settlement follows a stretch of river about 1,000 metres in length between two main roads and their bridges. The kampung is bordered on three sides by main city streets and their contiguous streetside properties and, on the fourth side, by the river itself. From early colonial times these streetside sites were occupied by businesses, government offices and the residences of the urban elite. The early kampung residents made their houses on land above the riverflat on the riverbank directly behind these elite properties and obtained title over this land, though refused title over the riverflat land that they were farming. In the early years of the New Order, it was announced that after a person had paid land tax on the riverflat land for ten years, the land would become theirs. Unfortunately, in 1968 a flood built up with cold lava from the nearby volcano and inundated the riverflat. Once again the municipal government withheld the granting of titles to what was seen as a vulnerable location. As a result, the ownership status of the riverflat remained ambiguous for many years, even as a residential population spilled onto it.

Population on the riverbank built up steadily over the years, from about 2,000 in 1940 to 3,449 in 1950 and 4,736 in 1979 (Guinness, 1986: 14–7).[3] Until the 1980s the riverflat remained an oasis of fruit and other trees, bamboo clumps, and water vegetables and fish farms, in sharp contrast with the surrounding settlement on the street and

Figure 2.1   Riverflat houses in 1979.

riverbank. Fronting the kampung on three sides were streetside properties, comprising city businesses and the homes of wealthy citizens
along three of the city's busiest roads.[4] Heavy walls protected these
premises from the mass of population behind and below, who were
assumed to be dangerous to these streetside residents. Kampung
people had a reputation as *kampungan* (uncivilised), a term which
connoted rough, boorish, uncultured, poor and potentially dangerous
and subversive people. For those who never dared to enter these
off-street neighbourhoods, kampung people were seen as an obstacle
to development. University students making their first visits to the
kampung as part of their obligatory community development course
assignment concluded that kampung people were dirty, irreligious,
lazy and uninterested in getting ahead. Whatever was happening in
the kampung was beyond the awareness of the city's middle class
and elite. Nor were they considered as worthy subjects of research by
local universities, which directed their attention towards rural society.
It was not until the 1990s that groups like Yayasan Pondok Rakyat
(Chapter Six) began to devote their energies to kampung matters.

There is no uniformity about kampung in Yogyakarta or any other
city in Indonesia. One of the first to write about kampung, Gerald

Krausse (1975), pointed this out over 30 years ago by calling attention to their geographical location as typifying their socio-economic diversity. Ledok, and other riverbank kampung, are located in areas where terrain complicates access and floods pose a danger to home and livelihood. Some kampung residents such as petty criminals and prostitutes made use of this inaccessible location as a protection against intrusive authorities; others took advantage of the special riverside location to pursue income-earning activities such as sand-digging, vegetable-growing and fish-raising. Many others settled in Ledok and elsewhere along the rivers of Yogyakarta because these areas were vacant, untitled state lands. Being unattractive housing locations for the middle and elite classes, they were cheap for poor migrants flooding in from surrounding villages. Those who had settled earlier in kampung such as Ledok attempted to instil in these later arrivals a sense of a moral community as a means of survival in the city.

Figure 2.2   Male and female sand-diggers in the 1970s.

During a visit in 2000 when residents were trying to recover from the financial crisis of previous years, I was made more aware of the drawbacks of the riverside location. One entrepreneur called it a 'dead kampung', because it lacked roads, schools and business to attract outsiders into the area. There were no roadside locations that would enable an entrepreneur to open a shop or a tailoring business to serve a wider population. Instead their clients were limited to those from the same neighbourhood. They encountered only the same people day after day, she said. However, not all these riverside kampung are seen as isolated. Residents of Ledok Macanan, along the same river, opened small stalls and service points called *kios* (kiosk) along a busy road bordering their kampung. Unlike in Ledok, where streetside land was occupied by prestigious private and state enterprises, kampung residents in Ledok Macanan had access to roadside premises, from where they sold petrol, cigarettes, videos and DVDs, tyres and stamps. When the city's economy slumped after 1997, many of these shop owners sold out, but when the city's economy improved in 2001, kampung youth re-established these roadside enterprises (Arifin, 2003).

Another Ledok entrepreneur in 2000 pointed out that residents were *malas keluar*, that is, 'lazy or reluctant to venture outside the kampung'. This of course provided an opportunity to petty entrepreneurs who were able to supply these 'lazy' residents with vegetables and other food items or daily necessities through small shops known as *warung*. However, the entrepreneur's comment also represented a criticism of his neighbours, who were quite isolated from the wider city society and economy. Another resident complained that outsiders were reluctant to enter the kampung, since to do so meant passing the scrutiny of the many groups of neighbours who lounged chatting along the many alleyways of the kampung and who confronted strangers to ask them what they were doing in the area. For this resident, such interference with visitors was an aspect of kampung behaviour that no longer accorded with modern urban living.

This was said to be the reason that students were no longer the main boarders in the kampung. During the 1970s and 1980s when major government and private universities began to locate to the north of the city, many tertiary students had sought cheap accommodation in nearby kampung. By the 1990s, however, many wealthier residents had begun constructing or converting large houses on the streets in the north of the city as dormitories. More and more students moved to rent a room in these lodgings, where they had the freedom to invite

Figure 2.3   The street-level entry to Ledok in 2000.

their friends home, where motorbike parking was directly outside their rooms, and where they were not under the scrutiny of neighbours. As a result, many of the riverside kampung lost their student clientele, replaced by other boarders working in the nearby shops and offices of the city.

The riverside kampung in Yogyakarta must therefore be seen as differing from other kampung in Yogyakarta and elsewhere, some of which have undergone such extensive capital investment in roads and houses and business premises that they are now little different from streetside locations. Indeed there is growing confusion over the term 'kampung'. Middle-class residents of Yogyakarta refer to their own neighbourhoods as 'kampung' and there are efforts to revive some of the cultural norms of kampung society, such as cooperation around rites of passage. City residents who originate from outside Java refer to their villages as 'kampung' and regard the concept of kampung being urban neighbourhoods as an aberration of their proper meaning. Other middle-class citizens suggested to me that people no longer talk of kampung at all — although my kampung neighbours certainly did so. This reaction may have much to do with the physical re-development that has occurred in many kampung. What were originally off-street, chaotic-looking urban settlements have been transformed by the construction of sealed roads, the provision of piped water, electricity and toilets to most houses, and the improvement of houses from bamboo to brick construction. Many former kampung areas now resemble middle-class neighbourhoods where residents can access their homes directly by car and where neighbours may put more emphasis on relationships beyond the neighbourhood than on those with their neighbours. Many middle-class residents resent the formal neighbour-hood RW/RT meetings they are expected to attend and prefer to form their friendships along lines of work or common interests. This may well apply to former off-street neighbourhoods and it may well no longer be justifiable to refer to these as kampung, except in the sense of 'homeplace' (*kampung halaman*).

Clearly 'kampung' does not have the same derogatory connotation as it used to. 'Kampung' has become more important as a symbol of identity, a nostalgic link to the past or to one's kin or *adat* (tradition). This would seem to indicate that public consciousness of socio-cultural distinctions between low-income settlements and the larger city have become less important. The kampung is now an address rather than a social tag. It may also reflect the disappearance of the Rukun Kampung, the administrative unit associated with the kampung as a low-income settlement. This was a formal designation of a city block, often including both streetside and off-street residences, with its elected committee of non-salaried officials responsible for the organisation of activities, especially within the off-street neighbourhoods. In this sense streetside residents were important donors of off-street activities but otherwise generally peripheral to RK activities. While the RK adminis-trative organisation existed, there was a sense of greater unity among kampung residents. The RK officials generally held great prestige within their neighbourhoods and the RK head, and sometimes other members of his staff, attended neighbourhood and family rituals and events throughout the area. In Ledok during the 1970s and 1980s, the RK heads were greatly respected. In 1989 the RK and its organisation were disbanded and replaced with several smaller RW units.

Among Indonesian scholars with whom I held discussions, there was indeed some disagreement as to whether 'kampung' was still an appropriate term. People no longer referred to their localities as kampung, they said, and no doubt that is the case for many kampung whose accessibility has been improved by internal lanes and infrastructure. However, riverside kampung remain 'kampung' to their residents, this term referring not just to a location but to a way of living in close proximity within community. This is not just a feature of riverside settlements. Norma Sullivan informed me (personal communication) that Sitiwaru, where she and John Sullivan worked, has remained this kind of dense, limited-access settlement, even though streetside business and the houses of the wealthy have pushed back into land formerly occupied by kampung residents.

Ledok could be termed a poor kampung. Limited access to the kampung makes it unattractive to those with cars and even those on motorbikes face some difficulties descending to the lower levels. They have to wind through the narrow alleyways busy with adults and children, dismount at certain spots, and find a spot to park the vehicle close to home but not to the inconvenience of neighbours. A majority of residents work in low-paid or casual employment in the city (for 1978 occupations see Guinness, 1986: 49). The kampung is on the list of various universities in Yogyakarta as a location of poorer people where students conduct their community development programs. When I first lived there in the 1970s, low-ranking civil servants (*pegawai*) constituted an elite, both in terms of their material resources and their contact and familiarity with the formal sector. Over the years most of these pegawai have retired, and some have died. A few pegawai have moved to *perumahan* (real estate complexes) constructed either by government or private business, although they in many cases retain their houses in the kampung. Some of the retired pegawai hold positions in neighbourhood leadership such as RW/RT heads. Nevertheless, by 2004 there was no longer the solid band of kampung elite earning a steady and moderate income as pegawai. By 2004 income was derived more from the informal sector of entrepreneurial activities, whose income was more uncertain but at times considerable.

Despite this characterisation of low socio-economic status, there are some in the kampung population and among the heirs of kampung residents who have emulated the lifestyles of streetside residents. One or two have excelled as entrepreneurs, such as a woman who in 2000 established a lucrative business selling alcohol and lottery tickets both inside and outside the kampung, employing eight kampung neighbours and purchasing for her household a car, mobile phone, computer, and refrigerator. A few two-storey homes in Ledok Code have been extensively remodelled, financed by former residents or heirs of residents living outside the kampung with an eye to retiring there or providing accommodation for their children while they complete secondary and tertiary schooling. Some of these premises on the very edge of the kampung have been made into student dormitories, imitating develop-ments on streetside. However, there is some local resentment of these large structures as being exhibitionist and oblivious to the needs of neighbours. They represent a lifestyle which, in its contrast, draws attention to the poverty of most of their neighbours and underlines their neighbours' inferiority in the wider economy and polity.

THE LIFE OF A LOCAL LEADER AND ENTREPRENEUR

Another way to introduce Ledok's story over the last 30 years is by tracing the life story of one of its extended households. The story of Sugi and his family illustrates the changes which Ledok households have experienced over the last three decades and draws out several of the key themes with which this book is concerned. Nigel Rapport has questioned the merits of focusing on individuals as the "corporeal constituents of the social world", the agents of history and creators of culture, rather than focusing on societies or communities as the real political actors in the world, the repositories of power and knowledge, and on culture as mediating the lives, insights and rights of their members (Rapport, 1997). I take the view that both are necessary to such an account. I want therefore to examine the validity of the concept of community and to explore the linkages between formal and informal economic and social perspectives from the perspective of an individual's life story.

As a central figure in the community, Sugi, over the 31 years I knew him, worked in both formal and informal economic sectors, negotiated the terrain of formal and informal social and cultural expectations and, by serving as RT and RW leader in various periods, negotiated the counter-claims on his loyalties and energy of a mili-taristic state and a local community. Such a neighbourhood leader is vital to the organisation and expression of community within the urban settlement as well as the administration of the area. However, the community may also at times build social interactions that ignore such leaders and reject their authority. The community is thus larger than its leaders, even as its identity is in part constructed by and through them. The life history of one of the more prosperous — though still low-income — families within kampung society, along with that of their home and business, may help to focus the issues of kampung community and the negotiation of household and community autonomy within the limits imposed by the wider society and economy. It is a story of experimentation and daring rather than passivity or apathy. It also shows the construction of local community under the guidance of local leaders but within an urban structure that often disadvantages kampung people of all income levels.

For low-income urban residents, there are two preferred options to secure a future for oneself and family. The first is to gain government employment, which carries with it the security of a pension after retirement. Government employees (pegawai) are held in high esteem in the kampung. Frequently they are able to arrange for their children to also move into government employment. The other option is to gain title to land. Ownership of land and ownership of a house provides another surety: it obviates the need to pay rent, it can be used as a guarantee for loans from the formal banking sector and it allows a family to stay together by adjusting their house and land use to accommodate all members. This chapter illustrates the flexibility with which a particular household negotiated formal and informal-sector employment and adjusted its economic enterprises, landholdings and housing and social expectations to survive the various crises they faced.

1970s

In 1975 when I negotiated to stay in his house, Sugi was a father of two young children. Sugi's mother, to whom I shall refer as 'grandmother', was a longtime resident of Ledok. She had grown up there and soon after her first marriage in the early 1940s, bought the house of their parents from her siblings, who were living elsewhere. It was a house of ten squares, 20 × 50 feet, with walls of plaited bamboo (*gedeg*) and a floor that was originally dirt but later was cemented over. Although she owned the house, she did not own the land, which was part of a block with several other houses, one of which was occupied by the landowner. Such an informal arrangement is termed *ngindung* — the land tenants pay the landlord a small rent each year for occupation of the land on which their house is built. Usually these rents are very small indeed, having been agreed to many years previously and not increased out of respect for the close ties that exist between the tenant and landlord. Tenants have obligations to lend help to their landlord at major family rituals or when labour is required to repair a house or improve the land. Sugi's father, referred to in this story as 'grandfather', came from a rural background in Wates, about 20 kilometres from the city, but held a job in the government service that brought him into urban employment. He was grandmother's second husband, and he kept spasmodic contact with a second wife he had married back in Wates. Thus their children came from three different unions and all occupied the house at various times. When I first met the family in 1975, Sugi, born in 1949 as the child of grandmother and grandfather, lived with them and his wife and two children (born 1972 and 1974). A son of grandfather and his Wates wife (born 1956) also shared the house while studying at the university. Later in the early 1980s the daughter of grandmother and her first husband (born circa 1940) moved in when her husband resigned from the military, bringing with them their three children.

From the 1960s grandfather nurtured his interest in farming in the urban environs. Below the house on the riverflat, where no formal land title existed because it was subject to regular flooding, he planted vegetables and fruit trees and kept goats and sheep over an expanse of land 50 metres wide that spanned both sides of the river. This land was termed *wedigengser*, which recognised state jurisdiction over the land but allowed his right to the land to be recognised informally within the kampung because he had opened it to farming. He became known as Pak Joyo Wedus ('goat/sheep Joyo'). Sugi remarked that this was potentially an insulting nickname but grandfather was an accepted member of the neighbourhood, even though he took little active part in the community. He had a passion for homing pigeons, which he released each afternoon to soar above the houses and river.

Grandmother kept a small warung selling household necessities such as soap, rice, tea, sugar, cigarettes, matches, kerosene, exercise books, pencils, some fresh vegetables, and fruit as well as a selection of food she cooked herself, such as curried vegetables, fried soybean cake (*tempe, tahu*) and biscuits. She invested grandfather's civil service pension in maintaining the range and quality of goods in the warung, and from this fed herself and grandfather, provided snacks for her grandchildren, and meals for those of her tenants who paid her a monthly sum for board. Like all warung proprietors, grandmother allowed her customers credit in order to retain their business, creating an informal network of credit relations. As a result, she was often short of capital. Without the monthly supplement of the pension she would not have been able to replace her stock from her suppliers in the formal commercial streetside world.

It was through the shop that grandmother gained ownership of the land. Many goods from the shop were purchased on credit.

Grandmother kept a tally of neighbours' debts in a small notebook and could become very surly with those who delayed payment for too long. Eventually she would refuse to sell them anything more on credit and hope in that way to recover the debt. Occasionally her debtor fled to another shop in the kampung but kampung gossip was strong and their reputation preceded them. It was therefore easier to pay the debt if possible. One of her customers was her landlady, who over the years had notched up a large debt but to which grandmother made no objection because she was her landlady. However, eventually it became so large that grandmother proposed to settle it with a transfer of the land title. That was agreed upon and the land was subdivided to give grandmother the title. A small triangular section of the house remained on an adjoining block, on which grandmother continued to pay land rent.

On the riverside of the house the ground was very unstable, dropping sharply by about three metres to the riverflat below. With Sugi's help, grandfather secured the soil with a high stone wall. Grandfather also made the acquaintance of Radi and his wife, *gelandangan* (homeless people) who were sand-diggers and sheltered in a shack of cardboard and tin on the opposite riverflat. Grandfather offered them shelter in his house, possibly in exchange for labour on his riverflat land. Having been accepted into the kampung, Radi began to improve the riverbank just to the south of grandmother's land by building a two-metre-high retaining wall and heaping river sand behind the wall with the aim of creating a house site. Wherever residents built a retaining wall in this way, it had the effect of converting lower-level riverflat *wedigengser* land to higher-level riverbank, thereby converting river reserve to land on riverbank level over which they could potentially claim title under formal state registration. However, Radi never finished the site, moving instead to the riverflat just to the north of grandfather's plot where another long-term resident had cultivated gardens.

Sugi finished his studies in 1968, when his father retired from government service. From high school he had gained admission to the Sekolah Tinggi Olahraga (Sports Tertiary College). Grandfather's pension, the greatest attraction of a government job, was withheld for a year and, because of the loss of family income, Sugi was forced to leave the institute to make a living. He became an itinerant trader, travelling by bus throughout Central and East Java with an assortment of goods such as clothes and exercise books and stationery. He rarely returned home. One day in his travels he saw a noodle-seller who

Figure 2.4 A riverflat dwelling below Sugi's house with foundations of the riverbank – retaining wall in the foreground.

looked just like his father. He was disturbed to see his father's likeness and returned home immediately to reunite with his parents. Within the year he was married to a Catholic girl from outside the kampung and, despite his parents being nominal Muslims, he was baptised into the Catholic Church.

He and his wife In gained a job in the household of a Dutch Protestant missionary sent to Yogyakarta as a lecturer in the city theological college. Sugi worked in the garden and as a security guard for the house, while In worked inside the house, learning to cook the Dutch way and caring for the children. Through his employers, Sugi later found a job in a cigar factory. He had thus successfully progressed to full employment in the formal capitalist sector. However, he was not content working on the production floor because he wanted to use his own initiative and enterprise and saw the informal sector as offering more opportunities to do that. In 1975, when the factory was downsizing its staff, Sugi applied for retrenchment and used the 'package' to start his own business in brickdust manufacture.

In the meantime Sugi and In had had two children, born in 1972 and 1974, and in 1973 they had added to the river side of their parents' home a further four squares constructed out of plaited bamboo walls on a sawn timber frame on a cement floor. In 1975 Sugi took advantage of demolition work at the cigar factory to bring home a lot of bricks, rebuilding the extension walls as half-brick, half-bamboo. He also extended their riverbank land by pushing out the wall he and grandfather had built by another ten feet, purchasing from Radi the soil he had collected in his aborted attempt to construct a house site. Sugi tells the story of how this new retaining wall kept collapsing, to the point when the artisan offered to resign in embarrassment and shame. Grandfather visited a *dukun* (spirit medium) back in his home village in Wates and learned from him that there was a cornerstone of the wall that "did not want to be there". The stone was described as round with marks on it, as though someone had tried to split it with a metal wedge. Hearing this Sugi demolished the wall, found the offending stone as described and removed it. Thereafter the construction proceeded without trouble. The former cornerstone was removed to grandfather's garden and for years grandfather made offerings of flower petals and burnt incense there to the spirit of the stone.

The history of Sugi's household economy was constructed out of the multiple linkages between the formal structures of the economy and state and the informal endeavours of kampung residents. While Sugi and his wife and parents moved between more and less dependence on the formal economy, their management of land and the construction of their family home demonstrated the complexity of their relationship with the wider state and urban society. They sought to convert land into property that could be recognised by the state, while the construction of their house gradually approached the standard that the state would recognise in terms of being a solid brick home with amenities of piped water, internal toilet and electricity. In part they depended on the formal economy and state services, as for the supply of recycled bricks or the provision of electricity. However, these were not obtained on the terms set by the state or formal economy. Instead the bricks were demolition materials from the factory site, the electricity was tapped by lines illegally connected to the city network. They continued to rely on wells for their water and community ablution blocks. In such ways kampung social relations are constructed out of constant interplay between the more formal aspects of city life such as government or commercial employment, government pensions, registration of land titles, establishment of streetside shops and registration of house construction, and the informal arrangements residents make to guarantee their survival, including street trading and small neighbourhood warung, informal credit, land reclamation, and informal rent arrangements. These are all constantly in flux according to household fortunes.

In 1975 Sugi was elected RT head. The length of the kampung between the upper-level pathway behind streetside properties and the river is split administratively into RT units, each a neighbourhood of originally about 30 households clustered around one or more alleyways. The RT head is elected for a five-year term, as are the other office-holders working within the RT administration, such as secretary, treasurer, women's convenor, youth convenor, and development and public works convenor. These positions are recognised though not paid by the state. All heads of households within the RT meet regularly, usually monthly, to deliberate on RT issues and be updated on state plans for their neighbourhood, as well as to conduct an *arisan* (rotating credit association). The RT head is also responsible for recording the movement of people into and out of the neighbourhood and, in general, for maintaining order. He or she intervenes in marital disputes, family violence, inter-household disputes and the like, as well as organising community relief for families suffering hardships. The RT committee is responsible for the improvement of public infrastructure and social welfare, particularly in the interests of youth, women and the aged. As detailed in Chapter One, John Sullivan suggested that RT, RW and RK kampung officers were authorised by the state to implement state programs and achieve the state aims of national development and social order (Sullivan, 1992: 37). In fact Sugi's leadership role extended well beyond such state initiatives.

At that time in 1975, Sugi and his family, like most of their neighbours, used the river as a toilet, with women often preferring to wait until after dark, particularly as the river was becoming busier with more people occupying the riverflat and sand-diggers operating in the river. In 1976, while Sugi was RT head, neighbourhood toilets and washrooms were built for the RT, with finance coming from the local population and a grant from the Foster Parents' Association, with whom Sugi had established contact. Sugi showed skill and perseverance in negotiating this outcome with the association. Residents provided all the labour and skills to construct the facilities beside a well, which was also improved. The facilities were located on grandfather's riverflat land, a not entirely suitable location because the water table was high and faecal matter drained into the river. However, the new toilet did at least protect people's privacy. Land provided for the toilets was surrendered free of compensation by Sugi's extended family to meet the needs of the wider neighbourhood and it has remained in public use until today. Later Sugi negotiated the construction of a biogas septic unit with a local engineering NGO, hoping to provide biogas for lighting and to ensure the discharge of cleaner effluent into the river. This experiment was less successful: the biogas unit had to be closed months later when neighbours complained about the odour.

The demolition of the cigar factory also gave Sugi the idea for his first business, which he pursued by using his retrenchment package to purchase a man-drawn cart with car tyres for Rp44,000. He used the cart to collect demolition bricks from building sites throughout nearby suburbs. Sugi employed a group of men, including several kampung neighbours and others from villages in the poor Gunung Kidul area to the west of the city, to crush the bricks by hand, using small hammers

Figure 2.5   Sugi's brickdust mill on the streetside.

and metal pipes swung on metal rods. The redbrick dust, used as a cheaper form of mortar in conjunction with sand and lime, was sold from his production site on the bank of the river opposite his home. The cart was also hired out to increase his income.

To supplement their earnings over the years, Sugi and In took in boarders, including myself and my wife, university students from Ambon and Semarang, and high school students. Later in 1980 Sugi obtained a loan from his former Dutch employer, with whom he had remained in contact, to add to his own savings, so that he could purchase a diesel engine and a brick crushing machine (adapted from a rice thresher) to replace the crude hammers. The machine roared to life each morning on the bank opposite the kampung. An expanded area on the roadside above the river was cleared to store the expanding production. Sugi and another two entrepreneurs who started similar businesses along the opposite riverbank were able to participate in the expansion in the city.

As the business expanded, so did the house. In was kept busy both supplying meals to the labour force from a cramped kitchen that spilled out into the backyard and in keeping the business accounts of the enterprise. Typical of Javanese household operations, In kept control of the finances for she thought her husband irresponsible with money. Sugi would ask her for all important outlays in the business. One such venture was to follow his father into tending sheep and goats, feeding them grass from the ample supplies along the river. Sugi built on the riverflat below a permanent brick pen, in which he also stored his brickdust equipment. Sugi was accumulating suitable bricks and timber for house extensions, as well as river stone to push out the retaining wall yet again. In 1979 he moved the wall another ten feet towards the river over the riverflat and contracted riverflat neighbours who were sand-diggers to deliver sand and dump it behind the wall, thereby extending his riverbank land. Nearer the river he constructed a separate building with two rooms and a toilet at riverflat level and a washroom above the toilet at riverbank level. A year later, in 1980, he constructed another building of two squares to the north of this on the riverflat and this he rented out. All of this income helped to finance the extension of his brickdust operations. As the business continued to thrive, Sugi and In built a kitchen and another three rooms as a north wing to his house where grandfather had formerly kept his pigeons. Costs again were reduced through using bricks, tiles and timber collected from demolition sites.

Figure 2.6   The riverflat in the 1980s.

1980s

In the 1970s and early 1980s many riverbank residents ignored the opportunity to move to riverflat areas. The riverflat was seen as the domain of sand-diggers, sex workers and transvestites. It was definitely not the place, in the view of these residents, to bring up children. Riverbank residents were concerned about their teenage sons and daughters associating with riverflat occupants. The riverflat population was seen to cultivate different ways of life, ones that promoted drinking alcohol, eating dogmeat, gambling, tattoos and scanty dress, but which also emphasised equality and the sharing of household equipment over respect for residents of higher social rank. They openly disdained snobbery based on social hierarchy, which they perceived among some riverbank residents, and cast aspersions on any neighbours they saw as belittling them as riverflat occupants or informal-sector workers. Among riverbank residents, riverflat occupants were accepted and even patronised, but only insofar as they adopted what were promoted as kampung norms of behaviour, showing respect for their social superiors and participating in community work projects and in neighbours' life ceremonies. However, as the 1980s proceeded, population pressure in the riverbank areas became so intense that residents began to move below, despite their concerns. There was a burgeoning hope that land title would be granted on the riverflat land and there were riverbank residents ready to sell or lease their riverflat holdings. In the 1990s city government plans would emerge to construct a river wall to contain flooding and better demarcate and enable the official registration of riverflat land. By 1996 the riverflat was as densely populated as adjacent riverbank areas and by 2000 even riverflat homes were being extended by a second storey as families desperately searched for room for their extended families and households.

Sugi's extended family also enlarged. During the 1980s grandmother and grandfather were joined in their side of the house by grandmother's daughter (from her first marriage) and her husband and three children, although two squares in the house continued to be rented out to long-term tenants. Their son-in-law had retired from the army, so the family had his pension to live off, but he remained aloof from community activities and was not happy sharing a house with his in-laws. Eventually the family moved to his village home where his wife, grandmother's daughter, died in the early 1990s. In 1990 grandmother and grandfather moved into Sugi's house and their house was subdivided into five different residences of two squares (3 × 3 metres) each and rented out to tenants. In 2004 each of these rooms was rented for Rp50,000 a month. After the death of grandmother's daughter, management and later ownership of this half of the house came into the hands of grandfather's son by his Wates wife, this son having graduated while in the house and found employment in the provincial government. He later married another university graduate and public servant and transferred to Wonosari, the capital of the Gunung Kidul district of Yogyakarta, but continued to visit at least annually to collect rents and renew ties with his extended family.

In the 1980s Sugi's business was not without challenges. There was competition among the brick dust producers, both for demolition materials and for sales, and some rancour among them when steady customers of one were snapped up by another producer. In her study of Javanese market traders, Jenny Alexander suggested that producers and traders of similar products prefer to be grouped together because this makes it easier for buyers to find the goods they wish to purchase. "Indeed, there appears to be a positive belief that increasing the numbers of households specializing in a particular form of production will benefit all producers. In other words, new producers are seen as increasing the overall size of the market, not as additional competitors for a limited number of sales" (Alexander, 1987: 104). Such may have also been the case among the brickdust producers of Yogyakarta, but there was still concern over the poaching of clients.

The more severe challenge came from the municipal government, which wanted to clear the riverbank opposite Ledok of all enterprises. This riverbank was located in a different administrative subdistrict of the city to kampung Ledok, being adjacent to a long-established elite housing and business area of the city. During the 1970s and early 1980s, the municipal government used the area as a rubbish dump, allowing the refuse gradually to build up on flat land below the bank. Each day clouds of acrid smoke drifted into the kampung as this rubbish was burned off. A settlement of gelandangan (homeless street people) grew up beside the dump, and these people combed through the rubbish to recycle anything of value. At night the riverbank was the domain of prostitutes, who operated from small makeshift stalls alongside the road. There was also a perception among police and city authorities that criminal gangs operated from this area. This led to recurring pressure to clear the area of all its 'less savoury' population. At the same time the municipal government needed to move a number of cut-flower businesses from in front of the nearby railway station in order to widen the road, which turned attention to the vacant land on this same stretch of riverbank. As a result, during the late 1970s and early 1980s, the police and army exerted heavy pressure on this riverbank population, dismantling the shacks of the gelandangan and transporting them out of town, raiding the prostitution stalls and taking the sex workers into custody, and regularly raiding riverflat houses across the river in Sugi's neighbourhood in search of stolen goods and criminals. The municipal government ended the dumping of the rubbish in the area and contracted the construction of massive stone walls to retain the extended riverbank land over the former rubbish dump. Here on the streetside above the river they settled the cut-flower merchants. They also announced plans to make the entire river bank area a nature reserve with the hope of winning the national Beautiful City (*Kota Adipura*) award.

The official pressure on the riverbank area was felt by Sugi and his fellow producers and each was warned to close down. They procrastinated for months while official attention moved elsewhere, but gained only a reprieve. Eventually Sugi found a substitute site beside the newly constructed ring road to the north of the city and in the mid-1980s moved his business there. The new site was not entirely successful, even though by this stage he had bought his own utility vehicle and was able to ferry materials from further away. To survive he had to complement his income by procuring building materials for construction businesses. The urban market was moving away from brick-dust as a building material. Impurities in the brickdust were making it a less attractive material and many preferred the more expensive but stronger cement, especially in the formal sector of housing estate construction. During this period of decline Sugi began to downsize, selling his utility, then his other equipment, as he made the decision to quit the brickdust business.

Instead, in 1985, he and In set up a shop within their home, investing in a set of glass cabinets for the purpose. Since grandmother also ran a shop next door, they negotiated with her for her to sell perishables such as cooked food while they sold manufactured goods such as clothes, books, soaps, medicines and sprays. This did not go entirely to their plan for grandmother continued to sell her full stock of goods, making it uncomfortable for them to compete within their own family. In the kampung, warung of various sizes are a popular means for women particularly to earn an income. These warung vary considerably in capital investment, ranging in size from, for example, a woman selling a few vegetables or hot rice porridge or other food-stuffs on the step outside her home to a well-stocked shop occupying a substantial home area on the ground floor providing all the neces-sities of daily life, from nails and needles to clothes, tinned food and possibly even offering a telephone service. In some neighborhoods, warung struggle to survive, given that they serve only the local popula-tion without much spare cash. Competition is unavoidable, although these Javanese shopkeepers do everything possible to avoid the public semblance of competing. They are well aware of the difficulty any neighbour faces when he/she is a regular client of another warung but wants to shift patronage. The community also commented on where a person was shopping. Some women who came to In's shop from other parts of the kampung served by other warung requested a plastic bag to conceal their purchases when they had to return home past shops owned by their more immediate neighbours. On the other hand, warung operators are often ready to point out the weaknesses of another warung — they do not give credit, or allow so much credit that they are in danger of closing down, or else they charge too highly or have poor-quality produce. Although In and grandmother could not indulge openly in such talk, there were moments of tension in their continued operation in adjacent premises. In and Sugi's shop business

was to last from 1985 to 1998, during which time grandfather died
(in 1990) and grandmother became too frail (in the early 1990s) to
continue her business. She died in 1996.

1990s

The shop was not able to sustain the family and from time to time
was shut when other income sources were available. Sugi and In continued to earn rental income from the houses on riverflat. In 1995–96
Sugi was away repeatedly on work projects with outside contractors.
He took contracts driving vehicles for the Department of Public Works,
while on other occasions he worked as an agent locating building
materials for large commercial builders. In did not always know where
Sugi was. He spent several days away at a time, leaving In under stress
trying to hold the household together. The shop was shut down for
a long period in 1995–96. While the shop was closed and Sugi off
work, they sold off real estate to survive. Sugi had built two houses
on grandfather's riverflat land, one of them was originally a sheep pen
where Sugi kept sheep and goats in the late 1970s, later converted into
room rental property. Both houses were sold in early 1996 to riverflat
neighbours, one for Rp5 million and the other for Rp6.5 million —
the remaining riverflat land was sold to another neighbour.

Using some of this capital, they reopened the shop in April
1996, intent on making it large enough to serve the whole RW of over
100 households by attracting customers with cheaper prices. In 1996
Sugi explained to me the rationale of running a shop in the kampung.
Women, he said, go to the city markets only if they can carry Rp5,000
or so. This is more than enough to buy their daily necessities but they
will not go without this margin of surplus and are thus often tempted
to buy clothes or other luxuries while they are there. As a result, those
with fewer funds prefer to make their purchases in the kampung, buying
smaller quantities of rice or sugar. On one day in November 1996
that I recorded, Sugi and In spent Rp170, 000 on purchasing warung
stock and grossed Rp60,000, attracting a clientele from throughout
the RW. Their aim was to turn over stock quickly by charging lower
prices. People were spending increasing amounts of money on petty
consumer items: bread and cakes in the morning for the children; rice,
cooking oil, kerosene, sugar, tea, cigarettes all sold fast; packaged snacks,
coffee, condensed milk, medicines, stationery, perfumes, deodorants,
cosmetics, hair colouring, soap, biscuits, mosquito repellent, thongs,

and tampons all sold well. Some customers would spend Rp6,000 at a time and many were not put off by a price of Rp500 on the newest range of snacks. In allowed people credit of up to Rp35,000, at which point they either paid their debt or stopped coming. However, In would ensure that community gossip pursued any bad debtors.

In 1995 Sugi and In's daughter married in a ceremony in their house. There had always been cases of a few residents hiring commercial places and contractors on streetside to hold wedding receptions. This trend was increasing because of the loss of open space in the kampung where cooking facilities and seating could be set up. Sugi and In were prepared for this eventuality. The interior of their house was stripped of all internal walls — bamboo panels were easily removed — to create a large space for the ceremony. Preparations took four days, with 100 women from the RT and RW taking part in preparing the food and making flower arrangements. Formal printed invitations were sent to 200 guests, mostly neighbours in the RW, but also grandfather's relatives in the village. On Friday packages of food were sent to neighbours' homes and snacks distributed to local children as an expression of gratitude for the support provided or expected. On Saturday women arrived to cook and make decorations, and these neighbours were also fed. Crockery and cutlery were hired from the local RT stock and special cooking equipment was hired from outside the kampung. A sound system was borrowed from friends. In the evening a Catholic prayer service was held for those of the local Catholic deaconate community scattered over three RW. On Sunday a wedding service was held in the streetside church and a buffet reception provided at home. In pointed out that the buffet was an impressive initiative because it allowed guests to choose their own food, thus avoiding the waste of food left on plates. However, it also reduced the host family's control on how much guests ate. In remarked that she had to provide three times the usual amount of chicken. It would have been the greatest shame imaginable to run out of food for one's guests, a situation which increasingly arose in subsequent years and was remarked upon as hosts adopted the buffet style. In calculated that the wedding cost her Rp3 million, against which she received Rp700,000 in gifts of money from neighbours and family to whose ceremonies she had contributed in times past. People remarked that it was the biggest and best wedding the kampung had seen.

Meanwhile their eldest child was attempting to put himself through university by trading. He borrowed Rp50,000 as capital from a friend to purchase 20 wallets and resell them in a distant town for twice the price. He could not sustain his studies, however, and after five semesters in the Faculty of Economics he quit his studies to concentrate on trading. Almost all his classmates, he related, were sent money regularly by their parents to keep them in studies. His younger brother completed high school in 1995 and, after failing to gain admission to the Gadjah Mada state university, declined to go to a private university because it would cost too much. He was critical of students from middle- and upper-class families who were only at university for status and did not take their studies seriously. In the next years he took various jobs as a cinema assistant, construction labourer, door-to-door salesman, and band musician, without settling at any of them.

By 1996 Sugi was looking for a new enterprise as a sideline, he said, to the warung business. To take advantage of the preference of many women to shop at their local warung, his plan was to purchase shirts, shorts and culottes and deliver them to warung in villages and small towns on the outskirts of the city, sharing the profits with the warung owner. He told the story of buying a jacket at a sale in town for Rp9,000, selling it to a friend for Rp10,000, who then sold it in a shop on the outskirts of the city for Rp20,000. Sugi began by buying clothes at sales in Yogyakarta — later also in Solo, the centre of the textile industry in central Java — and transporting these goods around the vast number of rural markets, sometimes from door to door in the villages. Soon he discovered a cheaper source of clothes from entre-preneurs who imported second-hand clothes from North Asia, mostly Taiwan, Hong Kong and Japan. These merchants were situated in Bandung in West Java, so Sugi began to make the 12-hour train or bus trip to select his wares and transport them back. This required a larger cash outlay, so Sugi successfully applied for a bank loan of about ten million rupiah on the surety of his land title. He also acquired a private loan of Rp500,000, which was repaid within weeks. He introduced his son, daughter and son-in-law, into the business, dividing the clothes with them until his son-in-law was able to begin to make his own trips to Bandung. His son, however, did not show the same interest in this business and reverted to selling children's toys and other items on the streets of Yogyakarta. The clothes business was a highly labour-intensive enterprise. Each time after Sugi's return from Bandung, the clothes had to be carefully inspected, repaired or washed as necessary, then all ironed and folded and packaged into plastic covers with labels attached. During these few days, two or three women neighbours were employed to carry out these tasks.

AFTER THE FINANCIAL CRISIS OF 1998

Through this business Sugi survived the financial crises of 1998–99 by selling his clothes with a minimum mark-up. Nevertheless, the financial crisis eventually destroyed his enterprise when in 2001 the government banned the import of second-hand clothes in order to protect local industry. Sugi's income disappeared. Sugi and In fell on hard times and during the next years ate into their capital. For a while Sugi traded shoes and sandals bought in Surabaya but they sold slowly. They pawned their motorcycle to obtain cash. By 2004 they needed Rp3.3 million to redeem the motorcycle and Rp12 million to redeem their land certificate. When the import of second-hand clothes resumed, though not with official permission, Sugi had unpaid loans to the bank and no capital to restart his business. In 2003 his friend lent him Rp5.5 million and in 2004 a further Rp3.5 million to begin his trading again and to repay the loans. The situation was further complicated at the end of 2004 when his half-brother proposed to sell grandmother's house in order to purchase a land certificate for a house elsewhere that his wife had inherited. Sugi was anxious to buy his half-brother's property, despite his adverse circumstances, rather than allow it to go out of family control.

His married daughter and her husband began their business life selling baskets from the main city tourist street. When the financial crisis reduced their sales, they resorted to a home business, selling noodles and fried rice from home, then creatively expanded this into baking cakes and biscuits in a tin oven set up over a gas flame, gradually acquiring a clientele of those who catered for large receptions. They continued to fulfil occasional orders, even as their business focus shifted. In 1998 they commenced trading in clothes. On his first trip to Bandung the son-in-law took capital of Rp400,000, made up of Rp100,000 of savings and Rp300,000 borrowed from family, but was too confused by the large range of goods on offer to fully spend his capital. Since the resumption of the used clothes business, he has become a canny merchant of women's clothes, in 2004 investing over Rp3 million on each trip. He employed a different pattern of sales to Sugi. Whereas his father-in-law took his wares to rural markets up to two hours by motorcycle from Yogya, he preferred to take his wares from office to office within the city. Each made independent trips to Bandung but they shared information on the best contacts there and the best means of transportation home.

The disruption in his trade for those years had their effect on Sugi's holdings. In 2003 he sold off one block of two rooms on the riverflat and the room above them at riverbank level to a school teacher who had lived with him for several years. Sugi and In also rented out two squares of the main home to two tenant households, in each case a married couple. The pressure on space in the house was relieved in 2000 when his daughter and son-in-law constructed a home above the riverflat rooms beyond the retaining wall. To do this they employed a certified builder from outside the kampung who demolished the rooms below and built a totally new structure containing tenants' rooms below and the daughter's residence above. Over the years they invested in tiled floors, Persian carpets, a DVD player, stereo, clocks and furnishings, an indication of the greater wealth and comfort they now enjoyed compared to Sugi and In. The space in Sugi and In's home was quickly filled when in 2001 their older son was forced by financial difficulties to return home with his wife and young child from where they had been renting near her parents in the north of Yogyakarta. Their younger son had married in 1997 and moved away to his wife's city in East Java. At the same time the well which supplied all members of this extended household was closed over and an electric pump installed to supply a cement tank above the well. Only after it was completed did old people inform Sugi that closing over a well brings bad fortune. This concerned him but he considered that it was too late for him to reopen the well.

AS A COMMUNITY LEADER

The transformations in Sugi's house and land — the extensions of riverbank land, the occupation of riverflat land, the extensions of the house, the building of additional houses and the subdividing of houses — reflected the family's changing fortunes over the years, while in turn reflecting the changes in the wider community. From a stretch of river characterised by trees, bamboo and horticulture on the riverflat in the 1970s, the area is now densely packed with houses, many of them apportioned off in rooms for tenants. In the 1970s many of these tenants were university and high school students from elsewhere in Indonesia. Since then students have moved north to other areas of the city to be closer to the several new campuses. Today's tenants are those involved in casual employment in the city centre such as pedicab drivers, shop attendants, construction labourers, carpenters, and petty traders. These new tenants have brought radical changes in the kampung population. Whereas in the 1970s community activities were in the hands of *pegawai negeri* (civil servants), chosen by virtue of the status of their government positions, since the 1980s there have been proportionally fewer of such pegawai and their influence over the cultural norms of the people has waned. Respect for the social ranks of pegawai, nobility or landowner had diminished. There was also less emphasis on social etiquette such as high Javanese or showing respect by stooping when passing higher-status neighbours. Part of this decline was due to the exodus of the next generation of pegawai, the children of retired pegawai, who moved away from the kampung to housing estates (*perumahan*) by taking advantage of cheap government loans. Several who remained absented themselves from community interaction. The more stridently egalitarian values once associated with the riverflat now began to assume more prominence in the kampung as a whole.

After a decade during which he held no RT or RW office, in 2003 Sugi was elected to the position of RW head for the next five years. This recognition was based on his previous record as RT head and his continued willingness to sacrifice his own interests for the good of the community. In Sugi's case this included providing his house as a venue for community gatherings of all sorts, as well as providing funding for community events. Neighbours recognised his community-mindedness. Entrepreneurs such as Sugi enjoyed some social prestige, especially the more successful and wealthy who displayed their success in the expansion of their homes. Like pegawai, entrepreneurs were considered by their neighbours to be more able to deal with the administrative complexities of the metropolis and to have the means and social standing to lead the community. On the other hand, they were seen as more amenable to community opinion because often their enterprises depended on the labour, resources or purchases of their neighbours. Although households became more inward-looking as television enticed residents out of the alleyways into the privacy of their homes, community was still deemed important for everyone's survival. People sought to maintain a sense of community through arisan and *simpan pinjam* (savings and loans societies) and religious worship, demonstrated through community building projects such as washrooms, bridges, meeting halls and mosques.

Figure 2.7   The monthly RW clinic for elderly residents.

The use of Sugi's house reflected his community concern. Over the three decades Sugi had held positions as RT head, Catholic deacon and RW head, the lack of a community meeting hall in this part of the kampung meant that his home was repeatedly used for community occasions. Some houses hosted RT arisan or simpan pinjam meetings, others were used for communal Islamic prayers, but Sugi's house proved the most amenable to hosting the more important and larger gatherings. The *kroncong* band rehearsed in his home, Catholic prayers were held there, neighbours used it for their weddings, a monthly health clinic was established there for babies and their mothers, as well as a monthly clinic for old people. While I was there in 2004, Sugi was approached by two men from an Islamic school (*pesantren*), who wanted to conduct a healing practice (using electric current and prayer) one afternoon each week in the kampung. Sugi willingly made his house available because he was the RW leader, his house could accommodate such a clinic, and he considered it would look bad if he as Catholic leader and RW head refused those of another religion.

When Sugi was RT head he occasionally had to mediate between neighbours, sometimes within households. This required negotiating skills rather than authoritarian discipline, the desired outcome being peace and harmony rather than the exclusion or punishment of a neighbour. He was very aware of the needs of neighbours. He campaigned strongly for the simplification of rites of passage to make them affordable to all who desired them. He considered the *kendhuren* ritual as too large a financial burden for many and encouraged people to hold a smaller celebration. He organised community members to paint the walls of the houses of their poorer neighbours. Sugi's earlier popularity had been based on his work among the youth of the kampung, where he organised sporting and musical activities. Later he became more involved in church activities and was elected as a deacon for the kampung.

His wife In was a strong advocate of these initiatives and was a leader both among the women of the RT and in the full RW community. She became involved in health programs, training as a health cadre, organising baby-weighing and maternity clinics, family planning clinics, the visiting of the sick in hospital, and visits for the sick to alternative healers. Her knowledge of the composition of each household in the RT/RW contributed to her husband's dealings with these households.

In their roles as RT/RW leaders, Sugi and In had to balance their obligations to government structures with their responsibilities to the community. In the main this was not a contradictory position (contra Sullivan, 1992: 170–1). The power that an RT/RW leader exercises does not originate in the threats of a New Order government associated with militaristic compulsion or administrative stonewalling, but in the ability to encourage conduct and induce residents to be self-regulating by appealing to their own interests within guidelines often, but not always, nominated by government (Foucault, 1977, 1983). As RT leader Sugi kept records of all movements in and out of the RT, records which allowed the government to monitor the population but which more importantly provided the means for individuals to travel to another city and residential neighbourhood and gain entry there because they carried the recommendation of their previous RT leader. The RT/RW/RK leader thereby assisted individual mobility as well as monitoring their freedoms. As RT leader, Sugi negotiated with an outside NGO to finance the installation by the community of public washing-places, toilets and public wells. He organised the community to build steps and ramps to provide access to riverbank and riverflat. He organised the building of a *pos ronda* (security post) on the streetside level alleyway. All these improvements were not at the request of state functionaries but on the initiative of community leaders or the demand of residents. In 2004 he coordinated the construction of a bridge across the river and the planning of an RW meeting hall.

In 2004 Sugi and In occupied a cramped bedroom in their extended house. Their son and family of four occupied another bedroom. A tenant and his family occupied another two rooms. Another square was crowded by a table and various cupboards where Sugi and In did accounts and ate. A large section of the house of four squares was available for meetings, furnished with easy chairs, and used to store various equipment belonging to the RW, such as the sound equipment and crockery and glasses. This comprised the main house of ten squares. Outside the back door was the well, the kitchen with two toilets attached and a further single room usually leased out. Facing his back door was his daughter's home of six squares. Gone were the riverflat expanses his grandfather once tended and the houses Sugi had built there. However, his enterprise over the years was reflected in the expanded area of riverbank land inside a three-metre retaining wall and the expansion of the original house and its improvement in bricks. He owned two motorcycles, although one remained in the pawnshop as a result of his desperate search for capital in 2003 to repay his bank loan. When he died in a road accident in 2006, he left a substantial mortgage on their house. Although many of his neighbours regarded Sugi as well-off because of his well-constructed home, he and In had struggled to survive over the years, their business successes interspersed with periods of hardship when they were forced to sell off real estate, to pawn their assets and to secure loans.

Sugi and In always regarded their house as an asset, not just for their family but also for the community, allowing it to be used for numerous community occasions. Indeed, Sugi was very conscious of his respected standing in the community and was aware that any refusal to allow neighbours to use his house occasionally for meetings or weddings would be seen as evidence of his financial misfortune and threaten his social standing. He was therefore committed to lending his house for these public purposes until the RW hall was completed, for which he was an enthusiastic promoter. He pointed out to me that if he refused his home for public use, meetings would shift to his daughter's house and then she and her husband would gain all the public credit that Sugi would lose. He was therefore prepared to pursue all financial alternatives to keep the home open in this way.

Sugi and In's life story is also the story of a neighbourhood over these decades as residents built community in the homes, through the good offices of leaders like Sugi. These leaders have gained prestige through such offices, but they have also made huge sacrifices of time, energy, home and resources to promote community. In this they were not so much the servants of government as the leaders of fellow residents, with a sense of the hardships, struggles and needs of their neighbours and with the initiative to create opportunities and space for them to survive. The story of Sugi and In's extended household illustrates the complex way in which kampung people negotiate their existence between formal and informal institutions. On the one hand are national and city governments and the regulated capitalist markets, on the other all the informal arrangements based around community and notions of mutual reciprocity by which they establish access to land and home, credit, material property, the assistance of others, and income generating pursuits. These formalisation/informalisation processes are the subjects of the next chapter.

3

State, Kampung and Development

The distinction between 'formal' and 'informal' generally applies to economic sectors or economic activities. However, the distinction is one that may also usefully be applied in discussing social, cultural and political activities. This chapter then deals directly with the question raised in Chapter One, that is the extent to which kampung communities are the construct of and under the control of the state and to what extent kampung residents manoeuvre within and beyond state programs to follow strategies of their own making.

FORMAL AND INFORMAL ECONOMIC ACTIVITY

Dualistic conceptions of 'developing' economies were given new direction in the work of Keith Hart distinguishing 'formal' and 'informal sectors' within the urban economy. In a paper first delivered at a Conference on Urban Unemployment in Africa at the Institute of Development Studies at the University of Sussex in 1971, Hart (1973) categorised informal-sector activities as marked by small-scale, family-type operations, with low capital, maximising family labour, operating in illegal or unregulated areas, marked sometimes by illicit operations, and with ease of entry and low skills. The International Labour Office adopted Hart's distinction and asserted that these operations were central to the economy and needed to be promoted in development activities (ILO, 1972). Following Hart's original formulation, observers around the world identified informal-sector activities in terms of the positive roles they played in economic development. One of the key features of informal activities was seen as their flexibility, this flexibility being the key to survival. While formal workers may work in the same operational area or the same office for all their lives, the informal

Figure 3.1 Food vendor carts parked in a vacant lot.

worker may conduct a number of different operations, even in the same day. The essence of the informal is that it defies codification and state control. It is based on local knowledge and experience more than formal training and skills and has to retain the flexibility to respond to limited opportunities as rapidly as possible for its agents' survival.

The simplicity of this distinction, however, has been questioned over the years. Joseph Gugler, for example, has suggested that "entry into much of the informal sector is far from easy, it is quite common for small-scale enterprises to employ non-family labour; illegal activities may be organized on a large scale ... skills are acquired in the formal school system and in formal-sector employment" (Gugler, 1992: 97–8). He pointed out that "the informal sector can be argued to subsidize the formal sector" in that it employs people, provides an income to those not in the formal sector, and provides cheap services and products like food to those in the formal sector, thus allowing the formal sector to operate on cheaper wages (Gugler, 1992: 99). While continuing to use the term 'informal sector', he emphasises the casual nature of this employment, that is, its instability and insecurity.

This chapter focuses on the recognition of economic activities that are not enumerated or regulated within the formal state system. As such they may represent alternative, local solutions that do not readily find a place within the state's development programs. However, just as they may represent a subsidy of formal-sector wages and production, they may also be written into development programs as the people's contribution to state initiatives, thereby becoming tools of state coercion, as Sullivan and others would argue (Chapter One). Thus it is essential to identify the place that these informal activities occupy within the larger economy of the kampung and city. In Ledok these have included digging and selling river sand, recycling used clothing, driving pedicabs, baking cakes for sale, producing handicrafts for the tourists, busking or pavement trading, to name a few. These informal activities also include casual labour such as short-term work in government construction or public works programs, including temporary work in the government employment schemes. When I began research in Ledok in the 1970s, just over a third of kampung household heads were government employees (pegawai) and another 14 per cent were employed as *karyawan* (employees) in the formal state-regulated sector of the economy, usually as shop assistants or hotel, factory or workshop employees. Both these groups were part of the formal economy, enjoying low but regular income, while pegawai could also hope for a pension in their retirement. For this reason, pegawai enjoyed high status in the kampung, even though they were seldom wealthy and often had to supplement their government wages with secondary jobs. Over the next three decades a small number of pegawai, particularly the younger generation, took advantage of government credit schemes to purchase homes in the burgeoning housing estates on the city outskirts, such that the proportion of formal-sector employees in the kampung declined. The decline was noticeable in another way as the positions of kampung officers held predominantly by pegawai in the 1970s increasingly fell to non-pegawai in subsequent years.

The other 50 per cent of household heads in the 1978 kampung survey were classified by local kampung leaders into the three groups: entrepreneurs (*swasta*), traders (*dagang*) and casual labour (*buruh*), all of whom sought their income in the informal sector of the economy. In an earlier publication I narrated the stories of five families who migrated to the city from nearby and remote villages to find work and who settled on the riverflat (Guinness, 1977). These life stories recounted their various attempts to make an income within the informal sector of the city economy in economic pursuits like sand-digging, prostitution and theft, all of which were outlawed by the city's formal regulatory institutions. As squatters they constructed makeshift shelters on riverflat

Figure 3.2　A breakfast food stall.

areas along both sides of the river, occasionally being offered more formal places on the riverbank under the patronage of a kampung landholder. A key to the success of their struggles for economic and social survival was their ultimate acceptance into the kampung community. Many of them began their city residence on the opposite riverflat, where they had no claim on membership in a city neighbourhood. As they became known to kampung residents, they were invited to occupy riverflat on the kampung side of the river and became recognised members of the neighbourhood community, participating in neighbours' life ceremonies, contributing their labour to neighbourhood work projects, and shopping and accumulating debts at local warung. However, while many of them succeeded in gaining acceptance for their economic pursuits and their residence and participation in kampung life from their kampung neighbours, they did not necessarily enjoy the same recognition from the state, which continued to outlaw their income pursuits and challenge their squatter rights.

　　Although it is convenient to present the informal economic activities as distinct from those of the capitalist-state economy, in Ledok the two broad categories of activity are intricately interwoven. For example, various shop and foodstalls serve the residential population. None of

Figure 3.3   A *sate* seller prepares his wares.

these requires a formal operating licence from the state, although in recent years it has become necessary to hold a licence to sell alcoholic drinks. Thus, while all would be characterised by family labour, small capital and operations beyond state licensing, a small part of the business of those who sell alcohol is overseen by the state. However, in terms of their continued operation, these shops and foodstalls depend heavily on income from the formal sector, and that not just from formal-sector employees who purchase daily necessities there. A well-stocked and solidly built shop, for example, may reflect the fact that its owner works as a pegawai and regularly invests some of her salary into the operation of the shop, from which she supports her better-off lifestyle. Alternatively, the pension of a retired male pegawai may be recycled each month through the warung, from which his wife feeds and provides for her family without ever increasing the capital investment in the foodstall. In the case of these household economies, there are a variety of intensive linkages between formal and informal economic activities.

By the 1980s, observers increasingly saw informal-sector activities not as the entrepreneurial triumph of economic agents in survival outside state regulation or financial dependence on private corporations but "as an attempt by formal-sector capital, acting with the complicity of the state, to reduce wage costs and enhance flexibility by making use of unprotected workers in the informal sector" (Meagher, 1995: 260). This was seen as a process of informalisation in which the state had been complicit (Castells and Portes, 1989: 134). According to this informalisation approach, "informality is analysed as a social and historical process, rather than as a sector" (Meagher, 1995: 264). Both informalisation and its opposite, formalisation, suggest that persons and activities may come under fluctuating pressures to conform to public regulations or state control. The dichotomy of two distinct sectors can obscure how informal and formal operations mutually interact, how individuals and families may combine informal and formal activities, drifting between one and the other. In her account of traders in Jakarta, Jellinek (1991) describes how street traders, long encouraged by officials in their provision of cheap and accessible food, were suddenly banned from the streets because they purportedly obstructed traffic. This redefinition of the formal, regulated sector of the city forced these workers into other income-generating activities beyond the formal sector. In a similar fashion, Jakarta had a history of tolerating, then banning *becak* (pedicab) operators as the number of becak increased beyond the control of municipal authorities to the point where they obstructed other vehicular traffic (Azuma, 2001).

The focus on informalisation and formalisation processes may thus show how state and kampung actors are constantly negotiating the relative weight that is put on the direction and control which the state seeks to impose on kampung residents and society. It may also draw attention to the flexibility and autonomy which kampung agents are able to gain in the process. More recently scholars have drawn attention within the urban economy to alternative economic representations to the dominant 'formal' capitalist-state systems. The interest of these scholars has been in repoliticising the economy, noting the linkages and resistances between alternative economies within a particular society. Gibson-Graham (1996) point out the diversity and contradictions within capitalism and the disparate relationships that characterise the links between capitalist and non-capitalist activities. These are particularly evident when we examine the economy of households whose members may be variously employed in formal and informal, capitalist and non-capitalist activities.

FORMALISATION AND INFORMALISATION IN STATE-KAMPUNG RELATIONS

This analysis uses the concepts of formalisation and informalisation in a wider sense than residents' flexible participation in the urban economy in order to address as well the political, social and cultural aspects of kampung life. During the period of the New Order government (1966–1997), state regulation and control became intrinsic to local organisation and development. Population surveys, family planning and health programs, local administrative structures, compulsory schooling, house fumigation, police control of criminal activities, political campaigns, and much else signified the incursion of state regulation into kampung affairs. Standards were established and procedures set in place to confirm those standards (Dick, 2002: 218–52). However, much kampung activity continued beyond the reach of these state controls, signifying an intricate relationship between more formal/less formal, more informal/less informal activities. In a kampung such as Ledok, for example, there are both formal and informal arenas for earning an income, formal and informal housing (the latter not subject to formal building requirements), formal and informal access to electricity and water (informal access where households have arrangements to steal or borrow these supplies outside the knowledge of the state corporations), and formal and informal associations of neighbours (the former to transact government business, the latter to serve the community). Seen in this light, there is always a range of options open to individuals and households and people may shift from a closer alignment with state regulations to a lesser one. The distinction remains useful in terms of categorising some activities as largely regulated, codified, and defined by the state and allied corporate business, as opposed to some other activities outside immediate control and regulation and often illegal, unstable and exploited by formal-sector operators. In terms of services or association, 'informal' refers to a range of activities where individuals or communities negotiate their own path beyond the knowledge of the state.

Within kampung society, there is a range of commitment to formal and informal social norms and cultures. Many of the RT/RW leaders are elected because their neighbours understand them to be more familiar with formal procedures and contacts, not only those laid down by the state but also those accepted within the urban elite of the city who administer the state and capitalist corporations. For these leaders, formal aspects of Javanese etiquette and the state expectation of bureaucratic formalities within neighbourhood meetings hold a larger importance, as does the paperwork that flows between their offices and the lowest rung of salaried administration, the kelurahan office. Among them there may be heightened insistence on formal codes such as the use of the Indonesian language, or perhaps the more formal language level of high Javanese in any public gathering, or strict etiquette in dealing with office-holders. In his study of a kampung in Solo, Siegel (1986) suggests that *Kromo*, the high-Javanese speech level, is used to suppress a lower level of language in which one could express one's real intention. With Kromo all is formalised, social hierarchy and order are maintained, and spontaneity and individuality suppressed.

However, the formal does not hold guaranteed precedence in kampung affairs. Stories are told of one office-holder in Ledok who would conduct business with residents only within designated office hours. He was not elected again to the office. The approved manner for RW/RT leaders to operate is in a more relaxed mode, making themselves accessible to residents at all hours. Similarly, kampung people recognize a diversity of moralities in social relationships. At one end of the scale are those who pride themselves on upholding the formal etiquette of a palace-style (*kraton*) Javanese culture, insisting on the proper respect being paid to those of more noble ancestry, higher education or formal office. This is a code designated in court documents and until the 1980s taught in 'manners' (*tata kromo*) classes within local schools. It is also upheld ostentatiously by certain prominent and long-term residents in Ledok's riverbank area. At the opposite end of the scale are those usually living on riverflat who pay scant regard to the 'formal' moral rules of social interactions accepted in elite social circles. They exercise a very different set of social relationships that allow neighbours to enter each other's house uninvited, borrow equipment, and indulge in gambling, cockfights, and the consumption of alcohol and dogmeat, which are formally disapproved of even in kampung society and culture. They are critical of their more 'formal' neighbours for their 'snobbish' lack of generosity, their inflexibility and their profit-seeking.

Riverflat criticism of formal procedures and manners, however, may not always be openly championed. For example, in the late 1990s when the state formalised title over riverflat land by surveying the local population and their practices of land tenure, Radi, a long-term

Figure 3.4   Riverflat housing on former garden land.

riverflat resident who had long privately expressed his rights to claim the riverflat land he occupied, absented himself from the process and knowingly allowed his wealthier neighbour and landlord, a university lecturer, RT office-holder and kampung property owner, to determine with the survey team the status and boundaries of the land. Perhaps he was aware that he was occupying part of his powerful neighbour's land, or that he had little influence over the survey process, and thus absented himself from the negotiations in an attempt to invite his neighbour's generosity. Any rights he might have had were thus overlooked in this process, leaving Radi to complain about how the formal process had marginalised him. James Scott refers to this as a "weapon of the weak" — "the prosaic but constant struggle between the peasantry and those who seek to extract labour, food, taxes, rents and interest from them. Most of the forms this struggle takes stop well short of collective outright defiance" (Scott, 1985: 29). It was clear in this case that Radi's struggle was against a neighbour who was more adept and more powerful within the formal social system of the wider urban society. Radi's best hope was to turn away from that formal code and appeal to values and perspectives that characterised the informal world of the kampung.

INFORMAL KAMPUNG SOCIETY

This analysis characterises kampung social patterns as informal in the sense that they are not regulated or standardised, are beyond state strictures and do not fit the state-sanctioned code. In this they contrast with the ways of formal government that impose, or attempt to impose, uniformity on society and culture. Just as informal economic activities remain to some extent outside government control and even knowledge, so these informal social patterns have their dynamic outside formal government procedures and become a point of identification of neighbourhood residents beyond the control of the state. This informality may be quite hidden to state and other outside agents in their efforts to reform, improve or develop kampung society. The lack of uniformity is a point of identification and of pride for kampung people. That is not always appreciated by outside agents, as I will demonstrate by discussing outsider projects that have undermined such patterns.

What continues to characterise kampung people's survival strategies is flexibility, often forced upon them by economic circumstances. This flexibility pertains to all aspects of life, from rubbish disposal, house construction and healthcare to rites of passage and neighbourhood meetings, leadership patterns, and savings and loans provisions. As part of informal culture, the strategies are always developed in relation to, but also additional to, formal procedures laid down by outside authorities and sometimes followed by internal authorities. These informal strategies may recognise that the standards or efficiencies espoused by the state or the formal economy have merit, but also that kampung residents need to take into account all kinds of other exigencies dictated by their low income and community way of life.

These informal processes commonly acknowledge the importance of communal norms and obligations. The strength of this community ethic is such that life is made difficult for those in the kampung who ignore the community. Certain long-term kampung residents regard it of prime importance to instil this informal, community ethic in their neighbours. Joyo, a retired government employee in the railways, is an example. His extended family occupies five adjacent houses in the centre of Ledok and its members have held various positions within the RT/RW administration, including RW/RT head, and women's and youth convenors. Joyo has a strong sense of a body of Javanese values and beliefs that provides an essential guide for himself and the next generation. He deplores the neglect of these values in more recent school programs and their substitution by curricula focusing on specific religions. He insists that parents have the prime responsibility for passing these values on to the next generation. Parents should begin, he said, by controlling their speech, even as early as when their child is in the womb. *Budi pekerti* refers to the natural ability, the disposition to good deeds that parents bestow on their children, which 'clothe' a person when he/she dies and which God rewards either through the person or through his/her descendants. Others in the neighbourhood commented that the success of Joyo's family was due to him being *prihatin* throughout his life, that is, sacrificing his own interests for the benefit of his children, for example by enabling them to get full schooling. Joyo's paternal grandfather was a medium and healer (dukun) who had been inspired through ascetic discipline and who passed on numerous Javanese sayings (*tembung Jawa*) to his grandson Joyo. Joyo considered it important for children to adopt *sopan santun*, a code of Javanese behaviour which, through overt linguistic and bodily signs, expresses respect for those of superior age, and/or social standing in the community. It is these values that Joyo espoused in the neighbourhood community, in earlier times insisting that those who had less regard for these values, such as the riverflat residents, come to appreciate the respect and deference on which community is based. He was a champion of the Javanese language with its refined Kromo level to express respect, even though he was and is equally at home with the more egalitarian Indonesian language. Within the community he represents a viewpoint that occasionally clashes with the strident egalitarianism that usually characterises riverflat residents' behaviour. There is a subtle distinction here between the egalitarian and anti-authoritarian values associated with riverflat and casual labourers and the values of a more hierarchical and more formal Javanese court tradition espoused by government employees and long-term residents of high social rank. This contrast between sets of values within the kampung rarely emerges dramatically into the public arena, because it would then focus attention on the socio-economic distinctions among residents rather than on their common interests.

The relationship of these informal processes to the formal urban world is always in flux, as the state introduces edicts and projects and as locals respond. As indicated in the previous chapter, there have been enormous changes in the kampung, though not always appreciated by outside agents intent on implementing their own vision of change. The most significant among these changes are those which challenge and transform understandings of the nature and operation of neighbourhood communities. Clearly the scope of community varies depending on each individual. Those with superior economic and social resources tend to have wider images of the community, encompassing the whole RW (an administrative unit of 100 or so households) or perhaps even the whole kampung. Others with little social capital see their community in a much narrower way, incorporating their children's or siblings' families who live nearby and their most immediate neighbours. In either case, people see the community as a social resource, to which they have social obligations and from which they expect benefits.

The individualistic focus of the consumer culture in contemporary urban society puts a heavy strain on kampung expressions of community and certainly dissuades some kampung people from looking to their neighbours for support. The younger generation is much more comfortable with that consumerist culture than the older generation. For example, the shopping mall less than a kilometre away holds no fears for the young, yet many of the older residents have yet to enter it and some have no wish to do so. This consumer trend does not necessarily point to radical changes in the importance of neighbourhood community for it is clear that as young people marry, settle into the area with their families and struggle to make a living, values of community become far more relevant to them. However, some youth do move out altogether, most strikingly to newly constructed housing estates that symbolise the emerging forces of consumerism and individualism. Other residents have moved back to the kampung after long absences on the streetside of other cities and bring back some of those more aloof and individualistic habits, to the condemnation of their kampung neighbours. There is a strong current of discourse in the kampung that upholds community values and condemns their detractors. Streetsiders, for example, are criticised by kampung residents for being individualistic — no one will come to your aid if you live on the streetside, kampung people say, there are no community forms of cooperation there, people don't even talk to neighbours. In comparison to such localities, kampung residents see themselves as enlightened and streetside society as sold out to materialist individualism. Villagers, on the other hand, are criticized for being clumsy in their practices of community, for example in holding rites of passage requiring huge expenditures that they cannot afford, while neglecting the basic rule of hospitality of welcoming guests with a drink when they have travelled long distances to attend such ceremonies. Prestige in the kampung is a reflection of the host's ability to invite the largest number of neighbours to the most lavish of ritual occasions without endangering the household's financial future. The villagers' ambition to imitate the rituals of the elite was not adjusted to their financial circumstances. As a result, they risked humiliating themselves by being unable to sustain the ritual.

Kampung residents sometimes tried to acculturate others into the informal ways of the community. For example, in regard to former gelandangan settled on the bank and riverflat opposite Ledok, kampung residents commented on their clumsy attempts to practise the art of community. They held large ceremonies for prestige, then ran out of food. They were making an effort to put communal values into practice, but needed advice from their kampung neighbours as to how to do that successfully by tailoring their ritual preparations to their household means. Kampung people therefore prided themselves on perfecting community practices, scaling down the expectations in rites of passage to cater for beleaguered resources, or tapping into available informal sources of finance. All this demonstrated their ability to tailor ritual practices to the financial circumstances of the household and community.

KRISMON: THE FINANCIAL CRISIS

The financial crisis (*Krismon*) that brought the downfall of the New Order government in 1998 severely affected kampung residents. It tested the capacity of formal state programs to provide for affected kampung residents and demonstrated the continued viability of the informal strategies of the neighbourhood communities. Large numbers of factories and small businesses throughout the country were forced to close down permanently, while in others working hours or employee numbers were cut drastically (Hardjono, 2000). By 2000 there was still little sign of a lasting recovery (Mackie, 2000), although the number of people living in poverty and unemployment was lower than had been anticipated in 1998. Continuing problems of corruption, collusion and nepotism continued to plague the country (Manning and van Diermen, 2000).

Contemporary accounts of the crisis provide more detail of the difficulties for kampung residents throughout Yogyakarta. In his eye-witness study in Kricak Kidul kampung in Yogyakarta, Hotze Lont (1999; 2005) notes that the Krismon first became noticeable in January 1998 after the exchange rate of the rupiah plummeted: "From then on the rising prices dominated conversations between neighbours, and it worried people a lot" (Lont, 1999: 9). Residents complained of the doubling of petrol and egg prices and the tripling of chicken prices. One informant said that many people ate only rice, *sambal* (chilli sauce) and tempe (soy bean biscuits). Kricak Kidul residents were less able to save and were forced to eat less, substituting tempe or tahu (soybean cake) for meat or simply eating their rice with vegetables. They began to pawn their possessions, televisions and radios if they had them, and their clothes. The electrical equipment could be pawned at the government pawnshop at lower interest but clothes were accepted only by private moneylenders. Even these moneylenders were stretched close to bankruptcy (Lont, 1999: 12). Lont notes that relatives were usually a source of assistance only of last resort, because they were in similar financial straits.

In Ledok the years 1998–99 were also the period when the crisis made the most serious impact. During this time, residents remarked that rice doubled in price to over Rp4,000 and sugar from Rp2,400 to Rp3,600 a kilogram. The national government released rice from stockpiles to kampung residents, much of it of poor quality and smelly. It was sold for Rp1,000 per kg with a limit of five kilograms in any sale but residents claimed they had to buy better rice to mix with it to make it edible. People sold what they could: motorcycles, bicycles, furniture, clothes. One riverflat man grew bananas for sale. Another couple dredged rocks from the river and cracked these into gravel as suitable raw material for construction concrete — continuing to do this work until 2004. The number of beggars and buskers on the streets increased dramatically. A group of Ledok youths busked by performing songs and instrumental music at pavement restaurants (*lesehan*) on the main tourist and shopping street; an old woman begged outside the nearby church and mosque; and a Ledok man with his young children begged from passing motorists at a major road intersection. There were stories of hardship in meeting school costs. Several families had to take their children out of school at this time and some students never returned to complete their senior high school education. A few gave up any idea of university education. In an urban economy that increasingly stipulated senior high school or university qualifications for even undemanding formal-sector employment, dropping out had serious consequences. There was reportedly a sharp increase in demand for informal credit. Many households purchased small capital items from roving traders (*pengecer*) such as kitchen utensils and clothes. These loans were paid back on a daily basis. In 2000 many households reported that they had substantial debts to pawnbrokers and neighbours and were in a never-ending process of taking loans to cover loans.

Lont (1999: 9–10) reported that the most seriously affected in Kricak Kidul were those who ran warung and could not entirely pass on the rising cost of goods; construction workers laid off from larger projects that ran into financial difficulties; and those who made garments at home, for whom the sale of such garments no long covered the cost of materials. Government employees also reported that their extra bonuses had dried up when special projects were stopped. Residents created new jobs for themselves such as washing the laundry for local prostitutes, making rings out of coins, searching for passengers for buses, establishing fishing boxes in the river, even digging up used coffins to sell the wood.

Writing of the impact on kampung in the city of Malang in East Java, Marianti (1999) reported that medical expenses increased by up to 400 per cent. People there died because their families could no longer afford the medical expenses. One asthmatic's medication rose in cost from Rp2,500 to Rp8,500 a month. Traditional medicines (*jamu*) and healers (dukun) became very popular as alternatives to the expensive biomedical system.

The effects of the crisis were still apparent during my visit to Ledok in 2000. Poverty is often hidden in such communities for few will admit to having nothing. In Ledok in 2000 various small informal income opportunities allowed residents to make do from day to day. Some dug sand when other jobs were not available, others went fishing. Women prepared cooked food such as rice porridge, noodles and tofu for sale in the alleyways in the morning or fried snacks later in the day. One man started making furniture for a friend instead of trading in used clothes. Another took advantage of a village visit to buy watermelons, which he sold back in the kampung. Another safety net was provided by pawning or selling goods. One pawned his television set, another sold his motorbike. A carpenter gradually sold all his tools. He went for two months without work; at other times work was irregular. In public he said that everything was all right and that the crisis had made little difference, but privately he admitted to me that it was an endless struggle. In his enforced lay-off, he had

Figure 3.5 *Becak* parked on the upper path.

improved the small 20-square-metre section of the house he occupied with his wife and three children as *pengindung* (land tenants) by using scraps culled from building sites such as tiles, lengths of teak timber, and a mirror. He was attempting to use his contacts to make a few real estate deals, offering his knowledge of houses and rooms for rent or sale. A single young man who worked in the construction industry admitted to being out of work sometimes for a month at a time. The main thing, his mother added, is that we still have rice to eat.

Employment in 2000 reflected the hard times, with a steady decline in the numbers of government employees. Many residents remained in multiple employments: as *satpam* (security guard) and becak (pedicab) driver; security guard and *padat karya* (government work scheme); sand-digger and padat karya; trader in fruit and in clothes; catering and satpam. Employment flexibility remained the key to survival. Residents took up other tasks on offer, picked up trading opportunities, and accepted labouring jobs in addition to their main occupation. Some reported much lower turnover in their business after the crisis. A becak driver whose main clients were foreign tourists reported he was so badly affected that he joined padat karya programs instead. Most shopkeepers reported that they were all but put out of business during the crisis because the prices of daily necessities rose so much on some days that they could not replace the stocks they had sold the previous day. Their stock became gradually depleted, until some of them decided they could not continue to pour capital into the business. Construction labour also found work scarce. Others, however, were able to move into other avenues of work or keep their business going by actively recruiting orders. A tailor kept his business alive by visiting factories to recruit orders for uniforms, while several others moved into the used clothing trade.

In this critical situation residents turned principally to informal strategies, but there were also formal-sector provisions made for them. The formal programs were instigated by World Bank loans to the Indonesian Government and other initiatives by corporate business.

SOCIAL SAFETY NET — THE FORMAL RESPONSES

The World Bank Programs were implemented by the Indonesian Government through a program labelled *Jaring Pengamanan Sosial* (JPS) or Social Safety Net. I will examine various aspects of the program as it affected Ledok and other kampung.

a) Food Distribution

As a response to the inflationary crisis, international bodies such as the World Bank arranged distribution of rice to urban areas, including Ledok. The food distribution was administered by the kelurahan office, from where it was directed to RT units considered to include needy households. Over 12 months, each household was issued monthly with a package of 25 kilograms of rice, sugar, tea and Indomie instant noodles, regardless of household size and, in some cases, of need. The list was compiled through RT and RW office-holders. The rice was called 'American' rice, which residents mixed with better rice to make it tasty enough to eat. This purchase of better rice incurred extra expense for residents and in consequence some residents rejected their quota while others sold theirs.

Commenting on the implementation of another JPS program in Sriharjo village outside Yogyakarta, Agus Dwiyanto (1999) observed that community members had different views from the government about who constituted households living below basic needs. This difference in opinion led to complaints to the village authority and, as a compromise, rather than the poorest households receiving ten kilograms of rice, every family received rice but of a quantity less than ten kilograms. The social jealousy generated by such programs of assistance "led to a process of social exclusion of the poor people in the community network" (Dwiyanto, 1999: 12). In rural West Java, Breman and Wiradi (2002: 30) reported "the immediate and down-right refusal by most well-to-do households to agree that the cheap rice should be set aside for the poor in the village", thus ensuring that rice was evenly apportioned among all. Reporting on a village in Central Java at the same time, Juliette Koning (1999) instanced a number of projects that supplied cheap rice for sale to villagers from the military, the National Family Planning Board and the district government, commenting that it was difficult to detect whether the rice was getting to the right people because richer villagers frequently purchased the right to the rice (in the form of a blue card) from poorer villagers, who could not afford the cheap rice, and then resold it. Villagers could not remember a time when the village had been supplied with as many aid programs in such a short period of time. There was much doubt in Koning's mind whether villagers shared the government's sense of crisis.

In Ledok there was also some community dissension over rice distribution. Some residents considered that all residents in the RT should receive a package; others thought that only the very poor should be targeted. Packages were uniform in size, despite the variation in size of household and level of need. This inevitably meant that the poorest were not helped as much as they might have been. In recounting these times, many recalled the poor taste and quality of the rice but acknowledged how desperately the food was needed at the time and that some residents would not have survived without it. Besides the national program, other local bodies offered help. In Ledok nearby businesses of Bank Bali and the state oil company Pertamina, both with headquarters adjacent to the kampung, offered similar packages through the kelurahan, while the local Catholic church and Muslim mosques gave assistance to residents. All such programs symbolised kampung reliance on the formal institutions of the wider society. In the end, no-one in the kampung went hungry and there were no major outbreaks of illness during the crisis.

b) Work Programs

Work programs (padat karya) were also instituted under the Safety Net program. These provided finance for labour on a variety of projects selected by kelurahan staff from requests submitted by RW office-holders. Each project was assigned a budget under a labour contractor, who employed the labour teams. In the padat karya scheme, labour gangs of ten workers, in the main unemployed kampung youth, were assigned to a particular task such as the laying of bricks along a kampung alleyway, the building of steps or the laying of pipes. They were each paid Rp8,200 per day and a set number of days was allocated for the completion of each project. A kelurahan office-holder supervised the work and sometimes an outside contractor was appointed. The money for materials was administered under another section of kelurahan bureaucracy and materials ordered through official suppliers. For example, the construction in October 2000 of the drainwater pipeline linking the top drain with the river was supported with a budget of Rp7 million, which did not include the padat karya labour costs. The formal aims of each project were achieved, that is the path or pipes were laid, but kampung residents were highly critical of the worth of the projects. In their eyes, the projects failed to recognise the capacity of the informal sector of the neighbourhoods. While physical infrastructure was undoubtedly improved, the opportunities to develop human skills and community resources were neglected. According to kampung priorities, work could have been contracted out to local entrepreneurs, not only developing their experience but acknowledging their local knowledge and social contacts. Kampung informants insisted that they would have made much better use of resources because their personal supervision of the projects would have lead to cost savings and achieved higher productivity among the workers.

These projects were generally acknowledged by residents to have provided work to the unemployed. Many were youth but among them were also casual workers with families such as Man, who was a sand-digger and keeper of sheep, and Radi, who was a security guard (satpam) and sand-digger. Residents were critical of the program, saying that labourers were given little training or skills, nor was there any thought of where such work would lead them when the program ceased. Moreover discipline was low and attendance irregular. Workers admitted that frequently several of their team of ten were absent on any one day. There was some discussion as to whether this meant that the labour contractor pocketed the absentees' wages. However, I observed one very effective session when workers laboured into the late afternoon to complete a set of steps. In their study of a Solo kampung, Musiyam and Wajdi (2000: 62) observed that padat karya projects tended to change work patterns in poor households because the poor took advantage of them when they had no other work. However, such

Figure 3.6 RT neighbourhood stairs.

projects did not guarantee permanent work and, once a project had been completed, the poor or unemployed were back just where they had been before. This was the case in Ledok, where many of the workers regarded *padat karya* as a stop-gap measure to be undertaken only if other more long-term employment was not available. This explained their irregular attendance.

Some kampung leaders expressed regret that the administration of such work programs was largely taken out of kampung hands. When Ledok RW leaders forwarded the names of unemployed residents and preferred projects to kelurahan officers, they received no further news on the process. Then suddenly, some time later, a project was 'dropped' on them, although financial and labour control was still out of their hands. They claimed that they could manage the projects more successfully if consultation was continuous and the kampung community retained control over the day-to-day direction of work and finance. They claimed that under such conditions they would achieve more with the cash available and, at the same time, enhance community capacity to manage their own environment. In February 1999 the Indonesian Minister of Labour, Fahmi Idris, recognised such weaknesses (Anon, 1999). He admitted that the padat karya program had merely taken over a program administered centrally by the National Development Planning Body, BAPPENAS. In the future he proposed that padat karya be channelled through community organisations, so that its planning would reflect the desires and needs of the community and finance be surrendered directly by the local bank to the community to prevent 'leakages'. The purpose of such a program would be to encourage the community to stand on its own feet, with the hope that it would grow economically.

The *Kompas* newspaper journalist who wrote this article added that such a hope rested on the target population having an entrepreneurial spirit (*berjiwa wiraspada*), as well as on there being a political and social climate conducive and supportive to small businesses and poor people. Such, the journalist noted, did not appear to be the case. However, the journalist accepted elite assumptions about kampung populations, giving them little credit for skill or initiative. Ledok residents did not agree that they were incapable of managing such projects. Instead they argued for the strength of formal programs to be merged with the informal activities and institutions of the kampung. As with the rice distribution, the padat karya project demonstrated the ineffectiveness of formal-sector provisions when divorced from the informal mechanisms of kampung society. These programs were based on elite assumptions about the nature of kampung community, particularly that residents would accept an identification and targeting of the poor. Although financial help proved vital to some families, overt targeting of the poor was potentially shameful to those households. Kampung community assistance to the poor is much more subtle than this, concealed in labour contracts, loans and credit arrangements. Secondly, the elite policy-makers assumed that residential communities would participate eagerly in programs that were essentially top-down with a minimum of consultation or cooperation. In consequence, these programs threatened to undermine community within the kampung, a result which might have surprised their elite sponsors.

c) Credit Programs

Another Safety Net program, a special loans program, modelled on the successful Grameen bank in Bangladesh, was set up with finance from the World Bank, managed through the *Kotamadya* (City), *Kecamatan* (Subdistrict), and *Kelurahan* administration. At the kelurahan level, the program was termed *Pengembangan Badan Keswadayaan Masyarakat*, or Promotion of People's Empowerment Organisations; at the city government level it was termed *Proyek Pengentasan Kemiskinan Perkotaan* or Urban Poverty Relief Project, administered as part of the Social Safety Net–Social Division. The first distribution to the local kelurahan was made in early 2000, with a sum of Rp100 million, 90 per cent of which came from the International Monetary Fund and 10 per cent from Indonesian Government contributions. These funds were divided among over 50 credit groups, including 23 in Ledok. Residents made applications in groups of between five and ten men and women, each member submitting a detailed plan and budget and rationale for their project. These were vetted by the rest of their small group and approved by RT and RW leaders before being submitted through the kelurahan office to a citywide selection panel said to include city municipal officers, students and religious leaders. The maximum that could be awarded to any group was Rp10 million. If selected, the group was then allocated a sum of money and it was up to them how to divide the cash. In the cases I observed in Ledok, the allocated amount was divided evenly among group members, even though they had requested different sums of money. The money was to be paid back in 12 monthly payments, including interest at 18 per cent a year. Each group appointed a collector of monies, whose task was to gather the individual members' repayments and deposit them in the name of the group in the bank. As initial loans were also distributed via the bank, no cash passed through the kelurahan office, although the selection panel at the city level took a percentage. The smallest loan in Ledok was Rp300,000 and the largest Rp2 million.

By October 2000, 70 groups in Ledok had received a loan. These and all the other similar group loans in the kelurahan were financed through the recycling of the original Rp100 million advance. This was seen by administrators of the scheme as a remarkable achievement. None of the Ledok groups had fallen behind in their loan repayments. Notably in this case, the effectiveness of this formal scheme depended on informal kampung processes. Social norms of behaviour among neighbours meant that members or RT leaders were rarely critical of individual projects and regarded it as an individual's responsibility to repay the loan, being bound by a legal contract to forfeit goods to the value of the borrowing if the loan was not repaid over three consecutive months. However, if any individual in the group failed to repay the loan, all members of the group suffered by being excluded from consideration for future loans. Despite this formal procedure, which was intended to harness community strengths as a guarantor of the success of these loans, the appeal to group members to watch over each other's loan arrangements was not enough to galvanise more critical action of the group towards each individual member's project. It was clear to many in the neighbourhood that some projects were not feasible, such as another small shop when there were already several, or a poultry-breeding project in an unhealthy environment. Six months after the initial loan, several of the businesses were no longer operating or showed little growth. The petty entrepreneurs admitted that they were repaying loans out of savings or other earnings such as their pensions.

In such cases, outside donors and government officials sought to formalise the informal relationships of co-residents, recognising in them a moral strength not present in regular government dealings with off-street neighbourhoods. However, these formal arrangements did not allow informal opinion and judgement of neighbours to play a significant role, thus bypassing important informal strategies of social sanctions. In fact, almost the opposite occurred. Residential groups contrived a concerted approach to the formal credit program, protecting each other from government interference. The way the program was instituted did not allow residents to feel involved other than as recipients of cash. For that reason, the community's informal strengths were not effectively tapped. In its report on such JPS loans, *Kompas* (Anon, 1999) reported one chairperson of a village council (LKMD) in Jakarta admitting that he felt "helpless, confused" (*bingung*) in his role of guaranteeing that these loans would be repaid. He wanted official sanctions to ensure that people would repay. A government official, a BAPPENAS (National Development Planning Board) deputy section head, on the other hand, asserted to *Kompas* that sanctions should be put in place by the relevant community as "agents of social control" (*pelaku kontrol sosial*). He opined that if sanctions were put in place by the government, it would merely extend bureaucratisation over the people, not support the emergence of the LKMD as a democratic community institution. *Kompas* pointed out that in the urban context many of the LKMD chairpersons were busy earning their family's livelihood and that LKMD responsibilities had to be confined to what time and energy remained after such daily responsibilities.

This discussion points to a tension at the centre of such programs. The central government's insistence that community strengths built on informal social arrangements be channelled into formal institutions marginalised the very same informal strengths that the government and outside donors sought to harness. Musiyam and Wajdi (2000) commented that the weakness of the JPS method, as pointed out by the World Bank, was the opportunity for government to intervene and in consequence to cultivate dependency and to undermine creativity among the targeted populations. The main problem, they said, was the government's inability to identify the appropriate local population and to understand the actual problems that they faced. They added that under conditions of careless administration, poor monitoring or poor integration among project agents, the chances of "cash going missing" was very high (Musiyam and Wajdi, 2000: 7). In the receiving community, such projects could lead to social exclusion and the weakening of social cohesion among the poor (Musiyam and Wajdi, 2000: 63).

In 2004 the Department of Social Affairs, formed under the new President Susilo Bambang Yudhoyono, introduced another program which was reportedly not credit but a direct gift. In this program, kelurahan officials with the help of RW office-holders identified 60 entrepreneurs in 13 RW and banded these together in groups of ten. In Ledok, one of these groups of ten was drawn from three adjacent RW. Each entrepreneur received a grant of one million rupiah in kind, not cash. I interviewed one RW office-holder who had been recruited into the group with the hope that he would provide stable leadership and regular reporting. Each group was under agreement to run a savings and loan fund (simpan pinjam) meeting each month. In all cases the entrepreneurs were consulted as to what gifts in kind they preferred — a carpenter requested tools, while a woman selling iced drinks and noodles requested a supply of noodles and a saucepan. An ice-seller was given a bicycle, a thermos and 50 kilograms of sugar, while a becak driver received a becak, a cooked food trader a quintal of rice and an ice-seller a refrigerator. However, the RW leader, Sugi, who had been persuaded to join the group because of his leadership qualities, said he was put under pressure to request goods, even though he had no immediate need of goods but instead needed cash to pay off a large debt. Finally the Department persuaded him to accept a gift of a clothes washer because of his involvement in a second-hand clothes enterprise. He calculated that the installation of the machine would require increasing the electricity wattage flowing to his house and would potentially raise conflict over electricity bills among those using the machine. He therefore preferred to store the machine for possible future disposal, for he knew that in a past program residents had been able to sell goods presented to them. His dilemma was summed up in his question to me: how could he refuse a gift?

This program became a political pawn during the election campaign of 2004, when promises were made that such gifts would be increased to three million rupiah for each entrepreneur. One presidential contender even promised to increase this to ten million rupiah. There were widespread rumours that the program was actually financed from World Bank loan money and would have to be paid back by the nation, if not by individual entrepreneurs. There was also concern among receiving entrepreneurs that the goods they received were not worth one million rupiah and that administrators of the program at the higher levels were benefiting corruptly. Kampung residents were prepared to report to the authorities on what they felt were irregularities in the purchasing of goods. As a result, participants confirmed to me that the kelurahan head had refused to sign off on the goods on behalf of the recipients.

In general then, the Social Safety Net was a formal solution with little ongoing importance for the community. It did represent an attempt to formalise the strengths of kampung community, building on already established expectations of gotong royong cooperation and RW/RT solidarity among neighbours. There was an assumption that at fairly short notice these community strengths could be harnessed, or perhaps be constructed, in these formal state programs of assistance, thus magnifying the effects of the programs. In most aspects, however, the Safety Net programs relied on office-holders at different levels of formal administration to make the decisions and control the implementation. As a result the real impact was to undermine the capacity of local communities and individuals. As noted by Breman and Wiradi (2002: 32), the program was "counterproductive in the sense of destroying or damaging coping mechanisms at individual, household and community level". In Ledok the program provided relief and charity, not recovery. It left the poor, the unemployed or casually employed, the asset poor, still much where they were before. There was little progress, only relief. Much of its failure lay in its inflexibility and its incapacity to build on informal community strategies to meet the immediate and long-term needs of residents.

4

Informalisation as an Alternative Strategy to State 'Development'

The downfall of the New Order government of President Suharto in 1998 and the installation of the interim Habibie government was linked to the promise of reform and brought a sense among the general population that change was again possible. The spirit of Reformasi (political reform, the term by which the new era became known) took hold in kampung communities, though not to the same dramatic effect as among students or journalists. There was an understanding among kampung residents that they could now comment publicly and could insist, albeit in subtle ways, on RW/RT office-holders and other leaders performing their responsibilities for the benefit of the community. This new spirit of local empowerment was demonstrated to me by a kampung woman who told me she could not stop yawning when the local deacon conducted prayers for the Catholic community in the kampung and she had immediately let him know that his manner only put people to sleep. She saw this as a bold thing to do but quite in line with Reformasi. On another occasion, neighbours at an RT meeting decided that they needed to assign specific people to follow through on group decisions at RT/RW meetings to ensure that the office-holders implemented them. In their view office-holders were now responsible to their constituents.

Under the New Order, economic development with its emphasis on industrial development and the consolidation of infrastructure, including roads, schools, and health centres, dominated the political discourse. The diversity and imagination of people was largely redundant to this process, although their entrepreneurial skills were vaguely encouraged. New Order policy-makers largely saw the challenge in terms of instilling and cultivating economic motivation and rationality through state programs of modernisation that were essentially unchallengeable, while overcoming the backwardness and ignorance of people who failed to back fully these programs. In her study of kampung-state relations in Jakarta, Alison Murray refers to the marginalisation of kampung people in this New Order "regime of truth": "the lower class community (kampung) is not only exploited by, but exists in opposition to, the 'regime of truth'. The internal community ... is very spatially limited and its members are aware of the basic antagonism of the wider society" (Murray, 1991: 83–4).

Although such opposition was evident in kampung talk and action during the period of the New Order, independent expression of ideas and autonomy of action gained greater public acknowledgement in the reform era. The formal programs through the Social Safety Net, for example, were criticised by kampung residents as insufficient and needing to be supplemented by local strategies of mutual assistance, with alternate principles of managing poverty. These kampung strategies largely arose out of people's desperation but they incorporated safety nets that were more grounded in social relations. In the kampung, the crisis did not lead to a mutually destructive contest among households in competing for government assistance, but rather a critical assessment of how those programs could be improved. There was some agreement that provision of rice should benefit some more than others, although that was not always easy to do.

Kampung residents instituted local strategies to mitigate the impact of the financial crisis. As described in Chapter Two, kampung leaders suggested that ceremonies were very taxing on poor households when cash contributions from neighbours did not nearly cover the cost of lavish celebrations. This led to social approval for the replacement of the expensive kendhuren ritual with less onerous alternatives (see Chapter Six). Similarly, instead of individual households preparing *apem* cakes for distribution to their neighbours during the month of *Ruah* as a memorial to their ancestors (Guinness, 1986: 72), women agreed to cook these together as a cooperative women's activity in the RT and each take home a portion for their own household, thereby cutting costs per household from Rp50,000 to Rp3,000. During the worst of the economic crisis, there was an expectation in the community that local entrepreneurs would employ neighbours in their business where this was possible. A catering supervisor recruited groups of neighbours whenever he was called on to provide labour to caterers at weddings and other ceremonies. Those in the used-clothes trade employed neighbours to wash and iron the clothes. When one riverflat resident received a contract to build a stone wall, he ordered sand and gravel from neighbours who worked in the river and employed neighbours to perform the work.

None of these strategies was unique to the period of the financial crisis. Such practices had been discussed and even implemented before 1998 to cope with situations of poverty. However, local energies intensified during the financial crisis as poorer neighbours struggled to survive. Kampung people looked to an alternative approach to living in the city, one that recognised that the formal provisions by the state or corporate business were never going to meet the specific demands of the kampung community.

The following examples indicate the scope of this contrast between the policies and practices of the state and the local initiative of kampung people and show how kampung residents accommodated the formal within alternative informal mechanisms and strategies to make their lives possible.

UNIVERSITY ASSISTANCE

For more than two decades, students from local universities have been obliged to enrol in a course called Applied Studies (*Kuliah Kerja Nyata*). While most such students were assigned by the university to work in rural villages, a minority who could not get away because they held formal jobs in the city and studied part-time was allowed to work in the poorest kampung in Yogyakarta. In consultation with RW/RT office-holders, they were required to devise a development program which they would implement during their three months in the kampung. For some of that time, they lived in the kampung. As their assignment, they were responsible for managing a development fund provided by the university, as well as raising extra resources themselves, and for negotiating with residents the investment of these funds in a development project. In general they emphasised formal and visible development outcomes such as walkways and safety fences, flower boxes or meeting halls, which they could erect with the cooperation of kampung residents. Students offered a variety of skills that were of potential benefit to the community, such as expertise in engineering, accountancy, law, the English language and teaching. In many of their proposals they stressed the upgrading of the skills of kampung residents and the formalisation of kampung procedures. These included setting up libraries and study sessions for school children, erecting noticeboards announcing RW/RT office-holders and local activities, naming alley-ways with identifying signboards, numbering every house in the kampung, and teaching bookkeeping, note-taking skills, the English language, law or accounting. All such projects were discussed with RW/RT office-holders, then announced at neighbourhood meetings. However, when the students held meetings with kampung residents, the RT community or PKK women's committee, there was little sense of inviting local residents to contribute to the decision-making process. Often the students regarded kampung residents as epitomising a 'culture of poverty', referring to what they considered a lack of initiative or forward-planning, social disorganisation, lack of education, immorality and poor commitment to religious ideals. When this was the case, community members sensed the students' condescending attitude and, as a result, the students were treated as outsiders who presented formal information or formal project plans and offered to residents large sums of cash, which residents sought to exploit to their own advantage. When the students cooperated more with residents' demands, such as running homework sessions with the children, or constructing a safety fence, or setting up a night-market where residents could purchase clothes and

Figure 4.1   RW newspaper board.

other items from outside traders in a festive atmosphere, the community welcomed the students' contribution. Those projects that imprinted a formality on kampung organisation were soon ignored.

The students' intrusion into the kampung community demonstrated the extreme contrast between informal and formal cultures. These students focused on bringing to the kampung a formality of organisation and development, emphasising formal meetings with hierarchically ranked participants and carefully formalised plans which distanced kampung residents. Many community members did not have the education nor the experience to prosper in such a culture and for that reason had continued over the years to elect public servants and retired public servants to positions of formal responsibility in the RW/RT, they being most competent in negotiating in the formal arena. However, residents always required these leaders to have the community sense to consult neighbours and understand local conditions and grievances.

Nevertheless, several student projects have grown beyond these formal strictures. One semester a group of engineering students helped in the planning and building of a bridge over the river (described below), while in 2004 a small group of students continued well after their formal project had finished to go to the kampung each weekday afternoon to tutor primary school children. Their enthusiasm was matched by the excitement of the children themselves. Because of the nature of the projects, these students had taken their involvement beyond the formal and demonstrated their commitment to work alongside kampung residents in activities of direct benefit to residents.

PUBLIC WORKS

The awarding of contracts to undertake kampung public works demonstrates the alternate strengths of the formal and informal. During the 1990s, a three-metre-high stone wall was constructed the length of the river on both sides to shield kampung houses from the floods that swept volcanic lava down the river every ten years or so. The river wall project (Guinness, 1999), an initiative of the municipal government in its successful bid to win the Indonesian Beautiful City (*Kota Adipura*) award, was awarded to contractors who had the formal requirements to tender for such work. These requirements included the financial capital and experience in similar projects, thereby excluding residents from tendering for the project. The tender was awarded to a group that included the local army command, which assigned army personnel to

Figure 4.2   Riverflat retention walls.

labour on the site. However, these soldiers showed little inclination to do any heavy work on the project, expecting instead to be provided with refreshments by kampung residents for merely attending. Kampung residents complained that their own qualifications to conduct the project were not seen as appropriate. Their qualifications were based on practical experience with construction within their locality, a familiarity with local conditions and social groups, and a personal interest in seeing the project done well. Having no means to intervene in guiding the project as it proceeded, even though it radically affected their lives, residents could only mutter about the poor workmanship and corruption that frequently marked such projects managed by outside contractors.

Residents had some justification for their claims. In the early 1990s a high wall was constructed on the opposite bank by a contractor to the municipal government, as a retainer for mounds of decomposing garbage deposited there by the Municipality over more than a decade. Large business premises housing flower shops and other enterprises had then been constructed above the site, further emphasising the need for a solid retaining wall. Residents who had witnessed the construction of this wall advised me in 1996 that the wall would collapse under the weight of rainwater, which would seep through the garbage. This indeed

Figure 4.3   The partly completed river wall in the 1990s.

proved to be the case in 1998, when the wall subsided, threatening buildings above and emergency reconstruction had to be done. Similarly, a contract to install household septic tanks in the kampung was awarded by the municipal authorities and an outside contractor installed the tanks in 1996. However, residents were powerless to control the implementation of this project, despite their observation that soil was mixed with sand in the concrete mix and the gravel was too coarse for the filter. As a result, the tanks became blocked or collapsed and a number had to be dug up and reconstructed, to the anger of those residents directly affected.

The construction of a small bridge over the river provided an insight into this interplay between formal and informal when kampung residents were, for once, able to manage the project themselves. This project was comparable with projects financed through government offices and contracted out to formal contractors. It grew out of the completion of the flood wall, a much larger project, but it required similar processes of diverting the river, establishing foundations in the riverbed and planning a structure strong enough to withstand floodwaters. The RT leader who led the project explained that he had the idea after a woman carrying her baby and a stock of vegetables had stumbled while wading across the river and lost her goods. This RT leader and two of his neighbours with building experience — but no formal qualifications — devised a plan. He approached the university administration where he worked as a security guard and an affiliated Catholic seminary and obtained from them a gift of 100 bags of cement for the work. Forty of these were used in the construction and the other 60 sold to provide funds. He found two discarded electricity poles and bought two coconut trunks and used these to span the river by laying them on steel uprights driven into the river bed. Apart from these resources, the bridge was constructed entirely from kampung resources — sand was dug from the river, residents contributed cement, steel, timber, and labour, and refreshments were prepared by kampung residents for the labourers. The bridge was designed and constructed under local leaders. The RT leader himself took on much of the labour, working on the bridge when he returned each day from his paid employment. He chose not to apply to the municipal government for approval of the bridge. That would take too long, he said, and they would insist on a far more substantial design beyond the means of the kampung. After a year the structure was experiencing its second flood season with no obvious failings. However, the bamboo walkway and softwood railings had begun to rot and were proving dangerous. These were replaced in 2002 with more durable materials. The RT leader rejected seeking outside assistance for the bridge unless it was in the form of an untied grant of cash or materials. He did not need any advice, he said, because he knew what was wrong and how to fix it. He certainly did not want any official intervention that would open the way for rejection of the community design and the labour and materials already expended. As he had rejected formal assistance, the conduct of the repairs lay almost entirely with him. Although some residents were critical of the leader's poor communication with them and the slow rate of progress, none questioned the RT head's ability to plan and implement the repairs.

Despite his efforts, the bridge only lasted 18 months. It was carried away when the flooded river carried down a huge log that lodged against the bridge pylon and dislodged it under the pressure of the swollen waters. Residents immediately made plans to replace the bridge with one of much sturdier structure and were assisted in their preparation by a resident who was an engineer and by a group of Applied Studies students from the engineering faculty of a local university. Once again, it was built without official permission, this time under the coordination of the RW head. The central pylon was built of steel and concrete and the bridge span walkway was also of concrete and steel. However, kampung leaders were aware that their design would not gain official permission because, in their endeavour to save costs, the design did not meet formal specifications. As a result, the kampung leaders did not apply for official approval. Eventually the bridge was opened on 1 January 2004 and, to the organisers' delight, by the subdistrict head (*Camat*), who entered into the spirit of celebrations by insisting that the opening coincide with New Year's Eve celebrations and occur precisely at midnight. Though the bridge was not officially approved by the Municipality, the Camat's endorsement was strong support for its existence and he promised that he would inform the Department of Public Works of its existence, that is not ask their permission but merely invite their tacit agreement to its existence. With this assurance, residents were confident that they would not have to fight to keep their bridge. The informal arrangements of kampung leaders and residents in this case found a way to provide for their own needs within the 'cracks' of formal government administration.

We can contrast this project with the story told by 'Pak Yudi' of Kampung Mergangsan Lor in Yogyakarta. He was concerned with the health risks associated with living alongside the Code River. After extensive community discussions, a design for a public septic tank/ toilet block was forwarded to the municipal government for financial assistance. In 1997 the Municipality began construction on the project but the design and implementation were not what the community had agreed upon. Instead, it had been replaced by a more complex design that cost more money and therefore required a higher commitment of government development funds. The consequence was that on completion the toilet block imposed higher maintenance costs on the community, being more suited to an upper-middle-class neighbourhood with their capacity to call on much greater financial and network support from their residents. Such a facility in Mergangsan Lor was therefore doomed to failure. Pak Yudi commented, "The government keeps on constructing them, but no-one uses them" (Yoshi, 2000b).

Another example of kampung residents successfully managing a project was in the Yogyakarta kampung of Kricak, where reportedly the RW residents were handed finance for the sealing of roads under community management of the project. After community discussions the minimum daily wage paid to labourers on this project was reduced from Rp8,200 to Rp6,000 on the understanding that an extra length of road could be sealed with the savings on labour.

Kampung communal work is termed *kerja bakti*. Sullivan (1992: 105–6) calls this "duty work" or "obligatory labour", that is "work that is entirely official and hence of the highest formality". The obligations are rigorously sanctioned by the community. According to his account, officialdom can virtually dictate what is and what is not kerja bakti, thereby obliging households to contribute labour. However, he also notes that "very few *wong kampung* (residents) in Kalasan would want to avoid the obligations" because they "generally find something of real value to themselves and their communities in typical kerja bakti projects". In Ledok, consultation and voluntary contribution of labour characterise kerja bakti rather than the heavy duty that Sullivan describes, which is why I prefer to translate the term as 'work cooperation'. The term can also be translated as 'honour work', 'respect work', or 'voluntary communal work'. Kerja bakti is called upon by RT or RW office-holders after community consultation in a neighbourhood meeting and generally involves improvements to public facilities such as washrooms, toilets, pathways and steps or, in the 1990s, the building of the flood wall or after that the construction of the bridges. It is not paid work and it is voluntary, although every household is expected to contribute a worker. It is generally held on Sundays when more people are free, but if it is a large project (such as the bridge) it may continue through the other days or at irregular hours when people return from their income earning. Some kerja bakti may be directed towards helping poorer households, such as whitewashing the bamboo walls or repairing the house of a poor widow. It resembles another form of common labour called *hajat* or *sambat*, which is when neighbours offer their labour to a person holding an important ritual. In this latter case, strict reciprocity is expected between neighbours. In the case of kerja bakti, there are no formal records kept of individuals' participation, and some may work for hours and days while others merely turn up for a few minutes to support the work. The social sanctions of gossip ensure that most do contribute. Those who cannot be present may contribute cash to provide refreshments or employ someone else to work in their stead. However, kerja bakti is often even less formal. In 2000 I came across a group of men building a wall to hide a community toilet from the view of the nearest house. It was a project that the RT head had announced to a recent RT meeting without designating a date for the work but this Sunday he had suddenly called a few together to implement the project and many in the RT were unaware that it was happening. The work scene was made livelier by the crowd of women and children

Figure 4.4   A well constructed by RT labour.

who gathered to watch and the passers-by who stopped to chat with the workers and even share their refreshments.

Over the decades, kerja bakti has been responsible for the construction of public wells, washrooms and toilet blocks; concrete steps and ramps linking the various levels of the riverbank; retaining walls, safety walls and fences; and drains. All have been constructed with voluntary labour and community donations of cash and refreshments, although sponsors have sometimes been found, such as the Foster Parents Association (PKAK), which sponsored one of the wells and washrooms, or the Pertamina or Bank Bali offices adjoining the kampung. It is exactly these kinds of projects that were financed and formalised through the World Bank padat karya program to relieve urban poverty, to the detriment of community kerja bakti institutions.

HEALTH CARE

Health care provided particular challenges to kampung residents during the crisis when hospital costs became a major cause of household perceptions of declining welfare. Hospital costs were usually prohibitive for most kampung households, but for some medical conditions kampung residents still needed the attention of formal medical practitioners such as cases of childbirth, road accident trauma, alcohol or drug overdose, infant fever, heart attacks, strokes, and breathing problems. The RW neighbourhood population where I lived could have kept one hospital bed occupied for the entire five weeks I was there during 2000. However, hospital costs were overwhelming and kampung residents complained that the hospitals were run as businesses to make a profit rather than as a service to the public. The Dr. Sarjito local public hospital was often rejected because of patients' lack of faith in its services. Hospital staff were said by kampung residents to distribute medicine or prescribe services for their own financial advantage rather than for the good of the patient. Hospital patients' relatives were sent out of the hospital in search of medicines that were available in the hospital and, if they were unable to find them elsewhere, were later charged an inflated price for the hospital supplies. Doctors, they claimed, had a financial interest in pharmacies. Private hospitals were also rejected because of the cost of the services. Kampung residents were not attending the local medical surgeries — one general practitioner had a practice in the kampung — because private medical practitioners were seen as self-seeking, both in prescribing medicines and in recommending services that were not necessary and for which they charged high fees. Even the local public health clinic (*puskesmas*), which in 2000 was known to stock few medicines and whose health personnel were often absent, was rarely attended. However, this was not a total rejection of the formal health services as represented by these institutions. Kampung babies were almost all delivered in state-registered maternity centres, whereas in the 1970s, by contrast, many babies had been delivered in the kampung by traditional midwives with no formal training or licensing.

The shift towards a mix of both formal and informal health practices was a response to financial difficulties but it also reflected a growing disillusionment of kampung people, and indeed other urban residents, in the biomedical system and a growing faith in alternative cures. Such alternate cures have been available for generations of Javanese rural and urban residents, but under the New Order the government had made great advances in persuading the urban masses to rely on puskesmas clinics, biomedical practitioners, hospitals and health clinics rather than on such alternative cures. With the onset of the crisis, kampung residents and urban residents in general turned back again to alternative cures. Even the formal sector began to recognise this shift in public sentiment. One private hospital introduced alternative health workers into the hospital to provide massage, acupuncture, herbal and similar 'traditional' medicines within the hospital ward.

Instead of formal-sector remedies, people sought alternative cures. The most accessible to kampung residents was the herbalist (*ibu jamu*), a woman who carried around various herbal remedies in bottles in a basket strapped across her back. She served these, sometimes mixing them on the spot in a half-coconut shell or a glass, for a vast range of complaints for both men and women. Some of the most popular cures were preventative, intended to keep people healthy, rather than to cure them of existing complaints. Other potions (*ramuan*) targeted the building of strength, the treatment of arthritis, or sexual potency, all of which could be purchased from the ibu jamu. There was also a range of commercially produced alternative medicines (*jamu*), usually sold in powder form for mixing with water or other liquids. Some kampung residents mixed these with alcohol to make what they saw as a particularly potent brew. There was also a wide interest within the larger society in alternative therapy, seen in terms of acupuncture, natural therapies, and massage.

Alternative medicines and therapies were also dispensed by alternative healers, referred to by some as *tabib*, by others as *battra*, seen as healers with spiritual abilities. The spiritual element was attractive but so was the fact that these healers generally did not charge a set fee but left it to the patient to pay what they could. Some healers even advised patients not to pay or suggested a donation to the mosque. These conditions put the relationship of healer to patient on an entirely different basis, whereby the healer assumed a familiar relationship with the patient and diagnosed not just their physical but their spiritual and emotional condition. This led in some cases to relations of extreme dependence, whereby patients would return regularly to consult the healer. The relationship with the healer often had a communal nature in that kampung neighbours arranged to make the trip together in a hired minivan to what was sometimes the remote location of the healer's practice and encouraged each other in undertaking the recommended treatment.

One healer (Pak Damin), whose practice I attended, prescribed both pharmaceutical products and his own herbal medicines. He and his helpers spent two days a week collecting the natural ingredients for these from the forest and fields around their remote mountain village and then prepared them themselves. Healers such as Pak Damin

generally acquired a clientele by word of mouth. Their becoming
healers was not by any formal process but by a series of incidents,
experiences, contacts and the like over what was often a long period of
time, which in the eyes of their clientele conferred on them a certain
mystical aura and power.

Muhammad Sobary describes one dukun who was told in a
dream early in her life that she would not become a healer until she
was 45 years old. All her efforts to hasten the process were thwarted
until she reached that age. This is a category of healer known as *dukun
tiban*, who "do not obtain their knowledge (*ilmu*) through the usual
study process but through a dream" (Sobary, 1997: 112). Another whom
he describes, Maruti, was approached in a vision by an old woman
who told her to become a midwife. It was such an unlikely command
— no one in her family had been a midwife — that she put it out of
her mind. She was recovering from syphilis at the time but the next
year the disease flared up again and only medicine from the puskesmas
nurse saved her. She dreamt again of the old woman, who asked her
why she had not obeyed the instructions and told her God would help
her. Thirteen days later a pregnant neighbour complained of a sore
stomach and appealed to Maruti for help. The birth went successfully.
After that Maruti became acknowledged as a midwife and with prayer
and massage saw many through birth and the post-partum period.

According to Sobary, dukun tiban are also called *dukun perwangan*,
one who has magical power, who calls on the help of supernatural
beings and the unseen world. Sobary (1997: 136) also uses the term
"possessed *tabib*", the *tabib* referring primarily to Indian, Arab, or
Pakistani dukun. Cederroth (1995) refers to the dukun perwangan
as a diviner. C. Geertz (1960: 103) describes dukun perwangan as
"mediums who become possessed by the spirits of the dead at will,
enabling one to present petitions to one's deceased relatives directly".
Geertz refers to the dukun tiban as marginal persons who have a more
direct relation to the "darker powers". Their power comes suddenly by
divine stroke, without any preparation. They are usually women, thought
to be somewhat unbalanced psychologically and from economically
depressed circumstances. Their power may disappear as quickly as it
comes. "There is sharp disagreement," he writes, "concerning both the
reality and the ethical character of the forces upon which the *tiban*
calls" (Geertz, 1960: 100).

On the day I observed Damin's practice, about 40 people crowded
into his consulting room and he treated each patient in front of the

others. He often joked with his patients, involving the audience in the conversation, as though to entertain them and relieve their long wait. His diagnoses of patients' conditions sometimes corresponded with those already made by biomedical practitioners for many of his clients were coming to him after visits to hospitals or other biomedical facilities. His knowledge of biomedical analysis impressed many of his patients. He also did not hesitate to recommend pharmaceutical products when he considered these relevant, but his treatment of conditions focused on his own techniques, drawing on his exceptional spiritual discernment and the remedies he had devised from natural and supernatural ingredients.

The alternative healers consulted by Ledok residents (and many others) were not as socially marginal as those described by Geertz. While they lived in remote or poorly accessible locations, some like Damin established themselves materially and socially in a way that reflected long-term success and social acceptance of their practices. They offered the attractive mixture of both scientific understanding, based on proven diagnostic techniques and remedies, and of supernatural or magical powers. In the latter, they contrasted with the formal modern medical practitioners and appealed to people dissatisfied with biomedical offerings.

Their practice was therefore boldly informal. Patients turned up rather than made appointments and there was no strict note taken of order. Patients were treated in public amid considerable banter with the surrounding clientele and no set fees were taken, although donations were encouraged. Much of their practice, diagnoses and treatments were in stark contrast to the scientific formal codes officially recognised by the Department of Health.

Five-year-old Adi was sick with swollen stomach. In 1999 he was admitted to hospital for five days, where all sorts of tests were performed on his stomach and colon. Finally the doctors declared he had a swollen liver. He was sent home but had to attend the hospital for regular follow-ups. These seemed to be going on indefinitely, because each time the doctors simply instructed him to come back again. His mother saw that there was no change in his condition and finally stopped taking him there. The original hospital treatment had cost Rp600,000 and each follow-up outpatient visit cost Rp50,000. She then took him to an alternative healer on the southern edge of the city. This man's unique practice centred on a long wooden pointer, on which were suspended a cross and a figure of the Virgin Mary, which he used in his diagnoses. In this case he ran the pointer over the five-year-old's body after a silent prayer, then probed with his finger until he suddenly stabbed the finger in. The young lad was startled, but the stomach receded to its normal size and remained like that. On another occasion this same mother took the lad to the healer when the boy was finding it hard to breathe. This time the mother did not bother going to the hospital but took him directly to the healer, who diagnosed a long-term pinched nerve in his back. He pinched the lad's finger to cure him. Another time he treated the mother for heart pain. She had already made one unsuccessful trip to the health centre. He massaged her with his fingers, then gave her a solution squeezed from pepper leaves to be drunk and rubbed on her chest.

This particular healer was a Roman Catholic, as were this particular mother and child, but religion was not a determinant factor in choice of healer. This same mother regularly visited Damin, a healer who was Muslim, though his health practices took place under the gaze of the Javanese deity Semar and two other *wayang* (shadow puppet) heroes of the Mahabharata epic displayed prominently on his wall. Not only did she visit him several times but also took others to him. Indeed, healing practices often run counter to formal notions of what constitutes the religion for religious authorities are unwilling to acknowledge such practices outside their formal religious codification. Damin was known to be a staunch supporter of the mosque — indeed payments at his practice were placed in a box marked *sumbangan mesjid* (mosque donations) — yet his appeal to Semar and other wayang figures ran counter to reformist Islamic views.

A woman in her forties was diagnosed with breast cancer by the local private hospital, where she had paid Rp2 million for largely unsuccessful treatment. She was introduced by this same mother to Pak Damin, who treated her by making several cuts in her skin with a razor blade. 'Miraculously' the bleeding stopped as soon as the 'operation' was over and she returned home with a herbal remedy he prescribed for her. For several days she screamed in agony while black matter oozed out of the skin of her breast, but she recovered and has not suffered the complaint again.

The results of alternate healing may be positive or negative but the positive stories tend to fuel the reputation of the healer, attracting others to try it out. One practitioner treated broken bones and, without the use of plaster or X-rays, reset the bones with often dramatically quick results. The sense of the miraculous was part of the mystique of these healers. Damin, the Muslim healer, had little formal education. He did not complete primary school but had learnt to read and write Arabic at a religious school. He issued most of his patients with an egg, the yolk of which they were to drink on returning home. On this egg he wrote in an Arabic/Jawi-type script, which no-one could read and whose characters differed from egg to egg. He had red scarves over which patients believed he had prayed, which he wrapped around the injured body part of the patient or hung round their necks, sometimes leaving them like that while he tended to other patients. Another healer known to kampung residents was said to have travelled away from home to other islands of Indonesia, where he acquired his healing skills. While away from Java he was told in a vision that if he was going to practise his healing he should do it at home. He returned home but part of his power came from the mystique gained from his unique experience in a strange land.

One informant, whose daughter had died at age 46 of cancer of the womb despite being taken to hospital and to various healers, explained that healers are not always able to bring results and they may recognise a particular condition as *berat* ('heavy'). A healer's powers come through *zihir* (prayer) or *semedi* (meditation) but healing, he pointed out, was in the hand of God. The particular healer whom he visited practised at Purworejo, his home town some 65 kilometres from Yogyakarta. He had travelled to Jakarta and to the Outer Islands of Indonesia where, he asserted, he was given the gift of healing by God. His diagnosis was conducted by running his hands over the body until they sensed the malady and began to tremble. He then massaged the affected area. He would call for medicine by flicking his fingers, at which it would 'miraculously' appear. This healer was called *kyai* (a term for an Islamic leader) because his ilmu (science) came through Islam.

Siti Sapardiyah Santoso and fellow psychologists (Santoso, 1999–2000) conducted research in Yogya on traditional healers, whom they termed *battra*. They claimed that alternative healing satisfied social, psychological, and organic needs that were not met by 'modern' doctors. Fifty-three per cent of their informants believed that battra could heal more quickly than modern doctors. There were still some informants, they reported, who believed that the cause of sickness was sorcery, the curse of God, or the visitation of a spirit or *setan*, and for these patients, battra were likely to be more successful than modern medical practitioners. One kampung woman reported to me that she had been knocked to the ground twice on her way to the market, feeling as though she had been pushed, although there was no-one around. She assumed that spirits were attacking her. The falls injured her shoulder but she went to an alternate healer who could deal not only with the shoulder but also with the spirit interference.

Alternative healers are usually not easily accessible. Some of the most popular are located in villages up to an hour's drive from the kampung; others are in out-of-the-way places in the city. The Catholic healer lived in a small, poorly lit house and was a high school teacher in the mornings. Only his close neighbours knew him by name. There was no fee for his services. Patients simply left some money for him in an envelope, as though they were attending a neighbour's life crisis ritual. The relationship was thus conceived as one between neighbours rather than between specialist and client. The remote or humble location of healers is part of their informality and appeals to people's faith in their services, rather than a government licensing of their qualifications. They are seen as healers who depend on psychic powers, spiritual powers, and keen insights into individual ailments and persons rather than formal training and book knowledge. Their place in the local community is part of their reputation. Some have built up substantial premises within the village or kampung and become patrons of the local community, contributing to the mosque, youth sport or music, and the like. The patient appraisal of their services is based far more on a holistic assessment of the person of the healer. In contrast, because the doctors or other medical practitioners servicing patients in a hospital or health service may constantly change, there is less interest in judging these modern services in terms of the individual practitioners.

Because the clientele of the alternative healers is built on a reputation for spiritual and psychic powers, they will be visited by people from a wide area. This contrasts with the government localisation of health services, particularly through the puskesmas clinics. Pak Damin, whose practice was 100 kilometres north of Yogyakarta, drew patients from as far away as Jakarta, Bandung, Semarang, Yogyakarta and Surabaya, that is from all parts of Java.

Visiting a healer is often done in a group. If the healer is some distance from the city, a bus is usually chartered and up to 20 kampung neighbours may make the trip. Generally there will a sponsor, who is able to organise the bus, collect the fares, and contact likely travellers. The sponsor may not even be seeking healing herself but simply go along for the ride, perhaps making a small profit on the side. On the way home on the trip I joined, patients talked about the medication they had been given and any return visits that had been suggested, while the sponsor again played a role in clarifying these details with them. Patients at this point shared their ailments and took a collective interest in the outcomes, encouraging each other with positive stories of the healer's success.

The following story takes even further this questioning of the formal biomedical system and reiterates the value placed on the informal. When riverflat dweller Radi's granddaughter of less than 12 months old fell sick with a high temperature, they rushed her to a 'children's doctor', who charged them Rp20,000 for the visit and Rp8,200 for medicine. When there was no improvement in her condition, they took her to a retired nurse who offered her services in the kampung. She charged them nothing except Rp2,000 for medicine. When there was still no improvement, they gave her a kampung remedy of honey mixed with the yolk of a kampung hen's egg. Her temperature immediately dropped. Next time, they averred, they would begin with the kampung remedy.

In this case, cost was a significant factor. However, it was clear that cost was not the only factor driving the increasing attraction to informal strategies. Kampung residents were seeking help not just from hospitals and health centres but also from alternative healers and alternative medicines not part of formal 'Western' medicine. These were not just the 'traditional' practices of Javanese 'peasants' not yet familiar with 'modern' practices but a conscious rejection of formal practices in favour of something that appealed more to the circumstances and attitudes of community residents.

FINANCIAL CREDIT

The community plays a key role in providing financial and material assistance to residents. Everyday needs are often met by neighbours, such as through the loan of equipment or food, or credit given at the local store, or labour assistance at ceremonies or life crises. The main sources of savings and loans for kampung people are informal community institutions, notably arisan, simpan pinjam and *koperasi*. They are termed here as 'informal' because they are not registered by the government and are not subject to government controls. Instead they rely on the strength and guarantee of the community for their success. While the arisan or 'rotating credit association' was common in the 1970s, the simpan pinjam or 'savings and loans association' has gained in popularity since the crisis (Lont, 2005: 206). In the case of the arisan, individual participants contribute a set amount of cash each period (week, fortnight, or month) to a fund that is distributed each time to one or two of the group according to a set order determined by the organiser at the beginning of the arisan. Once each member has received a share, the group disbands or starts again. In a simpan pinjam (save-and-borrow association), all members, commonly members of an RT or a RW, deposit a set amount each period. Any member may apply to borrow these accumulating funds. If approved, the loan has to be paid back within a year with regular set repayments of capital plus interest. What contributes to their informality is that both activities are seen not merely, or perhaps not primarily, as financial institutions but as social institutions. They are run by community members with no formal training in such services, they are audited by community members at regular meetings, and their continuation depends not on formal sanctions but on community social sanctions. That said, there are formal characteristics — office-holders, such as the treasurer, are appointed and records are taken of all transactions. However, these institutions are available to all households in the community or, sometimes, to those who are nominated or approached on the basis of neighbours' confidence in that person rather than on their material assets or documented income.

Simpan pinjam are organised within the neighbourhood, and community sanctions are important in making sure that loans are repaid on time and that financial administration is beyond suspicion. The purpose of the loans or, in the case of arisan, their distributions is not a factor in the granting of the funds — some will direct the money to a business venture, others to paying off other loans, school fees or hospital expenses, or for renovating a house or holding a life-crisis ceremony. Neighbours generally become aware of how the money is used but they do not need that knowledge for the cash to be granted. I once sat with a friend and his family when a neighbour arrived to give them Rp20,000. She visited other neighbours in the same way, distributing benefits from an arisan distribution she had received, as though it was a lottery windfall rather than a financial investment she had made over several months. The recipient in this case explained that these neighbours had helped her in small ways over recent months.

In 1996 one RW initiated a successful simpan pinjam association with a large number of residents involved in banking regular amounts and obtaining large loans. This project achieved much in the way of facilitating household business and investment and overcoming household emergencies. It was also seen to be a very successful means of ensuring community cooperation. In the following years, these simpan pinjam spread throughout the RWs and RTs and were found in women's, religious, neighbourhood, and even occupational groups. There were some very impressive stories of their success in accumulating capital. For example, among a group of neighbours who worked on a catering team, each member contributed Rp500 per job to the simpan pinjam out of the Rp15–25,000 they earned on each job. From this capital, members could borrow any amount they wished, paying it back over three months at 20 per cent interest. A further 10 per cent interest was charged if the payment was late.

In a Central Javanese village, Koning (1999) identified a variety of arisan that had either survived the worst of the crisis or even begun during it. She concluded that the arisan had a clear safety-net function, allowing members to access money for emergencies. Some arisan involved quite small amounts and generally accompanied women's village meetings such as PKK or Dharma Wanita, while others involved much larger amounts of Rp500,000–600,000 distributed each month to one of 30 members, and were organised by individuals with the express purpose of providing starting capital or larger sums for house renovations or emergencies. Koning also mentioned a simpan pinjam in the village, begun with capital from the National Development Planning Agency (BAPPENAS) and managed by the local state-sponsored cooperative (KUD), where people could borrow up to Rp500,000 at 10 per cent interest (no period stated).

Hotze Lont (1999; 2005) observed the functioning of simpan pinjam and arisan in Kampung Kricak Kidul and Bujung during the crisis of 1998 and noted that inflation posed a real threat to the survival of these associations. Those who received their turn in the arisan after the drop in the value of the rupiah and the inflation that accompanied it were not receiving the same value as earlier recipients.[5] However, he did not detect any desire among later recipients to default from the arisan. As one informant told him, "Really it is just bad luck. We agreed on the rules and these are the consequences" (Lont, 1999: 18). There was no consideration of any measure to compensate these later recipients, nor to defer the arisan until conditions improved. Despite his fears that many of these mutual associations would break down with the inflation of costs and the rising burden of debts, most continued to function as usual. He noted that:

> "The respondents...tend to mention the mutual associations as one of their fixed costs, together with food and education. It is not a luxury expenditure that can be easily stopped.... The dominant motive for participation is related to social relations and obligations. Stopping participation would not generate a substantial amount of money, and the social loss would be considerable. One may not only lose social status, but may also be confronted with restricted access to local sources of credit, simply because one has failed to show creditworthiness" (Lont, 1999: 17).

In Ledok there was no move to close down the arisan or the simpan pinjam for residents continued to have a high demand for loans. In his study of Bujung, Lont predicted that people would leave arisan at the completion of the current cycle and that they would take fewer loans from the simpan pinjam. However, on his return to Bujung in 1999, he found that most local self-help organisations were functioning as usual (Lont, 2005: 206). The evidence from Ledok is that the popularity of local self-help associations persisted, partly as a means of countering the crisis. During the crisis, the associations paid a dividend on the profits according to how much the member had generated for the association in savings and interest. In 2001 becak drivers established a community association (*paguyuban*) with 30 driver-members, meeting once a month to conduct a simpan pinjam. The association was on their own initiative, not the government's, but they were able to attract a government grant of eight becak, which the association rented out to drivers at Rp1,000 a day, half the usual rate.

A similar communal venture was a cooperative (koperasi) established among neighbours to purchase basic commodities such as rice or sugar. Buying in bulk, the cooperative was able to provide these commodities to those who needed them as a loan, which was repaid in cash at 20 per cent interest over one month. Cooperatives such as this were started during the crisis with outside funding through the Social Safety Net but these functioned independently. In one RW a cooperative was initiated in 1998 with capital of Rp300,000. This was used to fill members' orders for rice and sugar, which they had to repay within one month at 5 per cent interest above the cost price of the items. By 2000 capital in the cooperative had risen to Rp1.2 million.

Kampung people have always relied on informal strategies of savings and loans. For kampung residents, formal banking services have only recently become available. During the 1970s, only public servants would have been tempted to use banking services. The high interest rates awarded by banks on deposits reflected the scant interest in saving in banks. On the other hand, it was very common to save through the purchase of gold jewellery, which could readily be sold through gold and jewellery merchants, hopefully at a gain rather than a loss. Loans were obtained not from the banks, which required collateral in the way of a land title or house title, which few kampung residents possessed, but through pawnbrokers in exchange for valuable possessions such as a motorcycle, bicycle or, more recently, a televison set or other electrical equipment. Another common option was to buy on credit, either from a neighbour who ran a grocery store in the kampung or from hawkers who would return daily to collect dues on a client's purchase. All sorts of household equipment and furnishings were purchased by kampung residents this way.

To enable residents to reduce the inevitable costs of hosting life-crisis ceremonies, the RT holds a store of plates, bowls, glasses and cutlery for their use. A small hiring fee has allowed the RT to build up the stock. In 2000 the RT youth group purchased a sound system consisting of amplifier, microphones, tape deck and speakers for Rp850,000. At the RT meeting that approved this purchase, the youth group leader presented the youth budget and then said the youth wanted to spend the money on a sound system. Other RT office-holders encouraged the youth to augment their fund by approaching each household in the RT for a further donation as 'sponsor', which they did, raising the required amount. Such issues are raised at RT meetings and debated by a few speakers, but their success depends on the informal support of the community.

More recently, bank finance has become more available. Bank officers have introduced a system of lending generated by officers visiting people in their homes. More people have gained title to house and/or land as a result of recent surveying and government titling of riverflat land and been able to use this title as security for bank loans. One resident and his family recently gained their third bank loan on the basis of successful repayment of previous loans, each time gaining an increased amount, the last amounting to several million rupiah. Banks have also become far more accessible to the ordinary citizen through ATM machines and computer technology, which have reduced the amount of bureaucracy involved in providing personal services. Nevertheless, the inflexibility of repayment schedules has threatened to bankrupt several residents.

SHARING OF PUBLIC UTILITIES

By 2000 electricity was connected to almost all homes and piped water was available throughout the kampung. However, in regard to both electricity and water supplies, not all households could afford a formal connection to the city mains. In 2000 the state electricity supplier announced that it would supply new connections to private homes only at the level of 1,350 watts or above. This was a marked increase over the former minimum connection of 450 watts, later increased to 900 watts. The cost of such a connnection was set at Rp1.2 million for 1,350 watts, the equivalent of two years' rent on a single room or a year's rent on a house. Not surprisingly residents made their own adjustments, selling off electricity to neighbours who were not formally connected and charging them a set monthly fee. In one case, 900 watts at 220 volts was distributed between ten households. Similarly with piped water, many residents avoided the cost of connection by continuing to depend on private wells, which tap an ample ground-water supply in this area, in many cases installing pumps, overhead tanks and internal water pipes to complement the supply. Public wells were also widely used.

Formal electricity bills had a surcharge of about Rp8,000 as a contribution towards street lighting, which was a burden on residents of riverside kampung like Ledok that had no proper streets and therefore no street lighting. However, kampung leaders tapped into overhead lines at the nearest electricity pole to run public lights along all main alleys and for public facilities such as the badminton court. They knew that an official request from them for such lighting would be refused but that their informal arrangement was tolerated by the state electricity company. RW/RT officers were careful, however, to prevent any individual resident from stealing electricity in this way, because that would endanger the informal arrangement the kampung communities had with the company.

Although the state legally controls all land, either as state land or by granting and protecting title to private landholders, formal regu-lations and public space are always open to challenge by those living in the informal world of the kampung. For example, the completion of the river wall clearly separated residential land from state river reserve. Immediately, however, kampung residents began to challenge this by building structures overhanging the river from the wall and by planting out the river in bananas and vegetables, or by locating fish

Figure 4.5   River fish cages.

cages there. In these cases, RW officers appeared to be in a quandary. Their appeals to higher levels of formal government to set some rules or to police the area resulted in individual residents being brought to the attention of the formal kelurahan office. This spared the RT or RW leader the embarrassment of being seen to defend the state against the interests of fellow residents, even though their action in reporting it reflected a community concern that public space was being randomly privatised. On another occasion, however, younger residents appealed to formal municipal regulations to achieve informally what they saw as a good community outcome. In 2003 a group of youth in the north of the kampung decided that the river should be cleared in conjunction with a municipal Clean City campaign and proceeded to walk the length of the kampung, destroying all plantings on the riverflat. Although RW officers were repelled by this display of violence against fellow community members, they felt powerless to stand against this informal implementation of municipal instructions.

Titled land can also become the target of informal operations. One of the streetside properties bordering the kampung was used by the Department of Employment (Departmen Tenaga Kerja) until recent years, when the office was moved and the land sold to a private business. However, a prayer house (*mussolah*) had been built on the land while it was under government use, which Department employees and kampung residents attended for Friday prayers. On purchasing the land, the new owner in 2004 bricked in the door from the kampung leading to the mussolah, but irate residents broke down the wall and insisted that the mussolah be preserved from the demolitions on the block. The owner then asked for police to protect the site, but residents obtained at least temporary leave to continue using the mussolah. The land developer in this case faced the ire not only of the local kampung worshippers but even the much more outspoken urban Muslim population.

INFORMAL CULTURE, INFORMAL SOCIETY

Just as informal economic activities are squeezed and moulded by the dominant formal economy, informal social, political and cultural activities exist in an environment in which formal procedures of the state and capitalist business predominate. To some extent they exist because formal procedures cannot deal with the realities of kampung residents, but also because kampung residents espouse values very different from those of the formal rules of the urban society constructed by the city elite.

One of the determinants of kampung ways is the lack of material wealth and physical space, a lack to which residents have grown accustomed. Increasing density of houses has led over the years to many adaptations. In the 1970s housing pressure was already acute on the middle level of riverbank. In those years houses were being subdivided and spaces between houses, sometimes the narrowest of roof overhangs, were being covered and occupied. Population was beginning to sprawl out into the less prestigious areas of the kampung, along the top pathway and on the riverflat, both places at risk of expulsion by city authorities. These low-status areas were also seen as culturally rough (*kasar*), putting the children of riverbank residents more at risk of picking up unseemly or criminal habits, even if their only criminal behaviour was being a fellow squatter. Even so, the support for these squatters of their more established kampung neighbours was essential to survival, particularly in defending their right to occupy the sites. On the other hand, middle-level kampung residents saw it as important for the survival of their social practices to involve these new settlers as closely as possible in the ritual and communal activities of the neighbourhoods and to reform their more kasar ways.

Since the 1970s, as both the upper path and the riverflat have been completely built out, the density of housing has raised new problems. How do residents find enough sunlight to dry clothes? How do they direct drains around, under and between houses so that no dwelling is flooded? How do they resist the subtle and sometimes none-too-subtle attempts to expand dwellings into public spaces like alleyways and land adjacent to the floodwall, so that alleyways remain wide and straight enough to allow the bodies of deceased members to be carried away with dignity to their final resting place? By 2000 it was becoming more popular to build upwards, adding a sun deck for drying clothes, or an extra room. These physical conditions were beyond the scope of most formal government directions and required that residents construct their own social arrangements to cope with the changes. Much of this was negotiated in an informal way. For example, the wealthy returnee who built a two-storey mansion to the limits of his inherited block, thus depriving neighbours of sunlight and space in the alleyways, was never entirely forgiven in alleyway gossip. Neighbours were not sorry when he died soon after returning to the kampung. In the sharpest of insults, few of these neighbours attended his funeral.

Mutual assistance among neighbours is often of the informal kind that stresses mutual obligation rather than formal procedures. After a death in the neighbourhood, members of the RT and sometimes even the whole RW spontaneously gather at the house of the deceased to serve drinks to those who are mourning, contribute anonymously to a fund to help cover costs, and finally to join in the prayers and walk to the gravesite. More recently, kampung RT communities have instituted funeral funds to which all households contribute on a monthly basis, the funds drawn on by the RT head to help any bereaved neighbour with funeral costs. A community innovation I first noted in 2000 comprises visiting the sick, a practice said to have started first among the Catholic community. When someone falls sick, particularly if that involves a hospital stay, neighbours arrange a joint visit to the hospital. When an infant in my household returned home after a three-day, two-night stay in hospital, he was visited by crowds of women and girls over three days, to such an extent that he was reduced to coughing again. His renewed coughing did not seem to arouse any anxiety among his parents, or among the visiting crowd who were enjoying the social occasion.

The women were also at the forefront of another recent social innovation. When a neighbour's mother had a stroke and lay paralysed in her home because her poor family did not have the means to admit her to hospital, two different groups of women took up collections, which raised Rp50,000 for the household. As the women said, such an amount would not pay for hospital treatment but it did demonstrate neighbours' concern. As it turned out, the amount covered the cost of an ambulance to take the patient to her home village, where she died soon after.

Thus in kampung circumstances where finances are strained, an informal strategy is often preferred. Informal strategies address financial problems that the formal sector does not recognise and draw on very different principles of mutual assistance to those espoused by the formal society structures. For example, in the case mentioned earlier, women of one RT neighbourhood decided that individual preparation of apem cakes was an extravagance, given their financial circumstances, and that they could save costs without abandoning the ritual and the social sentiments by pooling their resources to cook together, carrying home a portion of the cakes. This reform of a cooperative activity was not even instigated by the formal leader of women, the wife of the RT or RW head, but by other women in the neighbourhood.

In an adjacent kampung, Beard described a group called Jumat Kliwon, named for the day in the 35-day Javanese calendar when the members met (Beard, 1998). The group began in 1969 when members' houses were inundated by flood waters and they met sporadically until 1983, when again they began to meet regularly. There was no formal leader but a charismatic member was named master of ceremonies. Meetings were conducted in the Javanese language rather than in the Indonesian used in RT, RW, PKK (Family Welfare Organization) and youth group meetings, further stressing its informality. The group meetings instituted an arisan and a simpan pinjam, discussed how the community could be improved and delivered announcements from the local government. Women became increasingly involved in administering the finances. The location of the meeting rotated throughout the neighbourhood and meetings were partially conducted outside in public open areas, where wives of men in attendance could listen from the periphery. Beard comments: "Interestingly, the informal social space of the Jumat Kliwon group has been more progressive than has the formal space of the RT/RW in allowing women to partake in the meetings and slowly breaking down the segregation of men and women in the planning process" (Beard, 1998: 226).

Beard goes on to describe two projects implemented in the kampung to pave neighbourhood paths, one by the Jumat Kliwon group and the other by the RW/RT leaders. In the first, the Jumat Kliwon members agreed in a public meeting to contribute Rp1,000 a month per household until all the paths were paved with *konblok* (cement bricks), which they would make themselves with the funds. A young community activist organised men into teams to labour each Sunday to make the bricks and lay the paths. When enthusiasm waned, he reorganised the teams around the hardest workers. Constantly over a period of two years, the men were encouraged both in the regular meetings and informally by the leaders to continue the work. Although progress was at times slow, by the end of two years most of the paths had been paved. In the second project, the work was planned by the RW leader, RW secretary, RW public works coordinator and RT leaders. These leaders chose to purchase the cement bricks and to pay day labourers to lay the brickwork. To raise the necessary funds for the project, the leaders determined that residents would pay Rp1,000 for each member of their household and an additional amount if they owned motor vehicles. However, the residents did not accept the plan. They had not been sufficiently consulted through RT-level meetings

Figure 4.6   An alleyway in mid-Ledok in late 1979.

and did not agree with the larger one-off payment. Despite a later agreement to pay Rp1,000 per household per month rather than the one-off payment, the project broke down because there was not enough money to hire labour. The RT leaders were widely condemned for not providing financial reports to residents. The project was completed only when the community decided to return to contributing voluntary labour and approached wealthier residents to donate additional cash to purchase the necessary materials.

As Beard concludes, "the cultural ethic of mutual cooperation (*gotong royong*) is not a Javanese urban myth: it is a powerful social structure that can support the implementation of community-based plans" (Beard, 1998: 245).

> In the end those spaces created by the Jumat Kliwon forum were more effective in terms of communicating, motivating and mobilising constituents than were those spaces sanctified by the state with their rigid leadership structure and strict social hierarchy. The space of Jumat Kliwon forum was more flexible, and as a result proved more responsive to the needs, desires and pace of its constituents (Beard, 1998: 246).

In this instance the knowledge of community members led to the success of the repaving project. This knowledge entailed understanding what type of plan, in terms of its scope, cost and pace would be acceptable to community members; how to keep community members motivated and working together; and how to revive a planning effort that had fallen apart. By contrast, where RT and RW leaders resorted to formal structures and formal contractors and in so doing under-mined community, the projects failed.

Beard recognised the vital role of women in these community activities. The national Family Welfare Association (PKK) was the key institution at RT and RW levels but Beard describes how this state institution was moulded by local participants. The PKK was an indigenous women's movement in the rural villages of Central Java before it was adopted by the state in 1972 and became standardised throughout the country. However, at the local level of Gondolayu Lor, kampung activities were largely conducted outside state administration. Although officially the wives of RT/RW heads (if they were male) were PKK leaders, "the work of self-appointed activists was often more visible than was that of the formal leaders" (Beard, 1998: 256). The key programs carried out by the women in Gondolayu Lor

Figure 4.7   Weighing of babies at the under-fives clinic.

were the Mother and Child Health Care Clinic (*Posyandu*) and the Family Planning Acceptors' Support Group (*Apsari*). The Posyandu was conducted monthly to record the height and weight of children under the age of five and to provide them with a wholesome snack. Local RT volunteers conducted the clinic and encouraged mothers to prepare healthy food. They also alerted a mother if her child was outside normal weight guidelines for its age and height. A similar program has for many years been conducted within Ledok. On the same date each month, women activists within the RT provide nutritious food and record the weight and height of children under five years of age, assessing whether the child has gained the appropriate weight for its age. It is a very relaxed occasion, enjoyed as much by the recorders as the participating mothers.

Beard noted that by 1995 the monthly Apsari meetings were no longer primarily focused on contraceptive use but on a microcredit program funded by a Bank Exim loan of Rp2 million. Local activists redesigned the program to offer loans at a modest 6 per cent interest. In addition to these PKK programs, local women also initiated a Health Care Clinic for the Elderly, which was conducted by local volunteers once a month and at which blood pressure and body weight were recorded and a meal provided. This clinic was very popular among the elderly because it provided health care and information and gave them an opportunity for socialising. Although this was entirely a local initiative, it is interesting that the main initiator was a government health clinic (puskesmas) nurse. She obtained the approval of kabupaten office as well as local leaders to establish the program because she did not want to be seen as undermining any government program. The clinic was approved by the government because there was no similar state initiative for the elderly. As Beard notes, "The question of whether or not these are 'state' poverty alleviation programs becomes blurred.... These programs are now organised locally by volunteers and are inevitably replanned, modified, or completely rejected according to the specific needs of the community" (Beard, 1998: 259).

Within the informal society of the kampung, the forms of the state are adopted and modified, or ignored as irrelevant or a nuisance. However, the local alternatives should not necessarily be seen as resistance, that is purposeful transgression of formal society structures. Instead, state forms are often seen as simply inappropriate. As an example, the secretary of one RW depended for an income on mediating residents' administrative requirements with the kelurahan office, such as obtaining identity cards for them. This was not an official position but an informal role he had created to earn an income. As one initiative, he was keen to widen the upper path in the RW locality at a point where the land sloped away sharply under a banana grove, this land being owned by a fellow resident. The RW secretary began to negotiate informally with this resident to cede some of the land in exchange for the construction on that land of a retaining wall which the community would build with kelurahan funding. There was no suggestion that land boundaries would be redrawn or contracts signed. It would remain an informal agreement that would benefit everyone.

Referring to another Yogyakarta kampung, Yoshi described the clash of formal and informal social institutions like this: "Kampung dwellers interact together to form their own socio-culture, with its own characteristics. The problem is that later on these traditional ties that have operated over the years within a communal territory confront ties of a new kind which are formalistic, bureaucratic and materialistic." (Yoshi, 2000: in translation). He refers here to those ties created by the state, capitalist market and advanced technology within the process of 'development'. He goes on to detail how residents of Sosrokusuman continued to resent and regret the administrative reorganisation of their RK into RW units. In their case, a single RK was divided into two RW. This undermined the identity and unity of what the residents felt to be a single community and, as a result, the original RK continued as an informal focus of their activities. However, Yoshi suggests that the identity of Sosrokusuman kampung will in the end disappear, though not without contributing in its enforced fragmentation to the rise in criminality and inter-kampung hostilities.

Musiyam and Farid Wajdi (2000) refer to a similar aspect of the informal kampung society in the neighbouring city of Solo by the term "local social institutions". An interesting instance they give of the perpetuation of local social institutions is a similar persistence of RK identity despite the 1989 government abolition of this kampung administrative unit. Residents continued to refer to their RK name as their primary territorial identity. The term was still used in mailing addresses and even the kelurahan office, the lowest level of formal administration under salaried government employees, continued to refer to the kampung by its RK name. Lont describes life in Kampung Kricak Kidul and refers to a mutual association called Paguyuban Warga Kricak Kidul (Association of Kricak Kidul Residents) started by leaders of the former RK Kricak Kidul "in order to preserve the unity of the community after an administrative redivision in the 1980s" (Lont, 1999: 16).

CONCLUSION

The distinction between informal and formal economic sectors by Hart and other social observers of urban life provided an important impetus for the recognition of the myriad income-producing activities that take place in the interstices of the formal economy. The danger in this distinction is that the two were seen as distinct sectors when in fact, formal and informal activities and institutions were closely interwoven. Similarly there is a danger in seeing kampung and its 'informal' society and culture as distinct from the wider city. Kampung institutions are constantly and intricately interrelated with the formal structures of the city, even as far as the formal leadership of kampung institutions and the employment of kampung residents in formal sectors. However, kampung society is not to be understood as an aberration of formal society, as a society that exhibits asocial or immoral behaviour and has to be put right by formalisation. As with the informal economic sector, 'kampung' responses are a response to the opportunities within the city in which people have to survive. That they do it in communal ways is both an advantage to the government and a thorn in its side. The lack of uniformity in the informal kampung society is not easily recognised in government development policy or implementation, but for kampung residents these informal institutions are a point of identification, a communal strength, and a potential resource offered in negotiation with the state.

The contrast between rich and poor is particularly marked in Indonesian cities. Although there is some disagreement in recent years over what constitutes a kampung, there is a common recognition of many kampung as the residential areas of the urban poor. Relations between the wealthy streetside and the poor kampung, government officials and the poor, middle-class NGOs and the poor, student activists and the poor commonly take the form of one side giving and the other receiving, one side with all the ideas and programs, the other with all the need. There is plenty of evidence in the analysis presented here that kampung poor have much to offer in terms of functioning social security networks, informal employment enterprises and strategies of mutual assistance that may provide the basis for a more reliable exit strategy from hardship and other crises. Formal programs of assistance to the kampung poor are likely to succeed only insofar as they can be incorporated within informal kampung social institutions.

5

Kampung Youth and Modern Consumer Lifestyles

Earlier chapters have represented the kampung not as a stagnant corner of a thriving metropolis but as a population tapped into the wider city and the national economy and society and as one that has experienced dramatic changes over the three decades in which I have known them. These changes are perhaps most marked within the experience of the youth. In this chapter I explore the changes that have taken place in kampung society through the experiences of kampung youth and social perceptions of these youth. While material changes in the kampung have affected everyone, I suggest that youth have often represented the vanguard of kampung residents seeking to come to terms with modernity. Over the three decades I have been associated with Ledok, kampung youth have changed in the way they express themselves and the way in which they are being absorbed into kampung society. They have adopted new styles presented by the global consumer world, such as alcohol, designer clothes, religious and music styles, but in a way that still allows them space to express their own identity and to live in the sometimes ambiguous spaces left to them within their neighbourhood communities. They are consumers of modernity — T-shirts and jeans, music, musical instruments, bus tours to recreational spots, DVDs, motorcycles — but struggle to meet the financial costs of that modernity. Yet they live as members of kampung society, a society categorised by the wider urban, middle-class society as boorish, low-income, lower-class, criminal and definitely not 'modern'. The behaviour of these kampung youth, and particularly the young men, can therefore be seen as reflecting both their position as members of a lower class within the wider urban society and their identity as a younger generation reacting to their parents' generation's values and occupations.

I will explore in this chapter why and how during the mid-1990s some youth became involved in excessive consumption of alcohol and extreme violence and how that condition contrasted with preceding and subsequent years. A sense of deprivation within the growing affluence of the mid-1990s led to extreme forms of alcohol consumption, radical music and violence, symbolising and consolidating these youths' alienation from kampung and wider societies. By the early 2000s youth were once again absorbed in ties of reciprocal exchange manifested in their service at ceremonial feasts, their respect for elders and their participation in music and work activities in the wider society.

YOUTH IN INDONESIAN SOCIETY

In pre-modern Javanese society, youth was a phase of life when males left their families to roam the countryside, often studying at religious schools or gaining esoteric religious knowledge in other ways (Siegel, 1986: 138; Anderson, 1972: 1999). This was a ritual phase for male adolescents, bridging the period between childhood and adulthood and marked by excessive tolerance, that is an overturning of the usual strict insistence on respect and conformity. Javanese regarded it as a vital period of individual development, an open door to take stock, focus one's thinking and prepare oneself to re-enter as an adult the world of sexuality, hierarchy and adult ways (Anderson, 1988; Cucu, 2002b). It was not however a period of total freedom, for youth were expected to make their own contribution towards the continuity of society.

School textbooks used in the 1990s attested to the historical importance of youth in the struggle for Indonesian independence. Indonesian students in the Netherlands formed Perhimpunan Indonesia (Indonesian Association) which called for independence through its publication *Indonesia Merdeka* (Independent Indonesia). These students were eventually arrested but later freed by a Dutch court as having no case to answer. At the Second Youth Congress in Indonesia in 1928, a pledge was formulated about the unity of Indonesian country, nation and language, a pledge that would inspire the independence struggle (Ricklefs, 1991: 183; Mulder, 2000: 41).

In New Order Indonesia, the role of religious schools was usurped by public schools but "it is still the case that students are seen to bear a special responsibility for the transformation of society" (Siegel, 1986:

139). In my account of Ledok in the 1970s, I wrote of the impact of education and other aspects of modernity on the kampung youth:

> Age is the first index of rank of which a Javanese child becomes aware. Kinship terms recognize seniority of age, and towards those senior kin a child is quickly taught to show the formal signs of deference .... Increased access of the young to education, television, films, wealth and high-ranked occupations in recent years has undermined the standing of older residents who never had the opportunity to appreciate these things in their younger years. The knowledge and experience of those senior in age is not necessarily relevant in the scramble for work and income in the city of 1979–80 .... The kampung youth ... complain of a generation gap between themselves and their parents and more senior neighbours. They claim that their seniors do not understand them, their interests or their opinions, even as they submit to the seniority of these elders (Guinness, 1986: 30–3).

During the struggle for Independence and then in 1965–66 preceding the emergence of the New Order, Indonesian youth (*pemuda*) earned a reputation as the people who dared to challenge the status quo. In the 1970s students led the protests against the corruption and excesses of the New Order and were silenced only by the government's Normalisasi Kampus decree of 1978, which prohibited all political activity on campus. For a decade thereafter, while student and youth political action was restricted to NGOs and religious reformist activities, youth became the target of consumer-oriented capitalism. Billiard halls, cafes, restaurants and numerous youth-focused magazines and tabloids grabbed their attention and sexual partnerships outside marriage became a part of their hedonistic existence (Cucu, 2002b). Then in 1989 students joined peasants in protesting against New Order excesses, beginning with issues of land dispossession. The protests joined those of factory workers, many of them single young men and women, and culminated in 1996–98 with direct challenges to the central government in Jakarta and the resignation of President Suharto in May 1998. From 1997 youth joined political parties and formed mass organisations and once again became a political force in Indonesian life (Cucu, 2002b).

Despite these radical roles in the wider society, Siegel suggests that there has been little change in the familial roles of kampung youth over the generations. Commenting on Javanese adolescence, Hildred

Geertz (1961) emphasised the strong difference in attitude towards male and female adolescent children. While girls were carefully controlled, boys were allowed complete freedom and were expected to be sexually experienced before marriage. Boys were considered to be irresponsible until after they reached their twenties. While some might well continue to stay at home, others left to find work or attend school. A boy did not marry until he could support a wife (Geertz, 1961: 119–20). This indicates not just the freedom and independence of adolescent boys but also the tolerance by the family and community of their freedom.

YOUTH SUBCULTURES IN THE CITY

In their theorization of youth subcultures, Clarke, Hall, Jefferson and Roberts (1996) suggest that there are many youth subcultures in any society and that each of these connects to both their 'parent' culture and the dominant culture of the wider society. Although the great majority of youth do not enter a tight or coherent subculture, those who do fashion distinctive cultural pursuits that feed off and appropriate things provided by the market (Clarke *et al.*, 1996: 15–6). These authors draw attention to the problems faced in Britain by working-class youth, who contribute the major proportion of what became known as youth culture, but they reject the theory that youth subcultures are best explained as a way of problem-solving. Rather they suggest that youth subcultures construct in an imaginary relation the contradictions which remain hidden or unresolved in the parent culture, along with the real relations they cannot otherwise transcend (Clarke *et al.*, 1996: 29–33). These subcultures are not "ideological" constructs, however, but designed to "win space for working class youth from the dominant cultures: cultural space in the neighbourhood and institutions, real time for leisure and recreation, actual room on the street or street-corner" (Clarke *et al.*, 1996: 45). These authors draw attention to the disposable income that allows working-class youth to adopt consumer patterns beyond the reach of their parents' generation, while still leaving them with a sense of deprivation compared to middle-class youth. The emphasis is therefore less on the dilemma of absorbing modern values or styles into traditions learnt from their parents than on a struggle to comprehend the limitations and frustrations of their class position.

Reviewing the literature on Western-society youth, Philip Cohen suggests that the "youth question is the site of singular nexus of contradictions. Youth is simultaneously constituted as a place and time of marginality and powerlessness and as the bearer of a whole series of special symbolic powers." He continues that "the construction of imaginary kingdoms of youth (mis)rule feeds off and reinforces real positions of powerlessness. Certainly the marginality of youth within the official body politic tends to sponsor a rival "body politics" centred on a culture of adolescent narcissism, which in turn even further alienates young people from organized politics" (Cohen, 1997: 225–6).

In the account that follows, I trace the role of youth in Ledok over the 30 years of my involvement in the neighbourhoods. Young people's involvement in organised activity, in schooling and university, or in the urban economy varied over these years with effects on their behaviour. Generally, however, within kampung society the youth were regarded as those most familiar with the life of the wider society. While other residents of the kampung might work in streetside society, for many this was no more than a place of work and they spent most of their time in the kampung. The exceptions here were the public servants and larger entrepreneurs, whose work demanded that they engage widely in city society. Many kampung youth engaged this wider society and its modernity both through schooling and, for some, university activities, as well as through the time they spent on the streets and in the shopping malls and internet cafes of the city. Their parents recognised that these youth were far more at home in the modern consumer city than they were. Many kampung residents of the older generation had never entered the larger shopping malls, nor eaten at Pizza Hut, McDonalds or other sites of 'Western' culture.

However, kampung youth in Yogyakarta still experienced marginalisation in diverse ways. Education, firstly, was generally recognised by kampung residents as essential for success in the city but schooling proved expensive and sometimes beyond the means of kampung parents. This led to youth dropping out of school and then sitting around the alleyways with nothing much to do. Secondly, unemployment characterised the lives of many kampung youth. They did not have the contacts with public servants or company officials to gain employment in the formal sector, even if they had adequate education. Nor did they or their parents have access to capital to promote their business aspirations.

The distinctiveness and importance of youth is recognised in Indonesian government with the insistence that every administrative unit, RT, RW, and RK, has a Seksi Pemuda (Youth Section), referring to a person elected by residents to focus on issues faced by youth. At the kampung level, these elected officers are responsible for organising activities for the youth, usually focused on sport, social outings, and music, for both young men and women. Although their focus was on recreational activities, these officers often reflected the concerns of the wider kampung community in providing youth with skills and resources to obtain a regular income and in involving them in responsibilities within the neighbourhood. Thus in one RT, the Youth Section provided musical equipment, which gave youth an incentive to seek work as street performers. In others, youth were persuaded to help out in household life-cycle rituals. One RW committee enabled youth to find employment under a government employment creation scheme; in another the RW committee engaged a local youth band as the main entertainment at an Independence Day concert.

Churches and mosques have also incorporated youth sections within their programs in the kampung. All mosques in the kampung run *ngaji* (Koranic recitation) for youth but it is recognised that youth in their later teen years tend to drop out of these classes. In one Ledok mosque, accommodation has been built beside the mosque to attract students from outside the Yogyakarta region who play a leadership and administrative role in children's activities. Catholic youth over the years became involved in a kampung choir that sang regularly at mass in the parish church located a short walk away from the kampung.

In the sections that follow, I identify from my participation and observation in the kampung four key periods that trace the changing experiences and expressions of kampung youth. Following Clarke *et al.* (1996) and Cohen (1997), I highlight the way youth articulate both to their 'parent' culture, in particular the culture of community, and to the dominant culture of the wider society. If Clarke *et al.* are correct, this will reveal some of the contradictions that lie unresolved in their parents' culture, reflecting the frustrations of their 'class' position in kampung. Feted as the bearers and wearers of modernity, they confront on a daily basis reminders of their own powerlessness, either in the wider economy and polity of the city or in the neighbourhood politics of the kampung. Their specific behaviours in these different periods of Ledok history reveal something more of the nature of kampung society and community.

LEDOK YOUTH, 1975–1980

During the 1970s when I first lived in Ledok, youth regularly participated in gamelan, volleyball, badminton and soccer, taking advantage

Figure 5.1   Youth playing volleyball in a 1970s neighbourhood.

of the still vacant spaces on the riverflat. Named youth organisations existed in the north, centre and south of the kampung. These were fully supported by RK and neighbourhood leaders and roughly corresponded in their membership to the later formalized RW neighbourhoods. These youth organisations were not organised around administrative RT units, but wider community neighbourhoods comprising several RT, thus underlining the community rather than government initiatives involved. In the central ward, residents recalled that in the 1960s a youth group organised regular sports activities and at the end of the year held a thanksgiving ceremony for which they cooked all the food, organised a band and to which they invited neighbourhood leaders. In the 1970s, a similar group competed in intra-kampung sports such as volleyball and table tennis and formed folk music and theatre groups. Their activities peaked on Independence Day, which was strongly promoted by the government as a day when each local unit could acknowledge the nation. Locally, however, it became a time when the community and community youth were celebrated. Each generation of youth created their own activities, supported by more senior advisors in the ward. In 1979 in the central ward, the youth organisation published on an alleyway wall a magazine consisting of poems and articles from members and ran an English-speaking course. A similar group in another ward organised bus trips for its members and celebrated national holidays with sack races, flower decoration contests and concerts. They also ran a savings group, whose meetings were addressed by kampung leaders. Another ward's youth group ran a library and had furnished a room with sewing machines for youth training. Youth in all wards also took part in security patrols (Guinness, 1986: 148–9). Youth were also strongly involved in church activities, forming their own choir and supporting church services under kampung deacons aligned to the local Catholic parish.

One example of the incorporation of kampung youth into neighbourhood rituals was their role in *jagongan*. These rituals were held in the evenings when men of the neighbourhood gathered to chat, smoke and play cards, generally right through the night, and were served with drinks and snacks by the male youth. The point of the ritual was to provide company to the household at a time of a life crisis, either a birth or death or after a kendhuren/slametan ceremony commemorating a marriage, the seventh month in a pregnancy, or a circumcision. The youth took this role very seriously. This made them an integral part of the population of the kampung and its component neighbourhoods and there appeared little ambiguity in their involvement in the community.

Youth were widely encouraged within kampung society. There was little or no condemnation of youth who could not find work and there was active encouragement of schooling as the means to employment. Since jobs were hard to find and many of the kampung youth in the 1970s had no more than casual employment in the informal sector, consumerism was modest in comparison to later years. There were no shopping malls. Youth bought cloth from textile shops to be made into clothes at a cheap price by neighbourhood tailors. Only a few families owned a television set, around which their neighbours, including youth, gathered at night. In the 1970s I noted a strong distancing between kampung and streetside neighbours, perhaps most strongly expressed by youth. A nearby streetside youth, for example, described how he had drifted away from kampung friends once he started high school and that on a visit to the kampung ten years later he had been ridiculed by kampung youth for his clothes and the way he walked and spoke. "They were spoiling for a fight," he said (Guinness, 1986: 23–4).

One way kampung youth sought to impress their peers was through demonstrating *ngelmu* (esoteric knowledge), which they claimed gave them inner strength or immunity from attack. To demonstrate this, they played with poisonous snakes, walking in processions with the snakes wrapped round their bodies. They claimed to inject their arms with mercury to provide them with immunity, or to use magical formulae to attract women or make their business successful (Guinness, 1986: 115). Older residents, however, dismissed these claims to ngelmu, claiming these youth did not have the self discipline to fast and meditate over long periods to acquire real powers. One group of youth who did demonstrate self discipline practised Orhiba ('new life sport') under the tutelage of a 34-year-old man imprisoned after the military coup of 1965 for spreading Marxist ideas among the youth. On his release, he returned to the kampung, where he taught the youth a special routine of physical exercises that aimed to provide resistance to the influence of dangerous spirits and which culminated in an ability to 'stop breathing' in order to reach a completeness in oneself. The more complete an adherent, the greater their power to control the world. These youth were attracted to the extraordinary powers that this 'new life sport' claimed to bring them. There was a sense of being different and wanting to be different in all this. One Orhiba informant reported that youth were in a state of *goncang* (shock), perplexed with the lack of guidance from their parents and from formalised religion. Their meditation exercises gave them eventually a power to defy or circumvent the conventions of normal society. The Orhiba leader boasted he possessed such great powers that he was once asked to leave a Christian Pentecostal meeting he was attending out of curiosity because "his power was disrupting the free movement of the 'spirit'" (Guinness, 1986: 123–5).

Among the adult kampung residents, there was an acceptance that youth should be free to find their own spiritual paths. This led to cases of families in which, parents proudly told me, there was one child who was Catholic, another Protestant, and another Muslim. Parents added that there were many paths to God. Circumstances were seen to have affected children's decisions. Attending a Catholic school persuaded one to become Catholic, marrying a Muslim persuaded another to become Muslim, but the decisions were seen as an individual choice that did not disadvantage the youth nor embarrass his or her parents.

This tolerance of youth individuality did not stretch to riverbank residents accepting behaviour propagated by riverflat squatters. At that time kampung society was clearly segregated into two strata, corresponding to residents' location on riverbank or riverflat. Riverbank residents comprised the original settlers, many with title to their land and/or house and who set the norms for kampung society and provided most kampung leaders. In contrast, the riverflat residents were squatters who worked in the informal economy, including illegal activities such as theft and prostitution. They were, in the eyes of some riverbank residents, permanently located on the margins by virtue of their lack of 'culture' and their poverty. In their marginality, these riverflat squatters occupied an analogous position to youth, and the two groups were thrown together by their occupation of riverflat space, the squatters occupying houses there and the youth gathering there for recreational purposes such as volleyball or soccer, music, or just socialising.

Many riverbank residents feared for their sons and daughters, associating as they were every day with riverflat occupants and allegedly being corrupted by them. This riverflat group did have an influence on kampung youth, particularly on young men looking for entertainment and company away from the home, as much as anything in the coarse riverflat defiance of riverbank customs that disadvantaged them. Riverflat dwellers cultivated a way of life that conformed to kampung patterns where it was important to their social and economic survival, but frequently in the hearing of kampung youth, they stressed the disadvantages they suffered, such as lack of access to credit at kampung shops, their silence at meetings because of their poor command of refined Javanese language, their dependence on kampung landholders for their home sites, and the arrogant attitudes of some riverbank dwellers in their behaviour toward them. Riverbank parents feared for their children associating with riverflat dwellers, not only because of their bad language and 'immoral behaviour' but because of their defiance of riverbank, that is 'kampung' standards of behaviour.

Although in danger of being corrupted by such 'immorality', kampung youth were also encouraged to be custodians of kampung morality. Among the incoming population during these years was a significant male student population, many from outside Java, boarding in kampung homes and taking advantage of Ledok's central location close to universities and high schools. These students were regarded with suspicion and some animosity by many kampung residents, who objected to their poor command of Javanese etiquette and their flirtations with young single women in the neighbourhood. Several accused of disrespect to community norms were confronted by kampung youth, even beaten up, and most were molested for money, cigarettes, or the loan of motorcycles or bicycles by kampung youth, who considered these boarders to be much wealthier than themselves. There was much effort from kampung leaders to ensure that these students conformed to kampung expectations of social etiquette, showing deference to their elders, contributing to neighbourhood work projects and family rituals, and curbing friendships with kampung girls. There were strong sanctions against students who did not cooperate and these were often enforced through kampung youth action against the offenders (Guinness, 1986: 37).

Deference between the generations weakened in the years that followed. As youth lost mastery of the higher levels of Javanese language, they were no longer able to express respect in subtle linguistic terms. The custom of stooping before an elder when passing them in the alleyway diminished, as did the custom of ritually asking for their forgiveness at the end of the fasting month.

The 1970s were therefore marked by the isolation of kampung youth from urban streetside society. In searching for a different identity from their parents' generation, they looked to distinctive spiritual identity or association with riverflat society and culture. At the same time, they also defended community norms against wayward students and contributed to community rituals. Administratively they were incorporated through Seksi Pemuda (Youth Groups) at RT and RK levels. Any youth resistance was contained within the local neighbourhood and was muted. Nevertheless, the older generations identified youth as a potential or actual threat to community morality and cohesiveness. Youth's enthusiasm for Orhiba, their association with riverflat, and the migrant students' neglect of kampung etiquette raised the greatest concern among the kampung elders. Youth explored change in areas their elders considered sacrosanct, but this era still demonstrated the ability of communal expression to contain youth energies.

LEDOK YOUTH IN THE 1980s

In 1978 the central government instituted the policy of Normalisasi Kampus, requiring university administrators to quell student political activity on campus. This was accompanied by increasing state control over political parties and a push for national development planned and managed from Jakarta. In cultural terms, the state also sought to impose models of national and regional cultures, promoted powerfully through television and government programs such as the Family Welfare Movement (PKK). Political stability took precedence over political participation and programs of national development facilitated the rise of consumerism and capitalism (Guinness, 1994).

During the 1980s, student and youth energies were expanded in two directions: into the consumer marketplace and into religious reformism. In Yogyakarta consumerism was epitomised by the new shopping plazas, which kampung youth eagerly explored, even though many of their parents refused to enter them, saying they felt completely out of place among the extravagant and highly priced boutique shops. This period of high consumption lasted through to 1998, during which time most kampung households acquired a television set and some of the wealthier, a DVD player, video, and refrigerator. Fast-food outlets such as McDonalds and Pizza Hut opened and became part of the youth image of modern urban living. As more kampung youth proceeded through to senior high school and some to university, they became more aware and involved in student activities.

At the national level, religious activities became more prominent. Leading mosques in Indonesia, such as the Salman Mosque on the Technological Institute of Bandung (ITB) campus and the Shalahuddin Mosque on the campus of Gadjah Mada University in Yogyakarta, promoted a more energetic commitment to Islamic ideals, encouraging this through small discussion groups. Karisma, the Salman Family of Muslim Youth, numbering 2,880 senior high school and university students in 1989, offered an Intensive Islamic Study course and a weekly mentoring program. On Sunday mornings hundreds of students divided into small groups and, guided by the group mentor, deepened their religious knowledge. Training for Religious Preachers (LMD) targeted university students who came from universities in Java and Sumatra to study Islamic scriptures, thought and morality. When these students returned to their home campuses, they initiated a religious resurgence. University mosques became a powerful network beyond state control for students to demonstrate their religious devotion (Hasbullah, 1999).

This movement eventually had an influence on national politics, culminating in the formation of the Indonesian Association of Islamic Intellectuals (ICMI) and President Suharto's pilgrimage to Mecca (Rosyad, 1995). Among the Indonesian middle classes, Islamic dress and Islamic music became increasingly popular (Hasbullah, 1999). Muslim activists declared that Muslim youth had become intoxicated by Western cultural infiltration, leading to moral decadence. They expressed dissatisfaction with the established social and political order, which suppressed Islamic social and cultural ideas and political aspirations (Rosyad, 1995: 26). Analysing another Islamic youth movement centred on a charismatic preacher Aa Gym and his Daarut Tauhid Pesantren (religious school) in Bandung, Solahudin suggested that young Muslims were attracted to such a movement because they felt unease that their 'delinquent' behaviour had drawn them away from religious piety and social orderliness. They now sought instead an inner happiness and certainty (Solahudin, 1996).

A similar movement took place among Christian groups in the 1980s and 1990s, as young people sought a form of expression for their religious faith and sentiments different from that provided through mainstream church liturgies. Pioneered through the activities of international organisations such as Navigators, this again took the form of small group discussions and worship, emphasising mutual commitment by members of the group, a sharing of personal experiences and study of the scriptures focused on a personal religious experience. Students were encouraged to express themselves through religious ritual and creed, not political goals, but group teaching emphasised the individual as a spiritual being under God and as a potential graduate within the growing urban, even international society. The cell groups that formed under this movement targeted both religious devotion and scholarly commitment. In Yogyakarta, Dhewayani reported 16 Christian prayer and study groups in 1996 and 84 in 2004 (Dhewayani, 2005).

Higher levels of education were not always accessible to kampung youth. In the 1970s junior high school was the highest level of achievement expected among kampung families, with only the children of public servants going on to senior high school or university. By 1990, however, the level of education required for employment had risen to at least senior high school but the parents of kampung youth struggled to finance that achievement. For example, in 1989 one parent mentioned to me that he would have to pay the equivalent of one year's rent on his house to meet the school building charges demanded for admission into senior high school (Guinness, 1991: 93). Kampung youth found themselves in a very competitive labour market place, in which their difficulty in gaining employment was their most severe form of marginalisation. Those youth who did complete secondary or tertiary education faced great competition for formal-sector jobs. In 1988 a large department store in Yogyakarta hired a sports stadium to process applicants for shop assistant positions; Gadjah Mada University received 20,000 applications for 1,000 places within its administration;

and the city government received 32,000 applications for 500 vacancies (Guinness, 1990: 14). Thus, despite their efforts at school, kampung youth had no confidence about securing a good job. At the same time their heightened aspirations dissuaded them from accepting menial work like their parents, as labourers, becak drivers, warung operators, streetsellers or hawkers.

During the 1980s, kampung youth did enjoy new opportunities for income-earning in the domestic and international tourist trade. Daily flights from Jakarta and Bali, improved bus and train services, and the mushrooming of international hotels and boutique shops in modern shopping plazas created a new local economy (Guinness, 1991: 92). For example, kampung artists and poets set up business on city pavements to supply shoppers with greeting cards crafted to their request or approached formal stores to carry their product. One of these was an economics graduate, unable to find employment in the formal sector (Guinness, 1990: 14). Some young people signed up for work in Batam or for international migrant labour to Malaysia, Singapore and Saudi Arabia, despite reports of mistreatment by foreign employers.

The 1980s was a period of marked economic growth in Indonesia which fed into a consumerist boom in popular culture. In the early 1980s, James Siegel observed and wrote about society in Solo, not far from Yogyakarta. He described the emergence of popular music among the youth as challenging the norms of Javanese society. Javanese traditionally stressed the importance of speaking and acting well, in which "to speak properly is to hold something back; to pay respect is to be reserved; respect is the basis of hierarchy; hierarchy is imaged in the state" (Siegel, 1986: 230). Siegel described the emergence during this period of a new social type of *remaja* (teenager, adolescent), which replaced the popular term *pemuda*. While pemuda had referred to the generations of youth who had struggled at the forefront of Indonesian society to gain independence from the Dutch, upset the Old Order and installed the New Order, and then challenged the excesses of the New Order, the identity of the remaja was expressed not in political terms but through consumer lifestyles. The popular music embraced by youth challenged the idea that everything good had been passed down by tradition. Instead, according to Siegel, this music emphasised surprise, creativity and individual taste, in contrast to the image of the socially and politically conscientious pemuda. While continuing to play more traditional roles within their family, remaja cultivated their own subculture, which was countervalent to traditions espoused by their parents. Similarly, in the Islamic resurgence of the 1980s, music also played an important part. The songs of Bimbo, Emha and others provided lyrics of religious contemplation and devotion that provided an individual space and collective religious identity for urban youth, distinguishing them from the more ritualistic practices of their parents (Hasbullah, 1999).

According to Siegel, for all their indeterminateness, remaja notions of person, music and fashion made it clear that they held the fantasy of an integrated self, distinct from its environment yet affected by it. Popular music depended on taste, a notion new to Javanese. In contrast to traditional music, which was mainly ritual background music, remaja emphasised the importance of getting involved in their music: "they listened to it, it 'passed through' them, they were affected by it, it mattered to them" (Siegel, 1986: 229). As with religious expressions, music became a means to express the distinctiveness of youth within the hegemonic political and cultural New Order.

However, Siegel also drew attention to the ambivalence associated with this independence. Clothing came to be the most important expression of an independent identity for youth. They had enough money to indulge themselves in such fashion expressions as jeans and message-laden T-shirts symbolising the new energy and independence of the youth, the clothing styles originating in local Chinese stores. Siegel described one dramatic period in Solo in 1980 when Javanese youth went on the rampage, looting these Chinese shops. In the riots, "what was demonstrated was the students' repudiation of their own desire to own what Chinese possessed ... they destroyed Chinese wealth not to shame Chinese but to show they were unlike them ... the aimless violence of the riots may have had the effect of breaking the identification of remaja and Chinese" (Siegel, 1986: 246–53). Siegel suggested that the remaja were repudiating the possibility of seeing themselves to be like Chinese because they wore what the Chinese sold. In Siegel's analysis, these Chinese shops were seen as responsible for introducing modern fashion and consumerism to Indonesian youth and, with their appeal to *pamrih* (personal indulgence), they were responsible for drawing youth away from Javanese practices of self-control. While the youth were avid clients of consumerism, they were also torn by their commitment to the Javanese values of self-restraint espoused by their parents. It was this ambivalence which found expression in the riots of 1980 (Siegel, 1986: 241).

The 1980s thus inspired youth in their search for distinctiveness, either through religious commitments or through a fascination with a certain style of pop music, clothing fashion and informal income earning linked to tourism. In all these they displayed an independence from the older kampung generations but were not entirely free of the moral expectations of that kampung community. The contradictions in their position were most evident in the Solo riot and similar disturbances, when the clash between the self-indulgence of consumerism and the self-restraint taught by their parents found violent expression. In Ledok youth in the 1980s were becoming increasingly absorbed into the consumer market, identifying with its fashions in clothes and music. They began to wander the shopping malls to indulge by gazing at the new fashions, also to form their own bands to play styles of music unfamiliar to their parents. However, they often struggled to find the cash to make their purchases. This led to aspirations for more secure and higher-paid formal-sector employment, but also to frustration when their hopes were disappointed.

The consumer boom of which Siegel writes was followed in the mid-1980s by the oil crisis, the weakening of the state, the devaluation of the currency and significant cuts to subsidies for energy and food. This generated hardships for kampung residents and the emergence of criminal gangs of young people called *gali* (*gabungan anak liar* or gangs of wild youth) (Barker, 2001: 23). Some kampung, though less so Ledok, gained a reputation for lawlessness.

URBAN COWBOYS AND LEDOK YOUTH, 1996

By 1996 kampung youth were observing acute contrasts of wealth in the world around them. The city was increasingly marked by public displays of wealth, much of it directed towards status. Universities, banks, shopping malls and hotels continued to construct opulent buildings to signify their standing in the new modern Indonesia. Many of these buildings used space and size to demand the attention of a public awed by opulence. The intervening years had seen the development of numerous housing estates, some even with golf courses, and the movement of the city's middle classes into these controlled and patrolled environments. Some of the kampung elite had joined this flow. The student boarders of earlier years had also largely gone, attracted to stylish *asrama* (boarding houses), which allowed students much more freedom and better facilities. Meanwhile, kampung spaces had become more densely settled. Residents had to negotiate crowded spaces to dry their washing, hold their life-crisis ceremonies and socialise. Though kampung living standards had improved in some ways, particularly in the construction materials of houses, the polarities of wealth were more and more obvious between kampung and streetside. Some of these discrepancies had even entered into the kampung as one or two outsiders or kin, returning from years of employment outside, took over existing riverbank titles and constructed houses more in keeping with streetside than kampung styles. Emphasising privacy, these homes were built to the very perimeters of their titled block, closed off at ground level but with large windows and verandahs at the upper level where occupants' privacy could be assured. Their owners attracted much hostility among adults and youth in the kampung for the anti-social attitudes reflected in such buildings.

In contrast, many kampung youths lacked self-esteem and confidence as a result of not having work. One day in 1996 I was asked by a group of the young men gathered in the alleyway what they could do to improve their situation. Thinking they were asking about finding a niche in the informal urban economy, I talked about the opportunities available in the tourist market. This was not what they wanted to hear. Instead they were seeking contacts with influential people in the city, from whom they could seek work in the formal sector. They saw their situation as one to be solved not through entrepreneurship and initiative but by recognising and overcoming the structural constraints of a hierarchical society that marginalised them. When streetside, middle-class university students in the KKN program held that kampung youth were lazy, not keen to find work, did not save, and did not cooperate in 'development' projects, kampung elders, some of whom were parents of these youths, tried to persuade the students to use their project to get alongside youth and pass on some of the secrets of success in today's world. There was a certain amount of realism in this for the parents recognised that success depended not only on skills but also on contacts within the larger urban economy outside. The university students and the kampung elders represented diametrically opposed views, one blaming the youth for a lack of initiative and commitment to the norms of the 'modern' society and the other seeing the young people as facing obstacles in the wider urban social and economic structures.

Kampung youth in 1996 loudly identified with two distinctive recreations: music and drinking. In Ledok the music scene among the youth was foreign music, often adapted to Indonesian lyrics. Those who had the means purchased guitars and practised regularly in make-shift studios or bedrooms, though the amplification of their rehearsals annoyed many of their close neighbours. While such music-making could include one or two friends, it was not conducive to building solidarity among the youth. Some who were keen on their own style of 'grunge' joined a band elsewhere. Each was jealously critical of others' music, both in its style and its playing. Such music was largely seen as anti-social in that other segments of the kampung were not invited and could not share with the youth in these passions.

Youth were also associated with a style of food and drink con-sumption epitomised in the *lesehan* (pavement food bars) and the *warung kauboi* (cowboy bars). Several prominent youth were drawn to these through their involvement as guides and companions of tourist backpackers. One who spoke with me boasted of his sexual conquests of foreign women whom he met in the hostel neighbourhood. He described a lifestyle he shared with them of chatting and drinking alcohol at bars, night clubs and restaurants on Yogyakarta's main tourist road. For him and his kampung friends, drinking alcohol had become a regular activity and one that he also pursued within the kampung, sitting in the alleyways with friends.

The warung kauboi were street stalls that opened at night and sold a variety of alcoholic drinks of local recipes. These drinks were often termed *ginseng*, a name derived from the term for the imported Korean root soaked in alcohol and sold in bottles from pharmacies in town. From this base, dealers produced their own mix in home breweries and sold it in smaller quantities to stall traders. A stall trader could begin with capital as small as Rp10,000 or two litres of alcohol and steadily build up his or her earnings. The stall trader sold the alcohol by glass in a variety of combinations with milk, eggs, or coffee, costing anything from Rp1,500 a glass.

Some of the stall traders came from Ledok. By one trader's esti-mate, 25 kampung men and women managed such stalls. The most successful of these traders ran a stall from inside a karaoke bar, where his drink sales were better than those of the bar itself. He was said to take Rp300,000 to Rp500,000 a night and to employ ten attendants and/or security staff, whom he paid Rp200,000 a month each, well above the minimum wage of Rp75,000 a month. He had begun in a small way only a few years previously and had already made enough to invest in a housing estate house and to purchase a car. At the other extreme, kampung residents had turned to *ginseng* stalls as a last resort because they required a minimum of capital.

The clientele of the stall were generally remaja or 'youthful' older men, that is, those who liked to have a drink away from home. They would sit around the stall, on bench seats or wherever they could find a place, and while away the evening hours in talk. In most cases the atmosphere was quiet and relaxed, though conversation could be animated. These were the 'cowboys', a term that referred not just to the lack of state regulation of these sales but to a frontier space where the old rules did not apply and new rules of behaviour took precedence. This behaviour was variously described as frank, open, freely expressing emotions, quick to engage in fights but not holding any grudge after the event. This was seen as largely in contrast with the more formal and hierarchical Javanese culture in wider society.

The ginseng and 'cowboy' stalls had not existed in the 1970s, nor when I visited in 1989. In those earlier years there was sly grog produced in a nearby kampung Sosrowijayan, but its consumption was largely confined to that kampung with its large flow of foreign and domestic tourists through home stays (Sullivan, 1980). Ginseng became popular in the 1990s, it was said, when the local government banned the sale of *beras kencur,* a traditional medicinal/alcoholic drink made from rice. Whereas beras kencur had been largely consumed at home and in the 1970s only by older men, by 1996 ginseng had become a profitable commodity for warung street stalls. It was not clear whether ginseng was necessarily the component in all drinks sold in these stalls. Whiskey, brandy and a variety of local concoctions were sold with little if any supervision from city government or the Health Department. To counter this image of 'cowboy' lawlessness, stall traders insisted that they were looking after their clientele. If anyone got too drunk, they said, he was escorted by the stall's security man to a pedicab and sent home. Stall traders were aware that if their stall became a site for open fights it would soon be closed by the police.

However, these were not the only places where ginseng and other alcohol were consumed publicly. Within the kampung, youth would gather nightly to share a bottle of home brew. One of them might purchase some ginseng from a local trader, generally sold in a plastic bag with straw attached, and this would be passed around the group of youth. More dangerously, one of the young men would buy a large bottle of sarsaparilla drink and mix with it crushed sleeping tablets and/or mosquito repellent or other substances purchased from the local kampung stall. There was keen interest in experimenting with such mixes and they would be shared around. Thus, with a minimal amount of perhaps Rp1,000, the group could get themselves drunk, this being the purpose of the activity for many of them. They would sit out in the kampung pathways after most residents had gone to sleep and into the small hours of the morning. Some would end up vomiting in the alleyway, some would fall asleep on the ground, while in a few cases some would lose consciousness and collapse. While I was living in the kampung in 1996, on a couple of occasions youths were found the morning after a drinking binge unconscious on the ground and ended up in hospital in intensive care. In one case a young father, sent from Sulawesi for studies in Yogyakarta, collapsed in a drunken stupor in the kampung and died. His pregnant wife and small child accompanied his body home to Sulawesi for burial. Sometimes fights broke out among drunken youths. In one case in the kampung a stall trader was slit in the face with a knife when he attempted to help his security man control a drunken client. In another case a fight broke out among a few youths after a gambling event and one of them was knifed to death. His killer, who already had a reputation of violence, was still on the run when I left in late 1996.

This consumption of alcoholic and other potent drinks enhanced the camaraderie of the youth who drank together and their standing among their peers. In nearby Ledok Macanan, where Arifin reported in 1993 that almost all youth were consumers of alcohol and marijuana, their frustrations with their economic situation as the decade wore on was reflected in the increasing numbers of youth who were drunk every night (Arifin, 2003). However, the drinking did more than create camaraderie or absorb frustrations. Bruce Kapferer, in reference to drinking at Anzac celebrations in Australia, questions an interpretation of drinking as merely an expression of camaraderie. In the Australian context, drinking is an ingredient in the formation of personal power. Drink is seen to have power and "bite, so that the ability to consume large amounts of beer or a very potent drink without being affected is a feat of prowess. To consume alcohol is to appropriate its power" (Kapferer, 1988: 156–7). In Yogyakarta kampung, there was a similar concept among the youth of the power of the drink and drinkers added components to their drink to increase that power. Pharmaceuticals or traditional medicines known for their potency were added to the already potent drink. However, it did not appear to me that there was the same emphasis on 'holding their booze' as with the

Australian drinker. The emphasis was on what was consumed rather than one's ability to withstand it. There was an awe, a fear, associated with consuming these highly uncertain mixtures. Potency came not from withstanding but rather from absorbing the potency of the drink. There was no embarassment, therefore, in sleeping off or even vomiting away the effects of the drink in public. It was assumed that friends would look after the inebriated during this time.

Despite the risks associated with drinking, it remained a popular, if not dominant, pastime among many remaja. While drinking these young men often got their arms and legs tattooed by drinking mates. Tattoos were not socially approved of in the wider kampung society and were generally interpreted as linking their wearer with criminal or deviant behaviour and gangs, yet many youth sported tattoos, evidence at least to some observers of their time on the streets among the gali (Barker, 2001: 34–5). There was some muttering among kampung neighbours about these youths' unruly behaviour. Neighbours were also critical of the cost of drinking for poor families and of the health costs of excessive drinking. Some in the kampung suggested that long periods of unemployment, dropping out of school, or the lack of caring family environment were the chief contributors to excessive drinking habit. For most of these youth, drinking was a form of relaxation and sharing with friends. Most who drank regularly were unemployed, either SMA (senior high school) graduates or senior school dropouts, that is they had a fairly good education but were without jobs. It was pointed out to me by several residents that university students and formal-sector employees were not in these groups. I observed one family's immediate strong reprimand of their student son, a SMA graduate, when he started drinking and their success in curtailing his drinking. Other families were not so successful.

There was widespread anxiety among kampung residents about the potential disruption caused by drunkenness. However, the issue of community action in relation to drinking, or rather in relation to dealing with the disruptions caused by unruly drinkers, was rarely discussed. Raising such an issue in neighbourhood meetings threatened to lead to conflict between neighbours and thus cut across the ideal condition of social harmony. Many residents considered that openly raising the problem of the disorderly conduct of some neighbours threatened cordial relations among community members. Instead the community put pressure on the drinkers themselves to censure raucous and disorderly behaviour. In the case of outsiders, neighbourhood leaders were quite blunt, telling outsiders who were drinking to go elsewhere and warning their kampung hosts to control the guests' behaviour. However, there was a reluctance to target directly kampung sons who drank to excess. Mosque leaders were willing to condemn a man coming drunk to pray but not to impose a blanket ban on drink. Residents commented that drinking was increasingly a public activity and therefore a source of public disturbance, in contrast to the past when people drank inside the home. Some admitted to fears that these 'cowboy' youth would steal to support their habit. However, there was a paralysis within the neighbourhoods about confronting this youth behaviour.

Extrovert and decidedly 'un-Javanese' behaviour was common within these drinking parties. These youth had a reputation for eating cooked dog meat with their drink, a food condemned by conservative Muslim residents. The number of dogs had increased in the kampung during the 1990s and although these dogs were seen as guard dogs and family companions, some of them were bred for the pot, while others had been known to disappear mysteriously. The cooked dog added to the excitement of the drinking parties. Those who drank regularly did so with some flair. There was little secrecy about it. It was not uncommon for drunken youth to loll about during the day, talking with family and neighbouring adults. The youth's drinking impressed neither adults nor the local girls, both of which groups commonly expressed their dislike of the youth's habit and concern for the youth themselves. Within their own peer group, however, these youth gained considerable prestige.

This youth behaviour reminded older residents of the riverflat culture that they had worked so hard to suppress over the years and raised the spectre for them of these youth becoming Yogyakarta's street children. In their pioneering work on the *tekyan* or culture of street children in Yogyakarta, Beazley (2000) and Berman and Beazley (1997) described how the 5,000 or so *anak jalanan* (street children) in the city were the victims of marginalisation — as young children they had found themselves on the street, lost to their families and with no official identity. They were forced into crime and sex and a variety of other informal income opportunities such as begging, shoe shining, and working as parking attendants. Their status as anak jalanan was largely determined by their sleeping place in shop doorways and other public spaces. In those living conditions they evolved a subculture that gave them identity as well as emphasising their separateness. Anak jalanan were condemned because they did many *haram* (socially unacceptable) things. Often they responded by changing their name and identity (Ertanto, 1994). They proved their masculinity by drinking alcohol, taking pills, gambling and engaging in 'free' sex. The very things seen as unsuitable for children were adopted to prove their adulthood. They lounged around on the street, smoking *ganja* (marijuana), playing the guitar, sporting dreadlocks, long hair and tattoos as a show of force and a symbol of toughness and masculinity, with rings in their ears, eyebrows, and navel. They adopted, sometimes through being drunk, a *cuek* or couldn't-care-less attitude towards legalities. Beazley suggested that these street children, marginalised by the wider society, attempted to assert their right over their own bodies and persons by these expressions of freedom and these symbols of creativity. She referred to the tekyan subculture of these street children as chiselling away spaces of control from the margins of power (Beazley, 2000).

Like the street children, kampung youth expressed their identity in ways utterly foreign to older residents. Kampung adults, particularly parents, expressed fear for what was happening to the young men. Some of these adults were too terrified by the youths' violence to confront them or order them to stop. Kampung leaders were also at a loss as to know how to deal with this new development. One former head of security in the kampung narrated how he had periodically summoned police to take the most violent of the drinkers away. He was critical of the weakness of present kampung leaders' response. Few leaders had any solution to what was seen as a growing problem, but still there was a reluctance to invite the formal-sector police to enter the kampung domain. From the youth's perspective, consumption of foreign music and drink provided a sense of power to young men frustrated with the lack of formal-sector employment and angry with their elders' marginal position in urban society. In the end their kampung elders were able to re-incorporate the youth only through re-invigorating community cooperation.

In her research in a neighbouring kampung along the Code River, Victoria Beard (1998) noted the importance of employment to changes in the behaviour of the kampung youth. In the early 1990s "groups of young men from the community were spending their evenings drinking and fighting". She describes how a newly elected RW leader focused his attention on finding them work. Firstly he approached the management of a local four-star hotel to find them employment, then assisted a local entrepreneur to switch his cottage industry from the production of batik to the more labour-intensive production of leather goods, thus creating more work in the neighbourhood. The RW leader said to this entrepreneur, "Help our neighbours who are still unemployed, who enjoy drinking, who do not yet have an opportunity to work, please include them, even if at first this is not everyone. Slowly." Beard observed how the level of employment increased, and with that the men began to think less about drinking (Beard, 1998: 217).

In 1996 neighbourhood leaders in the southern RW of Ledok claimed some success in providing unemployed remaja in the kampung with employment. Coordinated by the Youth Section convenor of the neighbourhood, the remaja in the RW arranged payment of neighbours' electricity and water bills at the city office, helped widows rebuild their homes, starred in bands and plays at neighbourhood Independence Day celebrations, raised money through a city walk, and organised picnics and bus tours together. All these activities supported a fund allocated for youth. The RW/RT leaders provided counselling for those remaja with a 'drinking problem' and encouraged and supported their parents to counsel them. In consequence the RW leaders in this southern RW claimed that there was no drinking problem in their neighbourhood, even though other areas in Ledok were experiencing heightened difficulties in controlling youth drinking behaviour, including fighting and violence among the young men.

Although youth drinking in the 1990s and the accompanying violence were linked to unemployment and perceptions of increasing disadvantage, it was also clear that drinking was not primarily a way to forget one's troubles but a means to construct a youth identity. Like the 'new life sport' and the snake handlers of the 1970s, the drinking patterns of the 1990s provided youth with a way to assert a power that would be recognised, even respected, at least by their peers. Significantly, this drinking behaviour appealed to habits associated with riverflat squatters in the 1970s and to street children in the 1990s. Both groups were tainted with criminal links and represented norms at odds with riverbank morality: they wore tattoos, ate dogmeat and drank alcohol, played cards and encouraged illicit cockfighting, and were seen as morally and sexually 'loose'. By the 1990s the riverflat element had virtually disappeared from the kampung as more and more riverbank families moved onto land on the riverflat, steadily incorporating the 'looser' members of the riverflat into the morality of the kampung community. In the 1990s it was the drunken youth, and outside the kampung, the tekyan culture street kids, who were most readily associated with a complex of behaviours targeted by the kampung moral elite. As Wearing writes, alternative behaviour is simply behaviour that is rule-breaking and different from what is normal. "This means we need to look at the kinds of rules that exist, who constructs them ... we also need to recognise that members of the reacting subcultures ... are not merely passive recipients of such controls and labels.... They resist, subvert, use and collude in their own interests" (Wearing, 1996: 137). Kampung youth were reacting not only to the political and economic conditions in the wider society but also to kampung norms of community that they no longer saw as satisfying their needs within the modern metropolis. It was this rejection of kampung sociality that represented the gravest threat to the kampung.

2000–2004, LEDOK YOUTH AFTER THE FINANCIAL CRISIS

In the local newspaper *Kedaulatan Rakyat* of 31 October 2000, Sultan Hamengkubuwono X, the Governor of the Special Region of Yogyakarta, was reported as saying that the spread of drugs in the city was serious, that Yogyakarta had become a city of violence (*kekerasan*), that Yogyakarta's reputation as a safe place for outside youth to come for education was under threat, and that parents would no longer want to send children to school and university there. During the 1990s students had been drawn into Yogyakarta by an ever increasing number of universities. Many of these students were sent from the major cities both in Java and beyond and enjoyed generous cash allowances sent to them by distant parents, allowing many of them to board in upmarket asrama accommodation and to indulge in drug use. Sixty-five per cent of drug users were students, 75 per cent of them were male and aged between 15 and 24 (*Kedualatan Rakyat*, 31/10/2000).

The wealth possessed by incoming students was in sharp contrast to the situation of kampung youth. After the 1998–99 financial crisis, many kampung residents struggled to make a living and the schooling of their children was cut short. The financial crisis added a new dimension to the youth's struggle. Casual work in the tourism sector dried up. Becak drivers, pavement sellers and lesehan foodstalls, hawkers and buskers were all affected. During the ensuing crisis, two projects funded by the World Bank and other donors targeted the kampung population — a food distribution program and an employment program (described in Chapter 4). The latter particularly targeted youth and casual workers as those who had lost their sources of income.

In this difficult financial environment, outside students doing their obligatory community service program in the kampung in 2000 instigated a night market, acknowledging the dire financial circumstances of many residents. The night market was coordinated by the RW Youth Section and raised funds for this section of RW government. It was set up in an open space of the kampung where traders, many from outside the kampung, could display their wares of cheap clothes and cloth and CDs. While adults found some bargains in clothing and children indulged themselves with sweets and drinks, youth gathered round the game stalls, where they competed for prizes of bottles of alcohol.

In 2000 the income of kampung youth continued to be spent on drink, gambling, clothes and food. However, the Ledok community's experience of tragedies, deaths, imprisonment and hospital admissions in the late 1990s had tempered youth behaviour and allowed neighbourhood communities to once again involve youth more directly in neighbourhood activities. Since my visit in 1996, two key troublemakers had departed, one to jail for theft and the other killed by his own brother in a drunken fight. Youth and a few older residents continued to gather to drink in the evenings or on Sundays but the situation was more in keeping with norms of sociality. The new river wall, designed to contain flooding of the riverflat, was a favourite meeting point, either at the several small warung beside the river wall or outside one of the drinkers' home. Several warung along the top path were also points for the drinkers to gather. As they shared the alcoholic drinks, they often played cards or enjoyed guitar music. Youth informants told me of the peer pressure that still prevailed to get their friends involved in drinking: "You first shout them a drink, then get them to contribute to the next round, and be ready to abuse them if they drop out." Such pressures were still noticeable in 2000. Drinking alcohol was an activity in which youth engaged in exclusive groups, with membership determined by a cash subscription and friendship. Drinking was not confined to youth. Older married men were also involved but these were older men who had begun to drink alcohol as youths. What had now changed was that the liquor suppliers had been recognised formally through licences issued by the Department of Health. Drinking was done more openly from recognised venues and with some community involvement in supervision. Drinking was seen as a recreational activity, sometimes done at home as relaxation in the privacy of home, sometimes as an evening or a Sunday group activity. Gone, however, were the extremes of drinking behaviour characteristic of previous years. There was general agreement that drinking was a more accepted part of social behaviour and that drunkenness and its attendant violence was much reduced.

On my return in 2004 there was general acknowledgement that alcohol abuse was no longer a problem in the kampung communities. I noticed little drinking in public, only once in three weeks coming across a group of men, young and old, drinking by the river wall. When I asked neighbours what they were doing about youth drinking, their replies were generally not of the panicked type I had met in 1996. "We watch them, when someone gets drunk we approach their friends to take him away and put him to sleep, when it is outsiders we tell their hosts they are not welcome." I asked several people to explain the change. A storekeeper mentioned that he had been raided twice on consecutive days, and his stock of *Anggur Orang Tua* ('Old People's Wine') had been confiscated because he did not have a licence. Some mentioned that the deaths through drink of several youth had changed the minds of many of their peers. A commonly given explanation was that one notorious drinker, a man aged 50 who had demonstrated a capacity to keep drinking and working when others had long succumbed to drunkenness, had become blind through drinking, a warning heeded by the youth. One producer of ginseng had stopped production when his own nephew died of alcohol poisoning. A kampung official gave credit to meetings he had organised among three RW to coordinate a campaign to warn youths about drinking. He admitted he had been motivated by his growing frustration with the habit of youth sitting up late at night outside his house, their conversation increasing in volume the more they drank, disturbing the sleep of his household and his neighbours. He finally took action when a fight broke out between youth from different RW over some small matter. At the subsequent meeting the RW leaders told the youth that drunken behaviour had to stop. An Islamic leader in the neighbourhood credited *ngaji* or Koran recitation programs run by the mosque targeting youth with the decline in drunkenness. Others suggested that those who had drunk excessively in the past had married and had accepted responsibility for their families. However, a particularly persuasive answer referred to new employment opportunities for many of the hardest drinkers.

Singaporean entrepreneurs, in partnership with businessmen in Medan and Jakarta, had established a casino on the streetside adjacent to Ledok. On its opening it was the focus of strident protests against gambling, largely from Islamic groups, but after some delay the casino went ahead. However, it did not advertise itself in any open way, occupying a derelict building whose street-level floor was completely vacant apart from a security desk. The windows on the upper floors, where the gambling activities took place, were heavily covered, so that there was no sign from the outside that these floors were occupied. Parking for the business was available in a disused adjacent block of land. On setting up the casino, the managers approached Ledok residents seeking workers and, despite opposition from some residents, a large number of kampung youth, both men and women, gained employment there. The men provided security at the street level while the women waited on the gambling tables and machines above. It was estimated variously that between 30 and 100 Ledok youth had jobs there and could earn about Rp600,000 (A\$100) per month for a five-hour shift. In addition, the casino supplied staff with a mobile phone so that they could be called back to work at a moment's notice. The casino operated from early afternoon throughout the night and was said to attract some very wealthy gamblers, reportedly ready to wager house and car on their games. The security guards could also earn additional income by returning to the casino when not on shift to give lifts on their motorcycles to any gambler anxious to get to the ATM to take out more cash. Kampung youth who spoke to me about their involvement had either been able to purchase a motorcycle or were planning to take advantage of this opportunity.

Among kampung informants, both youth and their elders, there was a strong view that new employment had helped diminish youth drinking. The casino had approached with offers of employment just those young men known to have a jago ('tough guy') reputation by virtue of their drinking behaviour. Getting a job had taken these youth out of the drinking circles. There was a recognition by the casino operators and by the kampung leaders whom they approached that a jago reputation was a bonus in providing security to the business. Similarly, kampung leaders recognised that sometimes the best security guards were those who had a reputation for criminal activities because they knew the field and were better able to apprehend those responsible. In both cases there was an assumption that those with a reputation for criminal activity or for violent drinking behaviour were the victims of structural inequalities within the urban economy and that, by offering them a chance of a legitimate income, their disapproved behaviour could be turned around. According to one informant, those who drank alcohol did so to amuse themselves, having little else to do. Without a job, they had no access to money but could beg or borrow the small amounts needed to join a drinking group. Once they began work at the casino, they no longer sat around drinking.

In the nearby Ledok Macanan, kampung leaders recognised that the nightly drunkenness among youth was a result of their frustrations with the economic crisis. A *padat karya* (government work) program was instituted by these leaders in 2000 to provide the youth with employment, paying them Rp8,000 for an eight-hour day's work to lay concrete bricks along the major pathways. This was the catalyst for change in their behaviour. In 2001 many of the youth re-opened kiosks on the main street outside the kampung to sell petrol, tyres, or videos, or found work as shop assistants or shop security staff. As unemployment declined, so did the drunkenness (Arifin, 2003).

Yoshi, a long-time activist with the non-government organisation Yayasan Pondok Rakyat involved in kampung community building, questions whether providing such deviants with jobs changes their behaviour (Yoshi, 2001). He focuses on the *pos ronda*, the neighbourhood guard post and whether this institution found in all kampung neighbourhoods actually contributes to kampung security. He suggests that the employment of known criminals to man kampung security posts and security offices confuses the notion of security for residents. On the contrary, it consolidates the government's intent to employ militaristic, strong-arm strategies in security and to place more emphasis on providing the form — a security post and security personnel — than on cultivating the content. Yoshi points out that many security posts operate outside the law and were frequented at night by men playing cards, drinking, following the lotteries and insulting passers-by, and during the day by women nursing babies, street-sellers, the homeless and loungers. According to him, pos ronda merely allowed those with criminal or anti-communal intent to legitimise their activities.

This does not appear to have occurred in Ledok, where those with a past record of pursuing illegitimate activities, including criminal activities, were incorporated into the community by providing them with respectable employment as security guards alongside other kampung youth and older residents. In some RW, all households were expected to contribute personnel to man the security posts at night. Security posts were not misused. Security guards played cards there at night to stay awake but also regularly patrolled the neighbourhood. In recognition of their services, neighbourhood families were rostered to provide them with tea and snacks each night. Their contribution was seen as diverse, not only to apprehend thieves, but also to warn guests who stayed past 11 p.m. and disturbed neighbours with their talk that they should leave the neighbourhood; to see out of the neighbourhood young men visiting single women or widows into the late hours; and even to escort to hospital or provide assistance to those who fell sick or those women whose labour contractions start during the night. Their role thus had a moral as well as security content. The youth who gathered under the auspices of the pos ronda had community recognition for their activities conducted there. Their task of patrolling the neighbourhood was welcomed by residents and their capacity to erupt into violence if the need arose was, on balance, a positive one for the community, which ostensibly avoided violence at all costs but on certain occasions were happy to see others dispense it. Because they were considered 'not yet adult' in the community, the youth could resort to violence, even while the community continued to prioritise the suppression of conflict in their adherence to social harmony (rukun).

The potential for violence may have always been a characteristic of youth involvement in the community. During the 1970s in the nearby kampung of Ledok Macanan, youth were banded together in Perhimpunan Pemuda dan Pelajar (Association of Youth and School Students) that took action against drinking and gambling in the neighbourhood, even against the youths' own fathers. With the knowledge of the RK head, they would escort a drunk man to the river and dunk his head in the water (Arifin, 2003).

By 2000 another youth activity of *ngamen* (busking) had become a focus for many youth. They mostly played at the pavement restaurants called lesehan not far from the kampung on the city's main commercial streets. These youth played *campur sari*, a combination of different styles of music, both Western and Indonesian, suited to the tastes of their diverse audience. They practised regularly as a larger group, then went on the streets to ngamen as smaller groups of up to half a dozen youth. Incomes were as high as Rp15,000 a day per player. The national newspaper *Kompas* (29/10/2000) reported that in Jakarta bands were so popular among kampung youth that studios were constructed for hire in the kampung with even band instruments provided for hire. One studio owner said he set it up to encourage youth to move away from drinking and *tawuran* (gambling). Some kampung youth were earning substantial disposable income through these performances. One of the Ledok youth, for example, bought a guitar for Rp250,000 (A$50) earned through busking. In several RW in Ledok, ngamen was seen to have filled the void. Remaja now found profitable ways of participating in society and drunkenness was said to have declined. The youth went about their performances and took their rehearsals very seriously. While I was there in 1996, one of the ngamen groups was invited through a kampung neighbour and RT leader to perform at a wedding at short notice. The booking of a more prestigious streetside band had fallen through and thus presented them with this opportunity to perform. They dressed as well as they could for the occasion, many in T-shirts and sandals, and performed admirably to the enjoyment of the guests. Soon after that occasion, band members bought matching T-shirts at Rp15,000 each for use in further anticipated performances.

Music provided more than a source of income. Both in 1996 and 2000, youth's passionate adoption of music as the expression of identity allowed them to link with modern fashions both overseas and within the wider urban culture of Indonesia. These songs expressed sentiments that were sometimes at variance with kampung morality. While in 1996 such music more frequently became a medium for resisting and resenting the obligations that kampung society imposed on youth, by 2000 such music had been integrated into kampung life and become an important source of income and community acceptance. The support from older residents for their activities was demonstrated in 2000 in the Rp850,000 that the youth were able to raise from neighbours towards a sound system in the central RW neighbourhood of Ledok. At the same time, neighbourhood leaders encouraged the youth to link up with older residents to play *kroncong*, a popular old style of Javanese dance music. While not all the youth stayed around for this, about five did and it was clear that both young and old intended to make use of the new sound system. In another neighbourhood of Ledok where lavish Independence Day celebrations were held, a youth band was incorporated as the main item in the program. Wearing (1996: 135) quoted Frith (1981) as saying that the expression of values, beliefs and ritual through rock music has proved the most distinctive feature of youth subculture: such expression shapes the self-definition of young people, giving them an identity and offering a haven with a very clear boundary, which is both inclusive and exclusive. It offers young people a means of dealing with contradictory and paradoxical relationships, especially those that bring pain and trouble; and it can define for them what youth and youthfulness means. Although some of their music activities were incorporated into the wider community, the rehearsal and performance of music constructed a space for kampung youth where they could explore their own identity, writing their own songs and experimenting with their own styles.

The campur sari group and the kroncong band had disbanded by 2004, following the departure of two boarders who were the main directors of the campur sari and the death and ageing of members of the kroncong. However, many of the youth continued to earn an income from busking. Noticeably there was acceptance in the community of busking as an income-earning activity. Men who had started their own families continued in this occupation, so that it was no longer seen as a purely youth occupation. It appeared though that music was no longer as central to youth identity construction in Ledok as it had been in 2000.

The largely successful reintegration of youth into neighbourhood communities during this period was achieved through community leaders instituting programs of employment and recreation and directly challenging the drunken behaviour of some youth. In addition, employment opportunities outside the kampung engaged some of the most abrasive young men and women. Community efforts to re-engage the youth consolidated cooperation between neighbourhood and religious leaders, between older and younger generations, and among neighbours more generally. These neighbourhood efforts were entirely independent of government programs in a period when both young and older generations had almost entirely given up hope of the state providing suitable solutions to local issues.

NEIGHBOURHOOD RESPONSES TO YOUTH

Much of the story of kampung youth revolves around their place within the wider kampung and city society. In the 1970s they were actively recruited into family and communal rituals. There was an acceptance of their 'new life sport' activities and their individualistic search for ngelmu as containable within kampung religious diversity. In the 1980s kampung youth were attracted towards a consumer revolution, expressed particularly in music and clothing styles and struggled to come to terms with this, both financially and in terms of the new expressions of youth identity it offered. In the 1990s, as outside pressures of wealth disparities and tourism increased, kampung youth were drawn into drinking behaviour, often sourced outside the kampung, which led to a tenuous relationship with kampung neighbours. By 2000 youth had found an acceptable source of income in busking and street-selling and their music was encouraged within the community. Youth were involved in ronda (security patrols) and played roles, sometimes of a potentially violent nature, in upholding the community values. I witnessed youths beating up a thief (*pencopet*) they had apprehended in the kampung and heard the story of how they had evicted a household of transvestites (*banci*) when their behaviour offended kampung standards of morality. By 2004 youth had found another source of employment in the casino and unacceptable binge drinking had disappeared.

Within the kampung neighbourhoods, there has always been considerable tolerance of youth activities, from the mystical activities of former years to the drinking and music of recent times. Youth are encouraged to pursue their own interests and there is little pressure put on the boys to take on adult roles until they marry. The integration of youth into the neighbourhood has remained a community enterprise rather than the responsibility of individual parents. Employment and income have been significant parts of such integration.

Over the decades, groups of youth have constructed their own self-expression and identity in a space discrete from both mainstream streetside society and culture and their parents' kampung society and culture. The key markers of that identity, such as gambling, drinking, tattoos, alternative religion or music, are ranged against the behaviour considered acceptable within either the kampung or wider urban society. The ambivalence and tension they subsequently experienced in the construction of self-identity derived on the one hand from their greater attraction and access to the consumer fashions popular on streetside but largely unfamiliar to their parents, and on the other hand from their awareness that they could not measure up to the consumption patterns of streetside youth. They had the time and freedom from familial and social responsibilities to explore the diversity of consumer styles but at the same time they were restricted both by their lack of purchasing power and by their need to maintain the parental identifications which supported them (Cohen, 1972: 26).

Do these activities of popular music, gambling, tattooing, and drinking express an oppositional culture, a resistance to the hegemonic culture? The youth alternate culture, so reminiscent of the challenges posed by the riverflat culture that I observed in the 1970s, was one that was created from familiar elements but put together in a confronting or contrasting form. Only in 1996 did this alternative culture almost completely alienate male youth from their parental society. At that time certain young men were rejected by their parents and by the community because they had abandoned any attempt at reciprocal obligations, showing no respect for their parents and elders, wasting resources needed by their families, and indulging in extreme forms of violence. This excess became their badge of identity. The "cultural and symbolic struggle, the contesting of meanings, is the means by which identities are given shapes that allow us to act" (Pred and Watts, 1992: 198). In the case of kampung youth, their acts were no longer within parameters recognised by the wider kampung society.

By the early 2000s these youth had been incorporated back into kampung community, even as that community accepted more of the drinking culture into everyday life. Alison Murray (1991) argued street subcultures have an ambivalent relation to the wider society in that they both reject the authority of wider society and embrace aspects of its spectacular consumption in the creation of their style. Friedman (1994) shows that this is not so much ambivalent as a creative reworking of fashion to achieve group identity and individual power. There is among the adult population of the kampung an ambivalence about youth, a fear that they will go over the top and destroy themselves, yet a wish to see them try new things, be given an opportunity, and use their considerable energies for the good of the community, for example, through pos ronda. There is a wish to harness what they may have to offer but a reluctance to give them free rein to make their contribution. In the Yogyakarta kampung, youth continue to provide dynamism and creativity and resistance, sometimes encountering stiff opposition from their elders and sometimes willing cooperation. Youth were engaged during all the periods I describe here in negotiating their identity and existence with and within kampung communities. These continued to provide them with a primary point of reference, even as they were themselves changing in response to outside circumstances.

6

Kendhuren and the Strengthening of Religious Community

Despite the poverty of many kampung households, the celebration of life events by Ledok families has always enlivened the neighbourhood community. It is with immediate neighbours that such rites are celebrated and families may choose from a variety of ways to do this, depending on their financial circumstances. The expense of rites of life ceremonies for poorer families has been a particular concern to neighbourhood leaders, who are aware of the stress this places on vulnerable household budgets. However, until recently households have regarded such ceremonies as vital to their standing within the local neighbourhood, measured both in the lavishness of the celebrations and the range of neighbours invited to participate. The ritual located the household socially among their neighbours and served to consolidate the communal support that the household could enjoy. In recent years, however, the key ritual of the kendhuren has largely disappeared from neighbourhood life, raising questions about the continuing viability of communal solidarity.

Kendhuren, kenduri or slametan is a ceremony conducted by Javanese households to celebrate or commemorate important occasions in the individual or family life cycle.[6] Geertz (1973: 110) stressed the importance of the slametan as a means of reinforcing social ties and perpetuating through ritual the social values significant to the group. In an earlier work (Geertz, 1960), he identified the slametan as the key ritual defining the category of Muslims he termed *abangan*, that is those who followed more animistic or Sufistic practices (Woodward, 1989: 52) as opposed to those of the *santri* or reformist Muslims. Peacock (1968) suggests that the slametan is the critical rite of community incorporation, sanctifying social harmony (rukun) and mutual dependence among neighbours. Koentjaraningrat, the pioneering Javanese anthropologist, identifies the slametan as the ritual expression of gotong royong, the social solidarity of cooperative work patterns (Koentjaraningrat, 1961; 1985: 146–7). However, both Geertz (1973) and Peacock (1968), whose observations were made in urban Surabaya, concluded that the slametan with its emphasis on neighbourhood was no longer relevant to modern Indonesian urban society. The slametan was no longer needed because the neighbourhood was no longer a corporate unit but an administrative division.

Mary Hawkins' work among the Javanese settlers of South Kalimantan challenges this conclusion. Citing both Guinness (1986) and Hatley (1982), she suggests that the ideal of rukun remains a "central ideological concept through and by means of which Javanese contextualise and apprehend their lives, their aspirations, their motivations and their social relations" (Hawkins, 1996: 226). Among these rice and clove farmers in the 1980s, it was considered *pantas* (appropriate) for the wealthier families to hold a slametan as a ritual that emphasised neighbourhood solidarity. The challenge she poses is not the tracing of the disappearance of 'traditions' such as rukun or slametan but rather to explain their continuing role in a modernising society.

Figure 6.1   Neighbourhood men attend a *kendhuren.*

Figure 6.2   A food basket distributed to neighbours.

In the 1970s when I first began to live in Ledok, I attended many kendhuren. A man, or usually his wife, would announce to neighbours their intention to hold a kendhuren. Neighbours would offer their services, providing money, goods such as rice, sugar or tea, and labour to prepare the food. Women played a dominant role in these ceremonies, organising the supply of glasses and crockery, managing the cooking and determining the guest list and the lavishness of the ritual (Sullivan, 1987, 1989). Men, as one informant put it, simply said 'yes'.

On the day of the ceremony, neighbours would turn up in the morning to cook the food. Mostly women were involved but a man might manage the large fire and pot for the cooking of the rice. Later in the day the food would be apportioned in small baskets to be presented to each guest at the ceremony. Just before the ceremony, a neighbour would be sent out to summon the male guests. The ceremony would be led by a community prayer leader, the Muslim *imam* or the Catholic deacon. Where the host was of traditionalist Islamic persuasion, a small offering was placed before the imam, consisting of some bananas, a small leaf of rice and condiments, a stick of burning incense, and flower petals — the imam in his prayers might mention that the offering was intended for the ancestors of the family. In all other respects, prayers were addressed by the imam or deacon to God, requesting the blessings of God on the household. Finally, guests would be presented with a plate of food to eat immediately and a basket of food to take home to their households. They would linger for a few minutes to smoke a cigarette or two and chat before returning home. The ceremony would be over within an hour.

The key occasion for performance of kendhuren was the commemoration of the death of a resident. For those households with the financial capacity, kendhuren would be held on the third, seventh, 40th, 100th, 365th and 1000th days after the death. In each case, neighbours would reconvene later in the evening after the kendhuren to play cards, and be served with tea and snacks by the young men of the neighbourhood. A kendhuren could also be held to celebrate a wedding or to give thanks, for example, for the safe return of a child from study elsewhere or recovery from a serious illness (Guinness, 1986: 73–5).

The kendhuren became in most Javanese communities an important indicator of social status. The variety and sophistication of foods offered to guests and the range of invited guests was a source of community discussion that assigned a measure of social respect to the host and his wife. The accepted minimum guest list was the neighbours in the immediate vicinity of one's house. In the tightly settled lanes of Ledok, such neighbours would come from the same alleyway, where neighbours would gather each afternoon and evening to talk. This was the same group that in the 1970s would gather to watch television in the sole household in the alleyway possessing such a luxury. By the 1990s every household had a television set but their immediate neighbours would remain those with whom they constantly conversed, who were there to lend a hand with children, emergencies and the like. The expectation, however, was that the host and hostess would invite to their kendhuren all those from the same RT, the primary unit of neighbourly identification for a household's kendhuren. A more prestigious resident, however, might invite neighbours from further away, in most cases confined to those who lived in adjacent RT, who knew each other and each other's family histories, who acknowledged each other and who would be drawn together on the death of any one of their number. This wider network generally corresponded to the territory known after 1989 as the RW. Neighbours then were the essential ingredient in the kendhuren — family or friends who lived further away were more likely to be found at larger kendhuren but not to the exclusion of neighbours.

The financial outlay for a kendhuren was not inconsiderable. The hosts needed to purchase and prepare rice and side dishes to feed 30 to 50 neighbours and their households, with additional baskets of food sent to key helpers on the day of the ceremony. The variety of side dishes reflected the prestige of the host. For example, whether the package contained egg, chicken and beef, or perhaps a variety of each, was the source of comment by neighbours, often even as they cooked and in the hearing of the host. There was social pressure to provide an acceptable standard of food, consistent with the host's social rank. In the 1970s a wedding kendhuren might be followed by a wedding *resepsi* (reception), held in the host home or the local community hall. This combination of celebrations would further enhance the host's social esteem.

After the 1970s, the frequency of the kendhuren declined. On my visit in 1996, residents acknowledged that only old-fashioned people (*wong kuno*) continued to hold them. Sugi claimed he was among the first to make the change, when in 1995 he decided that it was needless duplication to hold a prayer service and a kendhuren to mark his son's circumcision — his son having converted to Islam to get married — and, at the same time, his daughter's wedding. He chose to abandon the kendhuren, although he pointed out that he still sent packages of food to all households in the RW. In my visits during 2004, not a single kendhuren came to my notice.

At the same time, other rituals had become more lavish. Weddings were usually celebrated with receptions held outside the kampung in hired halls. Residents were quick to point out that there was no longer space in the kampung for holding them. In the 1970s, when families would hold both a kendhuren and a reception to celebrate a wedding, many hosts were able to remove one or more bamboo panels in the interior of their houses to create a space for entertaining their wedding guests while additional guests could be invited to occupy chairs in the alleyway outside. Wedding celebrations could therefore be accommodated within the neighbourhood. Both through the disruption they caused to community life and the cooperative work that they demanded, weddings became a neighbourhood affair. By 2004, however, houses had more permanent interior walls and alleyways were much tighter. One public hall (Balai RK), which in the 1970s had been available for kampung residents to use for receptions, was leased permanently as a mechanical workshop and thus no longer available to residents. As it became more difficult to locate the wedding reception in the kampung, some residents resorted to expensive locations outside, in one case locating the wedding 40 kilometres away at a mountain resort.

The commercialisation of kampung wedding celebrations was much more conspicuous in 2004. An increase in the number of guests was one aspect of this change, but in other ways the commercialisation undermined communal expressions of cooperation. At one wedding reception in 2004, when both bride and bridegroom were Ledok residents, 700 guests were invited and caterers prepared for an even greater number, knowing that invited guests brought others along. Guests, dressed in their formal best, arrived at this wedding reception at any time during a designated period of two to three hours. On arrival they filed through the hall, were greeted by a welcoming group of members of the bridal party and volunteers from neighbourhood youth, signed a guest book, made a donation in an envelope into a gift box, for which they received a small memento of thanks, then proceeded onto the stage where they congratulated the bridal couple and their parents, then moved on to serve themselves food from a buffet assortment supplied by a commercial catering company. As few seats were supplied, most stood to eat, entertained by four different music groups singing an assortment of popular and classical music. They lingered a few more moments before returning home. Although neighbourhood youth still had a role to play, the ceremony was marked by its commercialisation in the hiring of the venue, the contracting of a catering firm, and the performance of commercial musicians, all on a scale that dwarfed slametan and resepsi held in the kampung in previous generations or by poorer families.

The acknowledgement of community was not lost, however, for the wedding reception was preceded the night before by an Islamic prayer ceremony (*pengajian*) at both the bride's and bridegroom's parental homes, attended in each case by probably 200 RW neighbours. These were catered for by neighbourhood women who had worked cooperatively during the day and served by neighbourhood youth. The juxtaposition of these two rituals brought out clearly the two principles of commercial lavishness and community solidarity. Instead of conflicting, these were combined in innovative ways.

In some circumstances the community might withdraw their support for a neighbour's ritual. In another wedding reception in 2003, only three neighbours were invited, the reception being at the bride's home outside Yogyakarta. The night before, the bridegroom's family hosted Catholic prayers (*sembahyang*) in the kampung but failed to gain the cooperation of the youth in serving food and drink, nor many of the neighbourhood women in the preparation of food. Alleyway comment in this case was that the hosts had snubbed the community by contracting out the food preparation to certain neighbourhood women who were earning an income from doing it. Other women were thereby offended and did not volunteer their services. There was also criticism that only three neighbours had been invited to the wedding reception. The absence of youth volunteers was seen as a reflection of the bridegroom's tendency to disdain association with kampung youth and to focus more on outside networks.

By 2004 the costs of such rituals had escalated, affecting the nature of community involvement. One of these more lavish weddings in 2004 was estimated to have cost Rp12 million, of which the hosts probably recouped Rp6 million through gifts. If the host parents or the bridal couple themselves held well-paid jobs, generally in the formal sector, they were able to self-finance these receptions and recoup some of the costs through money contributions of the guests. In the 1970s, women had often contributed gifts of rice, tea or sugar to the neighbour's wedding preparations, but in recent years wedding invitations have sometimes stipulated that such gifts of goods were not required. In the 1990s when community catering arrangements were not always required, women neighbours would enquire of the hostess whether a donation (*sumbangan*) would be received, meaning whether the woman should bring a gift of money when she attended to help in preparations. The hostess might decline these gifts to avoid the task of preparing baskets of food to reciprocate such monetary gifts. However, monetary gifts were always welcomed at the reception itself and these were reciprocated with a token memento (in one case in 2004 a toy car, in another a notebook with a photo of the bridal couple on the cover). Residents welcomed the fact that gifts were presented in envelopes because some gave as little as Rp3,000 or perhaps even put in an empty envelope. A common donation by better-off residents was in the order of Rp20,000. Others, however, would contribute a large gift and write their name on the envelope to ensure that their generosity was noted and reciprocated when they themselves conducted such a ritual.

Weddings continued to be marked by the ornateness of ritual and ritual paraphernalia. One host family prided itself on the sophistication of its palace-style ritual. The wedding was marked by a ritual washing (*siraman*) of the bridal couple, the serving of a drink (*dawet*) by the bride's parents to symbolise the provision of financial capital for their future son-in-law, the presentation (*pasrahan*) of the bride-wealth by the bridegroom's party, the marriage licensing ritual (*akad nikah*) by a religious official, and finally the reception, these rituals over a span of two days. Different wedding clothes were worn for the specific rituals. However, even this fascination with ritual traditions in 2004 did not include a kendhuren. Even well-off residents were not encouraged to hold kendhuren. My informants acknowledged that kendhuren were no longer held and gave various reasons for their demise. Their responses indicate that the demise of the kendhuren was not evidence of the decline of community, as Geertz and Peacock had predicted, but rather the outcome of a complex mix of factors.[7]

EXPLAINING THE DECLINE OF KENDHUREN

According to some Ledok informants, the decline in kendhuren was due to the financial crisis because households could no longer afford to hold such an event. In Ledok during the years of the financial crisis, the income of the casual wage force and the petty entrepreneurs declined, while those who retained jobs at fixed salaries in government or private corporations experienced loss of purchasing power. As prices soared, salaries no longer covered household needs as they had before. Thus there is some evidence that it was the financial crisis that weakened the kendhuren ritual.

In fact, the kendhuren had been recognised as a drain on household resources from as early as the 1970s, when I noted RT leaders suggesting to their neighbourhood community that ceremonies could be simplified by restricting elaborate foods or perhaps subsituting a more economical ritual for the kendhuren. In the past some neighbours had commemorated an event not with a kendhuren but with a simpler ritual, such as the distribution of a snack to the neighbourhood's children or the sending of a small basket of foods to near neighbours. During the same period, some of those with financial means, such as prestige-conscious public servants, had preferred to contract women to provide food for kendhuren or receptions, thus bypassing the social obligations of involving neighbours. They suggested that it was less expensive to pay a few women to prepare all the food than hosting the whole community to work together. In earlier days this was condemned in neighbourhood gossip as arrogant, although the host in question defended her action by saying it was more efficient and ultimately cost-effective for it avoided the social obligation to reciprocate with material and labour at neighbours' rituals. These informants suggested that as the years passed the kendhuren was abandoned altogether as a cost-saving measure. This explanation was not entirely convincing, however, because the decline of the kendhuren was not mirrored in other forms of cost savings. Instead of simpler and cheaper rituals, many of the better-off residents opted for elaborate receptions with their attendant costs of venue hire, costume, food and entertainers. These events accrued much status to the host household, indicating perhaps that the kendhuren was no longer such an attractive status option.

Another reason for the decline of the kendhuren suggested by residents was that the RT neighbourhoods had become too large. By 2004 some RT numbered 40 to 50 households. Boundaries had remained the same but population had risen as vacant land became occupied, houses extended upwards to accommodate more families, and internal space was further subdivided. As all in the RT expected to be invited, it became more onerous to serve all in the neighbourhood with food. On the other hand, a wealthy host keen to gain the respect of neighbours could potentially turn this to their advantage, just as invitations could also be extended to larger RW populations. One informant suggested that there was now less urgency for associating with one's immediate neighbours because they no longer shared toilets, washrooms or electricity supply. Households had become more independent and their members' attention had turned inward to household entertainments like television and computer games, or outward to interest groups based on sporting activities, bands or drinking groups. Did the decline therefore represent a declining motivation among wealthier residents to seek prestige among their immediate neighbours? Such a conclusion was not borne out by the lavish and prestigious receptions I witnessed in 2004 when all members of the RT or an even wider group within the RW were invited.

An alternative explanation among Ledok residents for the decline of kendhuren focused on the rise in standards of living evident in 2004. According to these informants, whereas in the past, and particularly during the years of the crisis, chicken or beef had been rare on household menus, so that their provision in the kendhuren was a great delicacy, by 2004 chicken and beef were commonplace, meaning that the kendhuren was no longer the avenue for social prestige that it used to be. Other commentators stressed that it was pragmatic to drop the kendhuren because people were more involved in the outside world and had less time to spend on the organisation of such a complex ritual. It took a lot of trouble preparing the food and so much of the food went to waste and was thrown away. Again, this explanation is not entirely borne out by recent rituals. While beef and chicken were more common in kampung diets, it was the quantity of such foods provided at the reception buffets that caught residents' attention and contributed to the prestige of the occasion.

What these explanations appear to suggest is that the turmoil of the years of the financial crisis affected the continuity of community-based rituals such as the kendhuren. Whereas for some in straightened financial circumstances, the kendhuren may have represented too large a cost, others who came through the crisis with less household disruption were keen to celebrate that good fortune with even more lavish rituals such as receptions. The lavishness of some of the rituals in 2004 amazed many residents and drew attention to the increasing disparity among kampung residents while those still earning income in the formal sector recovered from the financial crisis.

Was the decline of kendhuren an indication of a general decline in neighbourhood sociality? Residents in 2004 still regarded their attendance or non-attendance at a ritual as indicative of the success of that ritual. Despite the lavishness of a wedding reception, neighbours would strongly dismiss it if the community had not been adequately acknowledged and involved. It was clear in 2004 that other forms of neighbourhood cooperation were continuing as strongly as in the past. Foremost among these were the savings and credit (simpan pinjam) associations and the arisan groupings. Both remained popular among Ledok neighbours as a way of binding together neighbours. The holding of an arisan or a simpan pinjam activity consolidated a women's group, or a youth group or even the whole RT community and provided the inducement to attend a meeting where the organisation of community projects such as building communal washrooms or repairing a flight of steps was conducted.

Thus if neighbourhood communities were still active, why were kendhuren declining? What were replacing kendhuren as the means to commemorate household and individual rites of passage? Were these rites of passage being abandoned altogether?

SEMBAHYANG (PRAYERS)

Although large-scale rituals in place of kendhuren were not as frequent in 2004 as in the past, the most common form of ritual to commemorate important life-cycle occasions had become the *sembahyang*. Both Muslim and Catholic groups congregated for such occasions. A family would invite members of their religious community to gather to pray and worship, then partake of drinks and snacks or perhaps a meal before returning home. In the most elaborate sembahyang, they carried home a basket of uncooked food (rice, eggs, noodles, oil) for the household. These occasions were held at night, often at 7.30 or 8 p.m. or among Muslims after the *Isya'*, the last formal time of daily prayer, rather than at dusk as with the kendhuren. Perhaps this reflected the increasing difficulties of gathering people together at the earlier time, now that more and more residents worked at a distance from the kampung.

However, it was the nature of the community that was the principal innovation. The sembahyang brought together members of a religious community who were spread more widely through Ledok. Most of Ledok residents identify as Muslims. As the kampung population expanded over the years, this led to the proliferation of places of worship. It was these places of worship that delineated the community that attended the household *sembahyang*. In the 1970s there were no mosques in Ledok. The obligatory Friday prayers were performed wherever possible at a mosque, so that residents crossed the river to pray at a streetside mosque, itself completed only in 1967. There were, however, two mussolah or prayer rooms that could be used for the five daily prayer times, for Koran recitation classes for children, for women and occasionally men to pray on Friday and for other meetings. In the following years, as the congregations grew, both these mussolah were converted into mosques, while two other mussolah were built and also eventually converted to mosques. Thus Ledok boasted in 2004 four mosques and two mussolah distributed through the settlement and serving populations the size of RW neighbourhoods. Moreover, the mosques had increased their activities in the community. All mosques offered regular instruction sessions for children, women, and youth, and one mosque provided a kindergarten, medical clinic, and a cooperative providing loans for petty entrepreneurs.

By the early 2000s, these mosques delineated the sembahyang groups that celebrated the household rituals. In his account of Yogyakarta society, Mark Woodward commented that "in a very real sense the Friday *salat* service defines the local community. Those who participate are members, while the status of those who do not is questionable at best" (Woodward, 1989: 141). With the multiplication of mosques in Ledok, the Muslim communities very closely corresponded to the RW areas, except of course that non-practising Muslims and non-Muslims within them were not part of these mosque communities. Some efforts were devoted by mosque leaders to incorporate nominal Muslims within the religious community, particularly at weekly sessions of instruction on the Koran.

Among the numerically smaller Catholic population, there were two deaconates formed in Ledok, each managed by an elected deacon formalised by the local parish priest. These groups met regularly for sembahyang, which included singing hymns and reciting the liturgy under the guidance of the deacon. This same form of worship became the medium for the celebration of household rites among these Catholic groups. The deacon provided the leadership of the prayers in which the particular household ritual event was declared and God's blessings sought.

The demarcation of neighbours into religious groupings therefore assumed a prominence it did not have in the past, even as neighbours of all faiths continued to cooperate together in other neighbourhood activities such as arisan and simpan pinjam. Most kendhuren of the past brought together neighbours of all faiths. The prayers at the kendhuren were led by the community imam, associated not with a mosque but with the community, and he would support the presentation of offerings to the spirits of the ancestors (*arwah*) as part of the ritual. He might directly address the ancestors, but most of his prayers, including Koranic recitation, constituting the large bulk of his offering, would be addressed to God. Non-Muslim neighbours would attend the ritual, bow respectfully in prayer, say '*amin*' at the end and otherwise participate fully in the occasion. The exception was where the family was Catholic and the deacon or outside priest was invited to lead the prayers at the kendhuren. In these cases the arwah were not addressed but the prayers would constitute more formal Catholic ritual. Muslim neighbours would not attend the prayers but would arrive later for the *jagongan* (evening gathering) to share in the food and talk (Guinness, 1986: 75).

The preference for sembahyang over kendhuren can be seen as a continuation of a trend noted by Robert Hefner and Masdar Hilmy. Hefner (1985) remarked on "a profound and ongoing process of Islamization" of the Javanese slametan; Hilmy (1998) concurs, suggesting that this has been driven by the reliance on devout Muslims (santri) to lead the prayers. In contemporary Yogyakarta, these santri have increasingly gained a secondary or tertiary education in an Islamic institution in which they learned to distinguish between Javanese indigenous elements and orthodox Islamic elements in local rituals. This led in later years to their advice to families that sembahyang was a more appropriate way of commemorating household events than the slametan/kendhuren. The increase in the number of mosques in Ledok also reflected residents' increasing concern with proper Islamic religious practice. The establishment of a mussolah required the allocation of land for this purpose, either through a gift from a resident landowner or through the allocation of public land, a former cemetery in one case, or land managed by the Department of Social Welfare in another, or marginal land behind streetside properties in yet another. Residents then formed a committee to collect funds from neighbours and from outside patrons, after which the community was invited to provide labour and materials to build the structure. The mussolah were used for daily prayers and for religious classes within the immediate community. They were also accessible for elderly residents who might attend Friday prayers there if they could not manage the longer walk to the mosque. To be recognised as a mosque, the mussolah needed to attract a sizeable congregation to attend prayers regularly. The establishment of a mussolah and subsequently a mosque therefore demonstrated substantial community support.

The growth of the mosques and mussolah also indicated a greater attention to 'correct' religious practices by kampung religious leaders. In Ledok, three of the mosques were associated with modernist tendencies in Islam. Residents referred to them as Muhammadiyah mosques, Muhammadiyah being the largest reformist Muslim association in Indonesia. Each of these had a religious leader who had received his education through a modernist establishment, either the Universitas Islam Indonesia or the IAIN (Institut Agama Islam Negeri, State Islamic Institute). In these tertiary colleges, classes took a critical view towards aspects of Islamic practices that did not conform to Islam as revealed in the holy books of the Hadith and the Koran. Students might also study *Kristologi*, which is a critique of Christianity and prepares students to contest religious practices that are non-Islamic. As these preachers and leaders asserted control of mosque instruction and ideology, there was pressure on kampung traditions diverting from the interpretations of Islam that the mosque leaders professed. In one kampung in Yogyakarta, for example, a newly returned student from IAIN asserted that non-Muslims could no longer participate in the washing of a Muslim corpse, an intervention that led to a serious rift among neighbours who were expecting to perform such a service at the funeral.

Islamic resurgence and increasing Islamic proselytisation began to have an impact on Indonesian society after 1979, reflecting growing Muslim activity throughout the world, including the Iranian Revolution of 1979 and the establishment of various Islamic institutions such as Islamic banks, organisations, and education and social welfare services (Rosyad, 1995: 5). The proselytisation (*dakwah*) movement in Indonesia originated particularly in two mosques, Salman in Bandung and Syuhada in Yogyakarta. Through their Sunday instructional classes, these mosques produced a new generation of students intent on reforming and revitalising Islamic practice in Indonesia. Their students fanned out to preach in mosques all over the country, particularly in Java. Moreover, during the late 1980s and early 1990s, President Suharto began to look to the Muslim political factions to support his flagging regime. Islamic banks were set up, the President went on the *haj* pilgrimage to the Holy Land, new mosques were built, and a network of Islamic intellectuals was set up (Ikatan Cendekiawan Muslim Indonesia). As a result, Indonesian culture took a more Islamic tone, with the Islamic greeting *Assalamu walaikum* replacing secular greetings such as *selamat pagi*. Women's dress increasingly featured the *jilbab* (headscarf). Haji in some circles acquired heightened status.

For two reasons one reformist target was the kendhuren. The reformists rejected prayer directed towards ancestral spirits and saw kendhuren as placating such spirits. Secondly, they criticised the holding of multiple rituals to commemorate the dead. Such patterns, they said, are not supported in the Koran or Hadith and therefore are not ordained by God. It is sufficient, they declared, to say prayers on the day of burial, with no subsequent rituals. Although this line is held strongly by reformist leaders, it has met with resistance from kampung residents. Community leaders have chosen to take a conciliatory position. Thus the pressure on the kendhuren has not been by direct frontal attack from the reformist mosques, although the position of the mosque leaders is widely known. The decline of the kendhuren has no doubt pleased these leaders but it is not clear they can take all the credit for its demise.

Reformists arguments were weakened by the more traditionalist line taken by the fourth mosque in Ledok, which recognised prayer to arwah and the multiple rituals after death and whose leader willingly participated in kendhuren. That mosque, centred on a charismatic spiritual leader who provided most of the entertaining and inspiring sermons on Friday and religious instructions on Thursday nights, also employed an *ustadz* (teacher) to lead the prayers. This young man was a graduate of a pesantren, a religious school that focused more attention on tuition in the traditional practices of Islam, often following the inspiration of a charismatic Sufi contemplative order. In Ledok it was observed that this mosque drew a congregation from a wider area in the kampung than its own neighbourhood, bringing in people wishing to identify with the more traditionalist positions taken by this mosque's leaders. Its spiritual leader was also invited to talk throughout the kampung during *Suwalan* (the month of *Suwal* when people paid formal respects to their elders) and thus exerted a counter to the condemnation of the kendhuren by reformist leaders.

In his study of Islam in Yogyakarta, Mark Woodward identifies two modes of piety based on divergent interpretations of a single set of cultural/religious axioms (Woodward, 1989: 6–7). Normative piety focuses on a set of behaviour which Allah, through the Prophet Mohammad, prescribed for the Muslim community (Woodward, 1989: 4), while mystical piety emphasises the mystical path by which the individual can attain union with Allah. Among those who practise normative piety, he distinguishes between reformists — both modernists and fundamentalists — and traditionalists, who support the practice of local traditions within their Islamic rituals (Woodward, 1989: 134–40). He thus recognises a diverse range of views and practices among the Yogyakarta Muslims. Woodward comments that the distinctions rest ultimately on individual interpretation, so that the two extremes of piety do not delineate two distinct groups of worshippers. Individuals may adopt aspects of both in their practices. In Ledok I encountered a range of views about the importance of mosque attendance, prayer to ancestral spirits at kendhuren or ancestral graves, and a mystical path to union with God. Informants were not easily categorised as reformist or mystical or traditionalist.

There is a popular saying in Ledok that there are many routes to climb the nearby Merapi volcano, reflecting the view that there are many ways to approach God. Among such who propound this view, there is condemnation of those who insist on their religious approach as the only way, the only truth. This, they say, is arrogant and thus against the principles of Islam, which preaches love, humility and gentleness in dealing with neighbours. Many regard such tolerance as one of the defining characteristics of kampung society and cite the kendhuren as one ritual that has promoted such views. It is a line taken by Sufi mystic followers, those who through contemplation (*tasawuf*) seek to know God's will. One such I interviewed was a leader in the reformist-oriented mosque who had also held positions as RT and RW head and RK official. Through *taqwa* (trust and obedience), he said, those who approach God will have God draw as close to them as the nerve in their neck. *Ikhsan* is the outward sign, the 'decorations' of such devotion, exemplified in thinking and doing good and in being kind, sincere, generous and honest with others. He declared to me that the Muslim must respect the non-Muslim. Part of being a good Muslim is accepting neighbours without judging them. One kampung kaum said to me that what matters in the kampung are *silaturrahmin* (ties of friendship). Despite different religions or different interpretations of Islam, these ties are never neglected or rejected. Silaturrahmin with others, of whatever religion, brings three benefits: friendship, long life and material reward. For such proponents, it is impossible for any human to know the mind of God and it is arrogance to condemn the sincere attempts of others who approach God in their way. According to my Sufi informant, those who reckon their way is right and others wrong are people who have not progressed in their faith to a true *taqwa* (trust in God); they still concentrate on *islam* (submission) and have not gone further in their religious journey. He and others like him were prepared to attend and support neighbours' kendhuren, though not necessarily encourage the practice. They admitted that such patterns can only change slowly and that outright denunciation of others' practices would only lead to conflict. However, the discussion in 2004 was clearly influenced by the religious reformists, who openly protested against the kendhuren as recognising and being directed towards ancestral spirits rather than God. It was a debate common in other parts of Indonesia, which had become increasingly dominated by the reformists (Bowen, 1993).

Tolerance of religious practice is high in the kampung. Catholics hold choir practices and worship prayers in private homes scattered throughout the kampung without complaint from Muslim neighbours, who must listen to them through the bamboo-thin walls. Similarly, Muslims use private homes for religious instruction and the recitation of the Koran in the hearing of non-Muslims. A disproportionate number of the administrative heads of RT and RW in the kampung are Catholic, despite the preponderance of Muslims in the population, because leaders are elected on the basis of their education, their employment or their moral authority rather than their religious affiliation. One of the present Catholic deacons in 2001 celebrated the 1000-day commemoration of his mother's death with a Muslim prayer ritual and, because she was a Muslim, invited a kaum to conduct the ceremony with 200 Muslims attending under the cross and other Catholic emblems hung on his walls. His family willingly cooked for days to provide their guests with food at the ritual. Sugi, a Catholic RW leader in Ledok, opened his house to healers from a local Islamic school (pesantren), who practised a healing based on electric charges to the affected area and on Islamic prayer. They openly pointed to God as the source of any healing that took place and were happy to attend to patients in the Catholic home. Sugi saw it as a good way to demonstrate his goodwill towards all households in the RW. In discussing the importance of promoting harmony between religious groups, he mentioned that their Catholic group had discussed the relevance of 'turning the other cheek', accepting without comment adverse comments about Christianity and not accusing the other religion of being false, thereby avoiding conflict between religious communities.

Among Muslims, meat donated on the Day of Sacrifice was offered to the poor of all religions in the neighbourhood. The poor were identified by mosque leaders and offered a coupon. They could make their own choice whether to pick up the meat from the mosque, as many practising Catholics and Protestants did. Parents boasted that their children followed different faiths, perhaps a result of the influence of the different religious schools they attended, or else as a consequence of their conversion at marriage to persons of another faith. For such parents, this was a source of pride because it reflected the value of tolerance they so strongly supported. One such parent said to me in 2004 that all members of his family had to show tolerance. He and his wife were Muslim, so they did not expect their Christian children to bring home pork to eat, but he was happy for them to eat pork outside the home. Similarly, if he was to entertain a Hindu, he said, he would not offer them beef or eat beef in front of them. He did not agree with anyone ridiculing another religion or claiming their religion was the best. This debased God, who created all people to fear Him. He added that if a mosque sermon or teaching session followed this intolerant line, he would reject it in his heart but outwardly say nothing against it. Tolerance did not entail denying the essentials of one's faith but rather allowing others to stand firm in theirs.

CONCLUSION

Religious tolerance in an environment of religious diversity allowed the RT/RW community over the years to attend the kendhuren as a neighbourhood group in support of individual neighbours. Despite the demise of kendhuren, that religious tolerance persisted in Ledok in 2004 and tended to counter the impact of the more forceful reformist preachers. However, the emergence of six mosques and mussolah in Ledok over 20 years and of two Catholic deaconates, constituted new communities based on a combination of religious practices and local residence. The formation of these new communities helped to bring about the decline in kendhuren. Reformist mosque leaders spoke out against kendhuren, while prayer gatherings were promoted as the more appropriate ritual. These religious communities were rivalling RT and RW neighbourhoods in their importance as the appropriate community of family rites of passage.

However, there is no single explanation for the decline of the kendhuren. Kampung residents found the alternatives more attractive in their pursuit of social status, or they were persuaded by religious arguments, or they counted the cost and sought cheaper alternatives. The nature of the neighbourhood society was changing as kampung population became denser, people worked further from home and the consumer revolution had its impact on individuals' lives. The financial crisis no doubt gave a jolt to the way people performed rituals, but the trend was in place before the financial crisis. Certainly there were increasingly strong religious affiliations that crosscut neighbourhood affiliation without, however, negating neighbourhood affiliations, which continued to be strongly expressed, both through the sembahyang and other activities such as arisan. Despite the potential for religious correctness to raise tension among neighbours of different faiths, harmony within the neighbourhood community remained a central ideological and practical principle of most residents.

Clifford Geertz and JamesPeacock both suggested that in the 1960s, slametan/kendhuren were no longer appropriate in urban neighbourhoods because these were no more than administrative units and no longer represented corporate communities. In this they anticipated the argument advanced by John Sullivan and others that RT neighbourhoods were creations of the state rather than constructions of local residents. Mary Hawkins in the 1990s countered these suggestions by demonstrating that slametan and the communities they constructed and reflected were still relevant among Javanese settlers in Kalimantan. Despite the demise of kendhuren in Ledok, this did not denote the end of community. Instead, neighbours worked through other rituals to express and strengthen local solidarity.

7

The Elections of 2004

Religious allegiance has always been part of the political arena in Indonesia. During the Soekarno period, competing Islamic parties emerged in the form of Masjumi, Sarekat Islam and Nahdlatul Ulama, although Soekarno banned Masjumi in 1960. The New Order state under Suharto sought to control religious political expression by fusing disparate Muslim parties into one party, the Development Unity Party (Partai Persatuan Pembangunan, PPP), and merging Catholic and Protestant parties with the Indonesian Nationalist Party into the Indonesian Democracy Party (Partai Demokrasi Indonesia, PDI), with office-holders in both parties appointed after negotiation with the state (Adnan, 1990). Throughout the New Order, elections were held every five years. *Pesta Demokrasi* (Festival of Democracy) was the term used after President Suharto coined the term in 1982. John Pemberton suggested that the term could be better translated as a 'Formal Reception of Democracy' (Pemberton, 1994: 5) and that these elections conformed to a New Order pattern, "an ideal absence in which nothing, as it were, happens." The New Order was able to affirm its rule through the construction of a general appearance of order, a routine political stillness. On the face of it, this is a surprising assertion because Pemberton also describes the noise and excitement that characterised every New Order election. However, he points out that the winner under the New Order was invariably not one of the two political parties but the government party Golkar (Golongan Karya, Federation of Functional Groups), whose victory quota of about 70 per cent of the vote was seemingly assured and defined the success of the election. Thus it became a national ritual to celebrate a certain result rather than the outcome of a contest to decide a winner. As a ritual, it was conducted on the city streets and incorporated huge crowds of participants. However, the state expressed some anxiety about these participating 'masses' because they constantly threatened to break out into uncontrolled violence and thus to invite security clampdowns on disruptive groups and disorderly occasions. Pemberton observed in 1982 the suddenness with which, after the day of the vote, the whole Festival/Reception was over and no longer worthy of further comment, "as if the whole business had just never happened" (Pemberton, 1994: 7).

Through the 1980s and up to 1997, only these three parties were allowed to compete. Golkar was officially not a party but a federation of functional groups. It represented public servants and they were obliged to vote for and support its campaign as the government party, which had brought the nation 'Development' (*Pembangunan*). The other two parties were creations of the state, conglomerations of previously independent parties. These parties were seriously disadvantaged over these years by the forced amalgamation of parties which differed in fundamental philosophies, by state interference in the selection of office-holders, by much poorer access to campaign funding, and by state insistence that they support the national ideology of *Pancasila* (the Five Principles of the Republic) and Pembangunan. Over five elections through to 1997, the vote for Golkar hovered around 70 per cent, a figure that reflected the ease with which the government was able to co-opt the votes of bureaucrats and other social groups (Castles, 2004: 7–8).

During both the Old and the New Orders, the President was elected not by the people in a direct election but by members of the Indonesian People's Consultative Assembly (Majelis Permusyawaratan Rakyat — MPR), which consisted of elected representatives of electorates and members appointed by virtue of their employment in the Armed Forces or their membership in community organisations. Castles (2004: 23) suggests that while President Suharto used elections to legitimate the position of his government, he preferred an indirect election of the President through a 'friendly' MPR over which he could exercise control.

People recognised the heavy-handed state control of the election process but still threw their energies into the Festival of Democracy. During each election campaign, the streets of Yogyakarta saw raucous scenes as the different parties staged their processions. Hundreds of motorcycles, some with three people on board, many waving flags and placards, roared through the streets and from all directions converged in the meeting arena, where participants were entertained by appearances from national artists and speeches from local and national leaders. With its superior resources, Golkar put on the largest 'parties', with many of the nation's top artists participating. The motorcycles roaring through the streets contributed to the party atmosphere, their riders and passengers dressed up in T-shirts and bandanas and waving flags advertising the party. Crowds lined the street, many offering drinks to the passing cavalcade.

Ledok residents recalled the heated campaigns that charac-terised the elections of the Old Order and early New Order periods. Clashes between supporters of different parties were fought out within the kampung as well as on the streets, and residents spoke strongly about the danger to community harmony (rukun) arising from political elections. In the 1982 election, supporters of the newly formed Partai Persatuan Pembangunan attacked a house in Kampung Tungkak, not far from Ledok, ostensibly to take revenge on someone from that kampung who had thrown stones at the PPP campaign parade. Residents recalled it as resembling a war, with attackers invading the kampung from all directions with a variety of sharp weapons. Many residents were injured, houses were destroyed and a number of families fled the kampung for several days, fearing that their homes would be burned. Only military intervention returned the situation to some sort of normality, although tensions remained high through to and even beyond election day. During that election campaign the government party Golkar used thugs to intimidate kampung residents thought to support other parties. Their tactics of pilfering kampung monies, stealing jewellery or even killing opponents were to guarantee Golkar's success in the elections through terror and violence. By 1985, however, Golkar no longer deemed such thugs necessary to its campaign and had eliminated many of them (Fauzannafi, 2004: 76–8). During later campaigns under the New Order, violence was kept to a minimum in Yogyakarta. However, in the freer atmosphere of post-New Order elections, physical clashes again became an issue. The local newspaper *Kedaulatan Rakyat* reported on 4 February 2002 that the celebration of the founding day of the PPP had led to clashes between its supporters and their detractors, which escalated into the throwing of Molotov cocktails and the destruction of motor vehicles. These clashes spread to some kampung when PPP enthusiasts from Notoprajan kampung attacked the home of a resident in the neighbouring kampung of Ngampilan, but security forces were able to prevent a full-scale fight between the two kampung from breaking out (Kusen, 2004: 52–3).

In his analysis of the 1992 elections, Budi Susanto (1992) refers to such parades by the two minor parties as anarchic. Youth, many of them students, defied the authorities by removing mufflers, persistently sounding their horns, removing number plates and standing up on their motorcycles. Many of their slogans were also defiant, questioning the importance or honesty of the elections. In his analysis, the *rakyat kecil* (the 'little people' or the public) of Yogyakarta, consisting mainly of kampung people but often given voice by students, used the election campaign to declare their boredom with the programs and slogans of 'Development', 'Unity' or *Yogyakarta Berhati Nyaman* ('Yogyakarta of the sound mind') espoused by the government. Their voices were given expression through posters and placards raised in the kampung and slogans shouted daily throughout the campaign. The region of Yogyakarta had been the origin of many new cultural trends and political initiatives throughout the New Order and the area was a breeding ground for militant student movements (Susanto, 1992: 19–25). Yet mass political mobilisation such as the huge rally against Suharto on 20 May 1998, which attracted over half a million people, did not result in mass violence (Mas'oed, 2001: 120; Aspinall, 1999). Yogyakarta remained a city where people still honoured their Sultan and the court traditions that valued social harmony, tolerance and patience. It was purportedly this respect, symbolised in the presence and words of the Sultan at that mass gathering, that prevented any resort to violence. However, the threat of violence was always a real one and there were occasions over those years when the city was rocked by clashes in the street between groups identifying with different religious groups or political parties. The burning of city churches and the training near to the city of the radical Laskar Jihad also kept in people's minds the threat of religiously inspired violence.[8]

Budi Susanto focuses his analysis on the so-called 'Yogya Incident of 1992'. Halfway through the 1992 election campaign, people across the city were roused one evening by a loudspeaker carried by a vehicle of the local government radio station announcing the decision by the governor of the province to ban all motorcycles from future campaigning. A subsequent announcement by the governor explained that the campaign of the Indonesian Democracy Party (PDI) had become brutal and high-spirited and thus in need of government control. This, he said, was not in keeping with Yogyakarta's reputation as a peaceful city. Two days after that announcement, the city was again startled, this time by the supporters of the two minor parties removing all their posters, placards and flags and announcing they were going on strike, mourning "the death of democracy" (Susanto, 1992: 29). On street corners burial cloths or coffins carrying the 'corpse' of demo-cracy were displayed, while incense was burned as a prayer to ancestral spirits. Hundreds of youth took to the street with white flags accom-panying a funeral coffin to the gates of the Provincial Government offices, progressing down the main road, which had been closed to campaigning. The demonstrators raised not only the spectre of ghosts and spirits, never far from the imagination of many urban residents, but also the threat of a potential invalid protest vote openly championed by various artists and intellectuals campaigning as the White Party (Golongan Putih, Golput), which was encouraging people not to mark their voting papers. In the face of this mass protest, the authorities relented and motorcycles were again allowed into the campaign. The Pesta Demokrasi was allowed to continue with all its noise and colour, with attention focused on the excitement of the campaign rather than the result of the vote.

The elections of 1999, the first after the heavy controls of the New Order state were lifted, introduced many new parties and the anticipation of political change. One of these new parties, Partai Demokrasi Indonesia Perjuangan (PDIP), led by nationalist Megawati Soekarnoputri, gained 33.7 per cent of the national vote. Golkar gained 22.4 per cent of the national vote, Partai Kebangkitan Bangsa (PKB), led by Nahdlatul Ulama Islamic leader Gus Dur gained 12.6 per cent, and Partai Amanat Nasional (PAN), led by former Muhammadiyah Islamic leader and Yogyakarta political scientist Amien Rais, gained 7.1 per cent (Castles, 2004). The votes for PDIP and PAN were particularly strong in Yogyakarta. As in previous elections, voters elected representatives to the national and provincial Parliaments. Although the parties nominated their representatives on the ballot papers, these were not necessarily the candidates who would represent the party in the parliament. There were many instances of national figures being featured as candidates in a party's pre-election propaganda, although the party and the proposed candidate had no intention for those figures to actually take a parliamentary seat. Voters nominated a party rather than a candidate on their ballot papers and it was left to the party to make its own nominations to the parliaments after the votes were counted. This led to a certain unreality in the whole procedure as voters saw their own preferences hijacked by internal party interests. That was to change in the elections of 2004. With past and recent memories to remind them, kampung residents approached the elections of 2004 with some trepidation, despite their excitement for the greater political participation promised within the Reformasi state.

THE APRIL 2004 ELECTIONS

As Indonesia prepared for the elections of 2004, the thoughts of kampung office-holders turned to the sheer logistics of organising three elections in one year. The waves of support for democracy assumed much higher levels of local administrative involvement in carrying out the elections and represented huge challenges to kampung leaders. The first election, in April, was for members to the national, provincial and district houses of parliament. It was contested by an astounding 24 parties, approved by the Electoral Commission from a list of 50 parties that had applied to contest the elections. This election was a huge challenge for all concerned, party supporters and electoral officials. Office-holders had gained some confidence by the completion of this election as they looked forward to the two rounds of presidential elections later in the year.

The 21 days of campaigning finished on March 31. In Yogyakarta the campaign went more smoothly than almost anyone could have hoped for. No-one could be certain what passions would be stirred by this election campaign. Police were more visible on the streets and among the plethora of campaign flags and buntings were large signs from the Electoral Commission encouraging people to put peace first.

The campaigns provided plenty of entertainment. With the drivers revving their engines in unison to a high pitch, cavalcades of motorcycles carried youth and sometimes families wearing T-shirts displaying the colour, symbol and acronym of their chosen party — the red-and-black buffalo of the PDIP, the blue-white square of PAN, the yellow crescents of PKS (Partai Keadilan Sejahtera) or the sacred banyan tree of Golkar. These were the most visible parties on the streets. In the stadium and public square, party organisers held meetings addressed by national leaders from Jakarta with entertainment by singers, dancers and comedians of national reputation. Although it was forbidden in the campaign speeches to attack another party, the government came under attack for its record on corruption and the lack of jobs for the unemployed and underemployed.

Despite the excitement of the campaign, there was an underlying pessimism among kampung residents and doubt that this election could bring any substantial changes. They saw it as a contest among an elite to gain access to the nation's wealth and power. Kampung people recognised that power had corrupted even the most sincere politician. The president was tainted, as were Golkar aspirants, and even their main rival, Amien Rais, the leader of PAN, former head of the national Islamic organisation Muhammadiyah and Speaker of the House of People's Representatives (Dewan Perwakilan Rakyat, DPR), was expected to fall foul of the same pressures. Despite their euphoria with Reformasi, people doubted that the election could bring substance beyond the ritual they still suspected it to be.

In the national and local press and in the local neighbourhoods, the election attracted as much interest in its logistics and administration as in its electoral outcome. It was recognised that previous elections had included many discrepancies of voter registration, giving rise to concern that every vote in the nation should count in this newly won democracy. For weeks the press drew attention to the failures of the Electoral Commission in meeting its targets — in the production of ballot boxes and election papers and their distribution throughout Indonesia's many islands. From its national headquarters, the Electoral Commissioner administered the creation of the Voter Registration and Continuous Population Data Collection (P4B) Program, the supply of re-useable ballot boxes and the installation of a communications network linking all 32 provinces, 440 districts and 4,167 subdistricts. Voters numbered 155 million and voted at 585,218 voting stations. The number of candidates was 460,000 across 2,057 electorates. The task of the Electoral Commission was daunting. The list of eligible parties was approved only in December 2003, the list of candidates was finalised in January 2004, and a final register of voters was produced in February 2004, the same month that 662 million voting papers were produced (Sjamsuddin, 2005).

The election posed huge challenges to electoral officials in a number of ways. Candidates were directly elected to four chambers, the House of Regional Representatives (Dewan Perwakilan Daerah, DPD), the House of People's Representatives (DPR), the provincial assemblies (Dewan Perwakilan Rakyat Daerah-Propinsi) and the regency or municipal assemblies (DPRD-Kabupaten/Kotamadya). Never before had people voted for all four chambers at once. The House of Regional Representatives was a new institution. Moreover, in this election, electors were able for the first time to cast their votes for specific candidates, knowing that these candidates were committed to taking up their seats in parliament.

These innovations resulted in the production of very large and complicated voting papers listing all the candidates for all 24 political parties. These papers were so big, in fact, that it was feared that the papers could not be laid out flat in the voting booths. Electors were expected to punch their mark against both the name of the party and the name of the candidate. Where only the party was marked, the first candidate on the party's list was deemed to score a vote. The voting booths provided a nail for electors to make their mark, seven times on four ballot papers.

Many residents of the kampung where I observed these preparations were poorly informed about these requirements. To make matters worse, preliminary ballot papers distributed for display had numerous mistakes. For example, one candidate's photo carried another candidate's name. Voting cards issued to each elector based on lists provided by local officials also contained significant errors and had to be returned. Older and illiterate residents particularly had difficulty understanding the complicated voting procedures.

All electors were assigned to a voting centre, one per approximately 300 electors. Each centre had a team of seven officials and two security guards drawn from the same community. This team set up the centre, registered and directed the voters and conducted the count. Each centre was assigned up to 24 observers, one appointed by each party, to scrutinise the voting process and the count and to verify the result. The centre team met for many weeks before the April election to familiarise itself with the voting procedures and protocols but they were hampered by the lack of vital information. For example, just two days before the election, they still had not seen the forms on which the voting results were to be recorded. The committee that I observed also considered how to ensure the elderly and disabled could be brought to the voting booth, whether seats needed to be supplied, and whether voters would need refreshments during what could be a long wait in queues. Since it was expected that voters would turn up early and register to vote and then wait before they could be called forward to vote, there was a concern that some voters who had recorded their arrival would return home to get a drink and then not be present when their turn came to vote. The committee considered what to do if it rained, as it was doing daily, because the voting centre was located out in the open on the only vacant space, a badminton court. In the end they erected a huge tarpaulin on a bamboo frame to provide shelter from sun and rain, all at their own expense. They also provided refreshments for the voters and meals for the invigilators and witnesses.

All these preparations were made without knowing how large a budget was allocated for each centre. The budget was finally determined as Rp300,000 ($A50) per centre. In the end, RW cash was used to supplement the Electoral Commission grant and wealthier residents made donations of Rp100,000 or more. Committees used RW equipment such as sound systems, glasses and crockery and chairs to limit their costs. Officials were also left unsure of whether they would be rewarded for this community service, with one report suggesting that they would be paid an honorarium over the three months that the three elections were held.

During the month of March 2004, party flags flew from high bamboo posts and were emblazoned on house walls and doors. Most prominent were the red of PDIP and the yellow and black of PKS, but there were also less commonly the flags of Golkar and of PPP. PDIP, the party of President Megawati associated with secular nationalism, remained the popular favourite, despite many admitting its ineffectiveness during the current term of her government. Her party continued to stand for a resistance to the authoritarianism of the New Order. Ledok had its own PDIP candidate who came from the southern RW and whose name was featured prominently on PDIP posters around the kampung. He was a highly educated man from the more affluent area of the kampung bordering the streetside, but he approached various RW leaders throughout the kampung to allow him to use their meeting rooms for his campaign. I heard of no objection to this request, although these meetings did not eventuate, perhaps due to his busy schedule elsewhere. When PDIP held its street campaign, kampung residents streamed out of the kampung dressed in the red T-shirts of the party, astride motorcycles that joined the parade. There was startling aggression in the way they rode those motorcycles out of the kampung, in vivid contrast to the care with which riders usually negotiated the alleyways. The other prominently advertised party PKS had done such a good job in putting up posters everywhere that I was quite convinced it was a kampung front-runner. Its campaign also featured an anti-corruption stance and an emphasis on good governance. PKS campaign meetings were held in the private homes of those particularly associated with reformist Muslim leaders. However, apart from the religious faithful who attended these meetings, kampung residents were quite guarded in their comments about PKS, commenting that the party stood for the steady imposition of an Islamic state and Islamic legislation. Two other Islamic parties had more backing in the daily conversations of the alleyways, PAN, the party of Amien Rais, who apart from his political accomplishments, was professor of political science at Gadjah Mada University, and PKB, the party associated with Gus Dur (Abdurrahman Wahid), appointed President after the last poll in 1999. He was a former leader of Nahdlatul Ulama, the traditionalist Islamic organisation, and his party's posters appeared most in the neighbourhood of the kampung mosque that espoused NU practices and values.

Within Ledok, the 2004 campaign passed without incident. Residents on the whole kept their preferences to themselves. Some, for example, supported other parties, like the Christian Party, but did not want to invite hostility or derision by stating their preference. Residents recalled past violence within the kampung between gangs of supporters and how kampung leaders concentrated on ensuring that no campaigning entered the kampung lest it endanger residential harmony and cooperation. Many residents recalled the fear they had felt in the earliest of those elections because of the violence of party followers. Under the New Order, campaigning had not been tolerated within the kampung, except in the form of posters and banners of the three political parties. After the fall of the New Order, in the 1999 and 2004 elections, some kampung in the city were declared by their residents to be 'party free', with no campaign activity of any sort allowed. In Ledok, posters and flags were tolerated as long as no campaigning was done. Although campaign meetings were allowed, few were held. The campaign was marked more by residents' pursuit of the monetary rewards of Rp10,000 or more paid by party organisers for flying a party flag or putting up a party poster or wearing a party T-shirt or cap. One party was known to give out Rp50, 000 to residents for such support. Such symbols thus often signified the resident's interest in the monetary incentive rather than their political support of the particular party.

As the campaign closed, there was increasing hope that the elections would be peaceful and free of administrative bungles. There was even some confidence among voters that the elections would be free of coercion. As it turned out, in the particular centre I observed, the voting went off without incident. Throughout the seven centres in the kampung counting was completed by midnight, the voting having closed at 2 p.m. In the polling booth of the area where I lived, PDIP obtained the highest vote, followed by PAN and PKB, while in Yogyakarta as a whole PAN scored the highest vote, followed by PDIP, Golkar, PKB and PKS.

The administrative success of this first election meant that these officials awaited their next test with greater confidence. Despite the un-certainty at times of instructions emanating from the central Electoral Commission and its regional centres, the different electoral teams had demonstrated the strength that lay in communities working with government to promote the reform of what had been an authoritarian electoral system. The success was not just in the administrative smooth-ness of the operation of multiple electoral administrative teams but in their avoidance of any harmful conflict among residents because of competing party interests. Residents had not been surprised by the results of the vote. Party allegiances within the community, at least in the aggregate, were now public and could be put to one side. While the presidential candidates electors scrutinised in the second and third elections were affiliated with political parties, they were seen as individuals and the elections were seen as less likely to lead to serious political schisms in the kampung.

THE JULY AND SEPTEMBER PRESIDENTIAL ELECTIONS

The 2004 elections were also the first time that voters could directly elect the president and vice-president, previously appointed by the People's Consultative Assembly. As a result, voters showed a lot of enthusiasm for this expression of democracy. Five presidential candidates and their vice-presidential partners were put forward in the July election and the two who gained the most votes ran off in the September elections. These were Megawati and Susilo Bambang Yudhoyono (popularly known as SBY), the latter eventually polling over 60 per cent of the final vote. Within the kampung there was a notable shift from voting along party lines in the April election to rejecting established party leaders in the July elections. Former general Wiranto, for example, was the official Golkar candidate, but the party had been tarnished in kampung eyes by its leader Akbar Tanjung's presumed corruption. Megawati, the current president and leader of PDIP, had disappointed many residents with lacklustre policies and programs and the lack of improvement in their living conditions over her term of office. On the other hand,

Susilo Bambang Yudhoyono, the leader of a minor new party, was seen as sharp and assured (*tegas*) and even-tempered (*kalam*). In television debates, he had shown no hesitation and had given clear answers to questions. Voters were aware that he was highly educated, having completed his doctoral degree in economics during the campaign. He was seen as a new face, untainted by party politics and the corruption of the past. One male kampung leader reported to me that women voters were attracted to him because he was handsome.

The number of voters registered and casting their vote actually increased by eight million from the April to the July elections. Castles (2004: 60–1) suggests that many were reluctant to take part in parliamentary elections because the role of these bodies was unclear or considered insignificant by many people. On the other hand, the additional eight million electors registered for the presidential election reflected the desire of citizens to determine their country's leader. However, in the booth in Ledok from which I gained information, the number of those casting their votes declined from 300 in April to 270 in July and 250 in September. The local explanation for this was that initially enthusiasm for the election was overwhelming and voters regarded it as an obligation to vote. Approaching the presidential elections, however, voters lost interest in the elections when their preferred candidate or party slipped out of the running.

The running of the July elections was marred by a national embarrassment. Because the voting paper was folded and two candidates' names and photos appeared on the front page, those wishing to vote for these two candidates did not need to unfold the paper. Subsequently, when they punctured the paper, the hole went through to the third or fourth candidate in the fold below. As a result, these votes were initially counted as invalid. As the day wore on, the National Electoral Commission realised the scale of this invalid vote and instructed polling booths to recount these informal votes and to assign these votes to the intended candidates.[9] This instruction was actually illegal but the decision was taken in the national interest to remedy what was a highly embarrassing situation (Castles, 2004: 59–77). At the local polling booths, kampung electoral committees soon became aware of the large number of papers where two candidates' photos were punctured, but they were reluctant to do anything until official written instructions were issued. Finally the votes in each ballot box were recounted, not at the polling station but in the kelurahan office, witnessed by all those witnesses and committee members of the earlier count. A third of the votes that had originally been designated invalid were validated in this process.

THE CO-OPTED KAMPUNG OFFICIAL

The implementation of the 2004 elections demonstrated a new form of co-option of kampung leaders into government administration. Elections are the concern of the state — shaping the parliament, deciding on the president and validating the elected political regime — and the government was under pressure to adequately finance and control the proceedings. Instructions were formulated at the centre through the National Electoral Commission and were broadcast throughout the nation. However, funding and instructions were laced with uncertainties. Kampung electoral committees were not sure how much funding would be available and had to spend their own funds when the funding was late or insufficient. Instructions were promised but did not arrive until the last moment, so officers had to make plans without them. The state was only a shadowy presence at the kampung level as leaders initiated their own arrangements, devised their own rules and funded the operations from their own pockets or RW funds. They added another dimension to arrangements by planning for not only the casting of votes but also the comfort of voters. Tarpaulins were erected to shade the voters and drinks were provided for the queues. These tarpaulins were erected over the badminton court no less than five times in 2004 — three times for the elections, once for the RW celebration of Independence Day and once for the commemoration of Idul Fitri, the end of the Muslim fasting month. Each time up to 300 residents attended the gathering at this particular location. Residents were recruited as invigilators for the count of each vote, which was held within the neighbourhood and witnessed by large festive crowds, celebrating each vote with shouts of encouragement.

The kampung leaders took on themselves much of the administration of the election and to them goes much of the credit for the success of the three elections. However, the events of the July recount revealed that these kampung leaders relied ultimately on the legitimacy provided by the National Electoral Commission to validate the election results. Though they were aware of the shortcomings in the electoral procedures, they saw their obligations as carrying out to the letter the instructions passed on to them from the national body. Only then could the elections be seen as free from the manipulation of results at a local level so common of earlier elections. The formal authority of the state provided a mantle of legitimation over the whole process, but that process was informalised in much of its implementation as kampung residents imposed their priorities on what could rightly be called a 'Festival of Democracy'. The celebration for kampung leaders and most residents was not so much for the successful candidate or parties but for the expression of community harmony and cooperation during what was seen as potentially one the most dangerous moments in its recent history.

8

Community and State Violence

In the minds of the city authorities and also of kampung leaders, the elections of 1999 and 2004 raised the spectre of spontaneous violence among the urban 'masses'. Such fears were given substance for kampung leaders in the youth violence that had emerged in the kampung during the 1990s, resulting in at least two fatalities and investigation by city police. These incursions by police or army units into kampung space are themselves seen as violent and are resisted by kampung residents whenever possible. In a society in which social harmony and tranquility are highly valued, the presence of such violence is especially threatening (Guinness, 1986: 119).

In post-New Order society, sporadic violence has punctuated attempts at reform. In 2000 crowds supporting President Wahid destroyed property in several towns in East Java as a warning to those in Parliament who wished to impeach the President. Conflict in Maluku, Aceh or Central Sulawesi was constantly in the news for several years. On occasions during my kampung stay in 2000, sermons from the nearby mosque, amplified to neighbouring localities, actually preached violence. These sermons began with anger over the Palestinian crisis and moved to condemnation of US policy, Israeli police actions, and Christian sympathies for Israel. However, some of these sermons also preached violence against Americans and Christians within Yogyakarta and used the cry of *jihad* or holy war. In nearby Solo, one group took up this challenge with a search for Americans throughout the main hotels in the city, a move that led the US State Department to advise its citizens not to travel to Indonesia.

Despite these explicit calls to violence, the congregations of the mosque adjacent to Ledok emerged quietly after such sermons and went about their daily business. Moreover, such sermons did not always reap agreement among their listeners. In the question-and-answer session that followed one such sermon in 2000, a member of the congregation challenged the speaker by saying that the 'West' often showed its superiority in being able to analyse a situation rationally rather than jump to sensational and mistaken interpretations of the Holy Book. A few years later, in 2004, sermons from this mosque appeared to be concentrating on matters of individual faith and no encouragement was given to acts of violence. Despite the immediacy of violence in state and civil action, which in 2000 was evident in anarchic forms such as incitements to jihad, crowd violence or public action on the streets, there were strong local curbs on its emergence, rooted in cultural priorities that valued cooperation and coexistence. These were particularly effective within kampung neighbourhoods.

SPONTANEOUS VIOLENCE

During the years after the New Order, stories of spontaneous violence (*keroyokan*) abounded in the media. James Siegel pointed out that keroyokan was recognised by Javanese as depicting a mass of people taking the law into their own hands, as when a "mob spontaneously chases, catches, and usually beats to death a thief or other culprit" (Siegel, 2001: 48). The following are some incidents of violence reported during 2000 by the local newspapers *Kedaulatan Rakyat* and *Bernas*.

On 4 November 2000 the police post in Penggung, Ceper, Klaten, a town 30 kilometres from Yogyakarta, was ransacked by a group of "irresponsible youth". The attack followed a highway incident in which two youths on a motorbike were passed (and endangered) by a tourist bus. They chased the bus and threw rocks at the bus, breaking windows. One of the youths was arrested by the public and surrendered while the other fled. Not long afterwards the youth who had fled confronted the police post with a group of young men in a truck. Beside breaking roof tiles, tables and chairs and a TV set in the police post, they severely injured the bus driver, who was rushed to hospital (*Kedaulatan Rakyat*, 5/11/2000).

On 26 October 2000 at a university campus in Yogyakarta, a male student stole the bracelet of a female student and was chased by the public, students and others. He was badly beaten up and the motorcycle he was riding severely damaged by the emotional crowd.

Only after the police intervened was he surrendered to the officers and rushed to hospital (*Kedaulatan Rakyat*, 27/10/2000).

On 9 September 2000 on a stretch of the Yogya-Solo road under repair near Jonggrangan, Klaten, a minibus collided with a motorcycle, throwing the rider into the ditch. Thinking the rider was dead, local residents set on the bus driver and beat him half to death. The driver was rescued by a passing police patrol who rushed him to hospital. There had apparently been a number of accidents recently on this stretch of road (*Kedaulatan Rakyat*, 30/9/2000).

On 20 September 2000 in Pogung village, Cawas, Klaten, a known criminal called Dwiyono extorted Rp150,000 from a resident Parno, who was preparing for his child's wedding. When Dwiyono again approached Parno the following day to demand more money and threatened him with a knife, he was refused and local residents chased Dwiyono into the rice field, beat him with timber and set him on fire using petrol. He was dead by the time police arrived (*Kedaulatan Rakyat*, 21/9/2000).

On 1 August 2000 four practitioners of black magic (*santet*) were apprehended by village security guards at 2 a.m. burying a package of nails, screws, knives, eggs and a water jar wrapped in cloth in the front yard of the home of Mrs. Slamet Rahayu, a traditional medicine dealer in Drono village, Ngawen, Klaten. When the guards could not obtain a satisfactory response to their questions, they beat up the sorcerers, aided by a crowd which grew to the hundreds and then set fire to Mrs. Slamet's store shed. Mrs Slamet was said to have invited the practitioners to sorcerise her distant relative Eko Haryanto, with whom she had a dispute over an inheritance (*Bernas*, 2/8/2000).

Two common explanations of such incidents or *keroyokan* were that either they reflected the breakdown in state and societal structures of law and order or, alternatively, that they mirrored and fed off state strategies of violence. In either case, these explanations recognised the key role that the state plays in the incidence of violence. James Siegel suggests that perhaps both explanations are valid. The militaristic New Order had both gained power through violence and established itself as protector against violence by its dramatic despatch of the state's enemies: "It is the Indonesian genius to make the state at once the chief source of murder and also the means of granting not merely immunity, but innocence as well, to its citizens" (Siegel, 2001: 66–7). This "genius" unravelled in the years after the fall of the New Order.

KEROYOKAN AS THE ABSENCE OF THE STATE AND LOSS OF CULTURAL CERTAINTY

According to the first interpretation, the 'masses' resorted to violence in and around the year 2000 in response to the state's invisibility or incompetence on the public stage, or to the breakdown of social order within social groups. Bridget Welsh (2006) confirmed my own observation that by 2004 reports of such violence in the press had greatly diminished. She found that there had indeed been a drop in both the reporting and incidence of keroyokan in the four areas where she did research — West Java and Jakarta, Bengkulu, Bali, South Kalimantan — although my impression was that in Yogyakarta the decline had been even more dramatic. Her conclusion was that the surge in the incidence of keroyokan in the years 2000–01 was due to political instability, particularly the perception that the police and judiciary were unable to provide the social control required by people, who subsequently took matters into their own hands in a premeditated way. Since then, according to her, mob violence had been replaced by vigilantism, while criminal gangs competed for control over a diverse range of fields from parking to drugs and prostitution. According to her account, then, violence persists but in a different form, with gangs becoming the principal agents of violence. Police and army personnel were reported to work with criminal gangs as a way to supplement their meagre incomes (Tadie, 2002). Whether or not these gangs were sanctioned by state interests, they confirmed people's perception that the state had lost its monopoly on violence, leaving people to take action into their own hands.

Siegel recounts that keroyokan is condemned by middle-class Indonesians. They condemn it as an act of the masses (*massa*), a derogatory term referring to the mob, "an incoherent group without a particular identity", its very spontaneity an indication that people have lost their cultural senses (Siegel, 2001: 52). They exhibit "savage" (*biadab*) behaviour by engaging in such violence (Siegel, 1998: 105). Siegel suggests that the violence reflects the failure of culture, the "collapse of structures that generate identities and the subsequent surge of untamed impulses" (Siegel, 2001: 49–52). In his view, the culprit is guilty of aggression by disturbing public harmony and threatening social order, this initial aggression triggering the response of keroyokan. The savageness of keroyokan and aggression itself cries out in middle-class views for a cultural/religious reformation to constrain the "cravings, wishes and erotic energy" of its perpetrators (Siegel, 1998: 105). Siegel rejects the idea that keroyokan is a response triggered by culture, asserting instead that it attests to a failure of culture. "In Java there are functioning modes of discussion and recognized ways to formulate community opinion. These are disabled when aggression appears on the scene" (Siegel, 2001: 48–9). Here Siegel appears to be referring to the hegemonic culture, the forms sanctioned by the urban middle classes and formalised within state structures, while recognising that the breakdown of cultural forms allows for mob violence to emerge. Although he admits that keroyokan is a "common reaction", given that there is a distinct Javanese language term for it, he prefers not to characterise this violent public response to what is perceived as aggression as a cultural response, referring to it rather as the loss of culture.

Siegel proposed that the collapse of state and other social structures providing people with their identities gave rise to the conditions for the outbreak of violence in Java in the late 1990s (Siegel, 2001: 52). The increase in witchhunts in East Java at that time, according to Siegel, was an attempt to reassert social control at the local level over uncertainty amid fears about the failure of the state at the national level in the post-New Order period (Siegel, 2001: 68. See also Sidel, 2006). Examining ethnic violence in Central Africa, China and Europe, Arjun Appadurai links the outbreaks of violence there to unacceptable levels of uncertainty about identity and rising suspicions about the deception of others' identities. Uncertainty raised by large-scale migrations, anxiety about state provision of goods on the basis of identity, or the erosion of social knowledge through rumour, terror or social movement give rise to violence as a "macabre form of certainty" (Appadurai, 1998: 290). Appadurai notes the "transformation of neighbours and friends into monsters" as people no longer trust the social identities that have bound them together up to that point (Appadurai, 1998: 298). The state is always involved in such uncertainty through its reconstruction of mass identities which become "significant imagined affiliations for large numbers of people, many of whom are resident across social, spatial and political divides" (Appadurai, 1998: 287). In Indonesia the New Order had fashioned national and regional societies and cultures that challenged 'traditional' social identities, which post-New Order decentralisation placed under further strain (Guinness, 1994).

As a result of rising confusion over identities, accusations of sorcery against fellow villagers arise throughout Africa (Geschiere,

1988) and in Java (Siegel, 2001; Campbell and Connor, 2000; Sidel, 2006). Campbell and Connor note that accusations of sorcery were frequently directed in East Java against those who had gained wealth or status 'unnaturally'. Such people were seen as ignoring the proper behaviour of reciprocity toward kin or neighbours, thereby abandoning their social identification with these significant others. Those accused were frequently dukun, whose acknowledged power over the supernatural was used in healing and re-establishing relations of reciprocity but whose powers could also be the source of wealth and power, alienating those with whom they had formerly been intimate. In Ledok a common accusation against those who suddenly or 'unnaturally' became wealthy was that they had gained their wealth by making a contract with a familiar spirit (*tuyul*). Such a contract was always on the basis that, in exchange for their suddenly acquired wealth, they had to sacrifice a close family member (Guinness, 1988: 103). Thus people watched for the unexpected death of one of their kin and in the event, were quick to condemn the immorality of their neighbour's newly acquired wealth.

VIOLENCE AS STATE MILITARISM

The New Order began with an enormous massacre, the killing of hundreds of thousands of alleged communists in a state-sanctioned act of great violence (Cribb, 1990). Barker (1998) illustrates how such violence became the essence of the New Order through its preoccupation with criminality, the incorporation of criminal elements into local security practices and the use of government-sanctioned violence as a form of "shock therapy" (Campbell and Connor, 2000: 81). The state drew up lists of suspected criminals who were monitored and later victimised through such operations as the imprisonment of suspected communist sympathisers or the mysterious killings of reputed criminals (*pembunuhan misterius — petrus*) of 1983–85. The local security system (*sistem keamanan lingkungan — siskamling*), according to Barker, was a state-initiated restructuring of local security with the aim of identifying and controlling the sources of violence. In this way, any source of opposition could be demonised as criminal and targeted by state-legitimated neighbourhood violence. Siegel (2001: 45) agrees that violence, although a means to the revolution in the cultural memory of Indonesians, under the New Order "was repressed, feared and built into the national memory under the form of fears of communist resurgence, sadistic criminals and social disruptors". However, by attributing violence to the unformed masses, the New Order redesignated the rakyat (common people), a social category with immense moral significance during the fight for Independence, as the (unthinking) 'mob', thereby gaining wide acceptance and justification for its clampdown against such 'mob violence'. The 'violent masses' were thus constructed by the state — and the middle classes who reflected that state — as people deprived of their moral sense, without goals and without form. Rather than the state being seen as a violent aggressor, which in many circumstances it was, the state was seen as the legitimate wielder of power to contain the violence of the common people.

In the post-Suharto period, the Indonesian New Order has been increasingly portrayed within Indonesia as being a violent state itself (Anderson, 2001). Marxist theories of the coercive state emphasise how states are fashioned through conquest and suppression and function to perpetuate the domination of the ruling class (Earle, 1997). In discussing the Haitian state under Duvalier, Cedras Bernat remarked that "the exercise of state power is always violent and that the state always claims a monopoly on force. The relations between the state and the civil society are power relations.... It [power] emerges as a particular arrangement of groups and institutions in the midst of social and ritual relations" (Bernat, 1999: 128). Quoting Foucault (1977) and Scarry (1985), he observes that state violence is a unique exercise of the state's monopoly on force — one that looks toward the terrorization of society into conformity. Taussig (1987) writes of a state "culture of terror", a "relentless assault upon a civilian population in which menace, torture, forced labour and imprisonment become endemic forms of socio-political control" (Margold, 1999: 63–4). Bernat points out that state use of violence is a:

> social project of creating punishable categories of people, forging and maintaining boundaries around them and building consensus about them that specify and enforce state-desired behavioral norms. It is a process of legitimating and de-legitimating specific groups and is a function of cultural violence ... becoming the precondition for the reproduction of civil violence (Bernat, 1999: 128–9).

In his case study, state-inspired social constructions by the Port-au-Prince community identified street children as dangerous social threats and denied human rights that would otherwise have been extended to these children.

The Institute for Research and Empowerment (IRE), an independent Indonesian institute, portrays militarisation and militarism in Indonesian society as a product of the New Order:

> The government has determined so many aspects of people's lives that they, the government, have lost sight of the basics of the nation state and a healthy society. Intervention has made them mentally sick, possessive, egotistical. Bureaucrats have lost their humanitarian feelings, and the bureaucratic apparatus favours the bureaucrats. They make use of the forces of police, army and the law to destroy the dynamism of the democratic life of the people (Supraja, 2000).

The Institute identifies militarisation as most clearly represented in the entry of the armed forces into civilian life, promoted by the government as *dwifungsi* (dual roles). Armed forces personnel ran businesses, took on corporate directorships, held civilian posts, financed and ran newspapers and conducted civilian projects. On the other hand, militarism also referred to the much more subtle process of the 'armament culture' seeping into the consciousness of Indonesians, an internalisation of military values, ideology, organisation and behaviour in civil society. The military invited civil society to enter the battle zone through their targeting of both external and internal enemies and their promotion of such traditions as marching and saluting the flag, wearing uniforms, neighbourhood night patrols and property guards. Films, both domestic and foreign produced, also provided a daily diet of violence and war for their audiences (see also McGregor, 2007).

In a hard-hitting review of intercultural contact in Kalimantan, John Bamba (2000), the Director of the Institute of Dayakology, documents how difference was eliminated by the central New Order government's attempts to generate oneness, unity of language, culture, thought, behaviour and ambitions. Education prepared children to regard local culture as backward and primitive and to condone the elimination of their longhouse homes on the pretext that they were communistic and encouraged uninhibited sex. Such education undermined solidarity and promoted individuality: the preaching of world religions damned local beliefs as satanic; television portrayed the good life of consumer luxury, through advertising lies sold the means to it, and promoted violence as the best way to solve problems; and laws and regulations marginalised local ways in the name of development. These changes were achieved through the force of law, ideology and arms. Under these conditions, forests were cut down, the poverty of shifting cultivators increased, and ethnic violence emerged as an expression of repressed anger and confusion.

These commentators suggest that Indonesia had been under the suppression of a militaristic and violent regime for so long that violence had become the accepted means of solution. Even when the New Order had formally been ousted, its influence lived on. Sutoro Eko, editor of the Institute of Research and Empowerment's journal *Flamma*, identified sports contexts or cultural evenings held as part of Independence Day celebrations as "mobilisation from above" (Eko, 2000b). The New Order government promoted such activities among the youth while banning them from political discussions and political activism, notably through the ban on student political activism, Normalisasi Kampus, in the early 1980s. Sport and cultural performances, Eko asserted, dulled their minds, so that they became less intelligent and less critical towards the authorities.

Eko (2000a) provides a lengthy theoretical chapter on militarisation and militarism. Militarism is defined as a set of values, ethics, ideologies, cultural paradigms and behaviours planted deeply in society, such as uniformity, discipline, obedience and order, force, loyalty, compactness, commando mentality, hierarchy, centralism, preference for physical solutions to problems, patriotism, warrior values and categorical notions of friend and foe. The list is expanded in various places in the book. In a section entitled 'The Face of Militarism in the Civil Community', the book lists the physical punishment of children in a family in the name of discipline, reinforcing hierarchical and centralistic relations among members of a family with the parents or the father at the apex, implying obedience, regulations and reluctance to dialogue. Beyond family, the book lists kampung activities organised within RT or RW (neighbourhood administrative units), such as Independence Day activities, which have abstract aims such as love of country, sacrifice for the nation, or warrior attitudes, and nightwatch activities in the kampung which "clearly imitate the way military organise patrols" (Eko, 2000a: 45). Militarism is so frequently found in everyday behaviour that, without people realising, it dominates community life: for example, in uniforms for school children, office workers or women's association (PKK) members, or the uniform painting of fences or the construction of entrance gates to villages. "Uniforms are seen as carrying the spirit of solidarity, meaning that there is no difference — a military meaning of solidarity" (Eko, 2000a: 45).

Militarism is also found in the acronyms common to Indonesian life and the appearance in television advertisements of muscle-bound and shortcropped males, or the wearing of military-like camouflage jackets by the general public.

Such critics of militarism and militarisation insist that the RK/RT structure in Yogyakarta residential areas represents the violent imposition of the state in order to pressure the people to do the government's bidding. Part of the argument here is that these structures were founded under military occupation. The RK/RT were modelled on Japanese military-inspired administrative units, *aza* and *tonarigumi*, introduced under the Japanese occupation during the Second World War (Sullivan, 1992: 34). For the first time, urban kampung neighbourhoods were formally identified as part of the state machinery. After Independence, the Government adopted this administrative structure with only a change in titles, *aza* becoming rukun kampung (RK) and *tonarigumi* the rukun tetangga (RT).

Ledok residents are very aware of the violent militarism that pervades the wider society. They are and, for decades, have been the daily victims of such violence. In the 1970s I reported how riverflat residents were the object of raids by police looking for stolen goods or known criminals (Guinness, 1977). Across the river from Ledok, so-called gelandangan (the homeless), who occupied shanties on the riverflat, were constantly hounded by authorities who destroyed their homes and trucked them out of the city (Guinness, 1983).

State 'violence' could also take much subtler forms. During the 1980s the government introduced a standardised structure of local government, abolishing the largest unit of communal administration, the RK (rukun kampung) headed by an elected but unpaid RK head, who was not a civil employee but a community representative. In its stead, the government instituted a new level of civil administration, the kelurahan, which incorporated several of the former RK, administered by paid civil servants. Within the former RK, the government established several RW, which in the case of Ledok corresponded to already existing informal neighbourhood communities (Guinness, 1990). This ruling had the effect of destroying one level of community participation, the kampung, while consolidating a much smaller unit of community. In another kampung along the Code river, the division of the former RK Sosrokusuman into two RW had disrupted residents' identification as a single community and had led to its gradual disappearance as a socio-cultural unit (Yoshi, 2000: 3). The loss continues to pain residents of many kampung, who recall the community cohesion under the former RK.

According to observers such as Eko and Sullivan, therefore, kampung were not characterised by autochthonous expressions of community but in their forms of communal order mimicked the militarism introduced by successive state regimes.

VIOLENCE IN THE KAMPUNG: RAKYAT OR MASSA?

James Siegel suggested that the kampung neighbourhood he observed in Solo was "founded on violence" (Siegel, 1986: 39–51). This kampung was in the centre of Solo, the bulk of the population was poor, and most households had been there for at least a decade, speaking of it as if they had been there for generations. It was a community because those who lived there "feel they have common interests and an important stake in each other's well-being and good behaviour", particularly valuing the security the community provided through ronda (nightwatch patrols) manned voluntarily by residents (Siegel, 1986: 39). He suggested that violence lies close to the surface of social interaction in Java and that cultural forms such as language levels and kampung administrative organisation help to suppress the outbreak of such violence (Siegel, 1986). Siegel witnessed the way youth patrols sealed off the neighbourhood during anti-Chinese riots in 1980, not only protecting Chinese co-residents but asserting neighbourhood solidarity and protecting neighbourhood identity in the face of external confusion. He defined the ronda as the strongest expression of the solidarity of the neighbourhood because it provided residents with the most pertinent sense of their community. The ronda acted to suppress the violence that existed just below the surface of social relations. According to Siegel, that violence was a form of language, with which residents addressed those they considered of a lower order than themselves. By controlling violence, the ronda maintained, if not created, the moral order of the neighbourhood. Order was founded on suppression — the suppression of violence, the suppression of self, the suppression of spontaneity in favour of culturally acceptable 'higher' forms of behaviour. Siegel's analysis of neighbourhood relations emphasised the suppression of violence and conflict in favour of "official" form, which included using appropriate levels of Javanese language to express deference for those of higher rank (Siegel, 1986: 79). However, this official form, according to Siegel, masked the more important unofficial activities of the ronda as the most essential component of neighbourhood community. Those involved in the ronda security patrols set the neighbourhood apart and against the incursions of outside confusion, hierarchy and authority, and they enforced community morality by enacting violence against thieves caught in the act, teaching them a lesson about respecting the property and persons of others in the community.

Although not usually of the physical sort, latent violence is also part of Ledok culture and society. The recognition of social hierarchy within Javanese society is one of its most noted characteristics, elaborated as it is in language, dress, occupation and ritual, most highly developed in the court culture of Yogyakarta. As such it predates by some centuries at least the militarism of New Order Indonesia. By dint of their superior social position, some Ledok residents attempt to dominate others, or are seen by those others to dominate them. However, as Siegel suggests, such latent violence is tempered in the softer symbols of local etiquette, including language levels, bowing and other expressions of politeness or, though rarely, the harsher expression of disdain. Overt pulling of rank is not condoned in the kampung. It is a point of constant negotiation among residents, as those of higher rank in the kampung insist on correct forms that express deference while those of lower rank at times belligerently express their disdain for all forms of social snobbery. Ledok communities are constructed on a fine and constantly negotiated balance between recognising all as common and equal members while acknowledging that some should be deferred to on the basis of their social rank. The violence of social status, as Siegel would put it, is suppressed through subtle uses of language and etiquette.

A hierarchy imposed by residential location and social ranking was particularly evident in Ledok in the 1970s. Kampung residents saw themselves as occupying either the slopes of the riverbank or the riverflat, associated respectively with higher or lower social status, particularly in the early years of occupation. Riverflat residents were most outspoken in their criticism of the autocratic ways adopted by some riverbank neighbours, particularly in relation to occupation of riverflat land and the sharing of resources. One riverflat resident summed up his perceived powerlessness against land claims by a riverbank resident in pointing out he was a mere buruh (labourer), while the riverbank man was a pegawai (civil servant).

Potentially a similar relationship of violence pertains between land-owners and those who occupy their land as *pengindung*, that is paying a low rent for the right to build their own home on another's land.

The landowner can refuse the houseowner permission to improve the house on the basis that improvements would need to be acknowledged in compensation payments if the landowner ever resumed the land. The landowner may also refuse permission for the sale or inheritance of the house, so that heirs may be denied further occupation of the land. Landowners like this are seen as *sadis* (brutal), 'with no heart', although they act entirely within the law. In one case in 2000, the widow of a pengindung was forced to relinquish the house on her husband's death with a mere Rp2 million paid to her in compensation for the brick home. That was *sadis*, according to neighbours, but the widow had surrendered (*pasrah*), leaving it to God to judge. It was a common response to such violence to leave it to fate or supernatural forces to avenge. Siegel notes the same acceptance by families affected by the lynching of witches in East Java (Siegel, 2001).

Violence was not restricted to men. One local woman frequently clashed with her husband, leading to public scenes in which the two argued verbally. He had lived for years in another city, returning only irregularly to see her and their children. Her language was seen as excessively rude and offensive, even though neighbours sympathised with the way she had been abandoned. She also clashed several times with neighbours, once with a woman who ran a warung when they argued over the purchase of goods, another time with a man who asked her not to discard solids into the drain that flowed directly under the rooms of his house. Once she even fought another woman with stones in the alleyway, drawing blood. She was thus recognised as one who allowed emotions to emerge in violent behaviour, contrary to accepted social norms of behaviour.

However, it was generally assumed that men were more likely to resort to violence, especially when drinking alcohol or when taken by surprise. During my stay in 2000, an outsider from a local non-government organisation spoke to the RT women's group about violence in the home, claiming that women were often the object of sexual, financial, physical or emotional violence within the home by men who confined their wives to *dapur, sumur dan kasur* (kitchen, well and bed). Although his presentation attracted little discussion among the women at the time, they all must have been conscious of cases such as those he presented. I was witness to a number of cases over the years of domestic violence. However, rather than seeing such violence as permeating kampung life, residents were more conscious of the community environment that helped to thwart and control such violence. The speaker was publicising a Women's Crisis Centre set up by an NGO. In fact the kampung community provided its own crisis response involving close neighbours, overseen by elders in the community including RW or RT officials. Kampung residents were very reluctant to refer such violence to authorities outside the close community, both because of the effectiveness of such community measures and because of the uncertainties of involving outsiders. Violence was seen as aberrant behaviour that could be controlled through communal measures.

There were incidents of communal violence in Ledok. I witnessed this once in the 1970s, when a young man of the kampung was caught stealing a pair of shoes from a neighbour. He was a youth whom neighbours suspected, or perhaps knew, had stolen before and he came from a family that was of low status and considered ill-equipped to discipline the young man themselves, the father having died and the mother struggling to provide for her family. The youth was set on by a crowd that increased rapidly into a spontaneous *massa*, beating and kicking him as he cowered on the ground. Then, as suddenly as the violence had emerged, order again prevailed and he was released to kampung office-holders for further admonition, at the same time saving him from further violence (Guinness, 1988: 103). After a reprimand, he was released back into the community without any thought of handing him over to outside authorities. In 2000 he was still in the neighbourhood, married with children and earning an income. In Siegel's account of a similar incident the *ronda* security guard was the executor of this community violence (Siegel, 1986: 47).

In 2000 I was told of several other incidents when violence had been used like this against local miscreants. When I enquired what had happened to the transvestites (*banci*) who had lived in the neighbourhood in 1996 and worked as sex-workers outside the kampung. I was told that their behaviour had become less and less respectful of kampung norms, that is they dressed skimpily, used rude language, and were disrespectful to neighbours. One day the young men of the neighbourhood, apparently high school youths, beat up the transvestites and forced them out of the kampung. I do not see this as condemnation of their sexual preference for I witnessed many occasions in 1996 when these transvestites joined circles of kampung women discussing at length use of makeup, haircuts, or analysing male behaviour. Several transvestites practised as hair and beauty specialists in the kampung. Rather the youths seem to have been aroused by what was seen as anti-communal behaviour. After a period of putting up with this behaviour, the youths resorted to violence and this was accepted by the community as the right strategy. The youths were praised, but I did not get the impression that they were directed to be violent. It was rather accepted that youth are more likely than the older generations to become violent and, in this case, it achieved the result the community wanted. It might not have been possible for the RT leaders to achieve the same result through non-violent means. In these extreme and rare cases, violence was an expression of community and an affirmation of the moral order of community.

There is an obvious parallel here to the ronda, which Siegel suggested is the most potent symbol of community solidarity expressed through violence. The *Warta Kampung* magazine put out by the non-government organisation Yayasan Pondok Rakyat (Chapter 9) devoted a cover story to the *pos ronda* (Yoshi, 2001). There the writer pointed out that the origins of the post are found in the colonial government's provision of security over cash-crop estates and the Japanese war administration's concern for controlling the native population. Its origin was therefore, like the RT and RK administrative units, in the violence of foreign occupation over local populations. From that beginning the patrol post has become an essential piece of neighbourhood infrastructure, a product of 'development', a symbol of modernity, linked through the formal siskamling (local patrol) system to the security sections at the kelurahan office as well as local police and army control posts. The ronda is thus securely located in a wider system of population control that is identified through the New Order with militaristic strategies. In addition, according to Yoshi, within the neighbourhood the pos ronda is further implicated in violence. The mostly young men who patrol the neighbourhood from the post have a licence to confront suspicious persons in the area, to beat up criminal intruders, to monitor male guests of single and divorced women in the neighbourhood, and to challenge any residents seen to be acting criminally or immorally.

However, in a bizarre twist pointed out by Yoshi, many of those engaged in neighbourhood nightwatch have a reputation themselves of being criminals and 'tough guys' (jago). This reputation of being at least knowledgeable in the criminal world provides their kampung neighbours with some sense of security for, by involving the criminals in security, they counter any inclination of these persons to resort to criminality within the neighbourhood, while encouraging them to

Figure 8.1 A neighbourhood security post.

employ their knowledge of the criminal world in identifying potential threats to the neighbourhood. Yoshi claims that the paradoxical status of the guards undermines the value to community represented in the ronda. If criminals man the nightwatch posts, he writes, and if they work in close collaboration with bureaucrats, the police and army, how are residents able to distinguish between right and wrong behaviour, and how are they to trust the city authorities who are meant to be protecting them? As a result, he suggests that the morality of community represented in the ronda is being seriously undermined. The youth who lounge there through day or night are not model residents but threaten the construction of community as they heckle passers-by, make lewd comments at passing women, or stir up a fight with passing young men.

Yoshi (2001: 11) is sceptical about the possibility that engaging petty criminals in kampung security will render them useful for that purpose. However, in his account the pos remains a central element in community life. It becomes a place where men play cards and drink, where young men sleep for the night, where hawkers set up their wares, women nurse their babies and neighbours gather to chat. It is a central location of the neighbourhood community, used for providing security and companionship as well as occasionally serving as a base for more nefarious activities. In Ledok every RT neighbourhood had built a pos ronda in which similar activities took place. These were manned throughout the night by neighbourhood males on a rostered basis, from which they regularly moved out through the alleyways, sounding the post's wooden slit-gong (*kentungan*) as they did so, and to which they returned to spend the night hours playing cards. During the day and the night, the posts were community gathering points.

In Ledok, those with criminal reputations were also engaged in the siskamling (local patrol) of neighbourhood administration. They were appointed by RW officials and approved by local police, army and regency officers. They were given rudimentary training on maintaining security, provided with uniforms which they wore when providing security at community events such as Independence Day celebrations and election days, and were included in the planning of major RW events. They performed this role with pride and it earned them respect in their neighbours' eyes. It was also a small source of income and as such invited them to curtail their criminal activities. They were not seen as violent people in daily life, or as threatening to their neighbours, though residents expected they would employ violence if forced to accost an intruder or deal with others' violence. However, unlike Yoshi's account above, these criminals did not constitute the core of the ronda patrols. These were recruited from all adult males in the community and rostered on a nightly basis.

Elsewhere I have taken issue with Siegel's dismal interpretation that violence and its suppression is the foundation of kampung community, suggesting instead that deference and mutual obligations, tolerance and harmony provide the essential elements of neighbourhood community (Guinness, 1988). Community involvement through cooperative work (kerja bakti) and savings and credit associations (arisan, simpan pinjam), to name only the most overt activities, was considered a more effective way to maintain social order than the threat of violence. However, residents were aware that violence posed a threat to community and they relied on communal forms to control that violence. When neighbours or household members fought, either verbally or physically, neighbours intervened if there was a risk of physical damage to property or person. The community elder, the male (*Bapak*) or female (*Ibu*) RT/RW head was expected to sit down with the combatants, reason with them, and admonish them in the most *halus* (sensitive) way. The elder or RT/RW head could call on

Figure 8.2   A working bee on the RK meeting house in 1976.

any respected member of the community to help in these dealings. For example, in 2000 a recently arrived man from Sumatra made no attempt to socialise, thus threatening community solidarity. He forbad his children from playing with neighbours' children unless he had specifically approved of those children. He passed along the alleyway without acknowledging anyone in conversation. One day he was observed to douse with boiling water a neighbour's dog in the alleyway — by way of explanation, he stated that his Muslim beliefs made it intolerable to have dogs around his house. His actions were soon known throughout the neighbourhood through gossip chains and neighbours further isolated him and his family. This behaviour was condemned by neighbours as *tak lumrah* (not right/usual). In this situation, the RT community referred the matter to the RT head, who negotiated with this man to accommodate to community demands.

STATE VIOLENCE IN THE KAMPUNG: IS COMMUNITY LOCAL?

In the analyses of Eko (2000) and Sullivan (1992) cited earlier, the for-mation of neighbourhoods units such as RT, RW or RK, the organising

Figure 8.3 The completed RK building in 1980.

of gotong royong/kerja bakti labour, or the kampung celebrations of Independence Day all bear the unmistakeable marks of state dominance. They posit that community is not of the people but of the state and is violently imposed on the state's most vulnerable citizens. In Ledok there was some support for this argument. My informants stated that the disbanding of the former RK and the introduction of kelurahan administrative units had undermined local communities by introducing this extra level of bureaucratic intervention and had provided the New Order political machine with a base close to the people. The division of unified kampung into smaller RW had dissipated community strength and undermined residents' capacity to initiate action themselves.

In Ledok, the effects of this 1989 legislation was a lack of coordination between the various segments of the kampung. The path that ran the entire length of the kampung on the upper level and was the main route for residents leaving or entering the neighbourhood, whether by car, motorcycle, bicycle or on foot, came under the control of a number of RW instead of being seen as RK infrastructure. Each RW exercised its separate control in distinctive ways. The path was paved and lined with a concrete fence in some parts; in others, houses had intruded onto the path to such an extent that an ambulance was unable to pass. What would have been a fairly easy task for RK leaders in standardising the maintenance of this path had become impossible once the state had disbanded the overarching RK administration. The RK community hall, built in the 1970s at the expense of and with the cooperation of RK citizens through kerja bakti, became virtually abandoned and in serious need of maintenance because of the demise of the RK. It had been the site for large meetings such as Independence Day celebrations, concerts, weddings and other functions and remained the only venue within the former RK domain that could meet such needs. Independence Day celebrations, a time of much enjoyment in the past, when residents from the whole kampung competed in sport, cooking and other activities or participated in concerts and dramatic performances, were now conducted in much smaller RW gatherings. Because residents of the wealthier RW were no longer under any obligation to support the activities of residents of the poorer RW, the celebrations were conducted at very different financial levels. For example, the purchase of expensive equipment such as sound systems was possible for only some RW, whereas previously the larger RK community resources had made these available to all member neighbourhoods. Similarly, the river wall constructed in the late 1990s was completed under the watch of various RW, so that there was no uniform policy in regard to controlling the path that ran alongside the wall or the public use of land created in the environs of the wall. As a result, local leaders felt powerless to ensure that the wall contributed to community development. All these changes were largely seen as the consequence of the forced imposition of the model structure of the central government that had disbanded RK community coordination and replaced it with more distant and bureaucratic kelurahan units.

The militarism of the New Order was most directly represented in the construction of this river wall. The army became the director of the project. It contracted builders to erect the wall but introduced army troops on a daily basis in platoon rotation to provide labour to the contractors alongside kampung volunteers. Each day kampung residents, mainly women, would prepare food and drink for the military labour force. The project came to symbolise a burdensome imposition on kampung residents and administration.

John Sullivan asserts that in kampung society the RW/RT exist largely to ensure the government's bidding. "Ultimately the state seems

Figure 8.4   Space created by the floodwall.

to supply, control, or structure all major occasions and opportunities for the celebration and reaffirmation of community, all critical foci at which the community recreates and replenishes itself" (Sullivan, 1992: 11). Sullivan describes how RT and RW authorities intensify RT group solidarity with inter-RT competition through sporting and cultural contests: "competitions to stimulate greater achievements of state-defined targets in tax contributions, acceptance of family-planning methods, kampung cleanliness and sanitation, participation in various state-favoured bodies — Scouts, Volunteer Defense Forces, marching teams" (Sullivan, 1992: 147). Sullivan suggests that RT and RW functionaries are communal leaders serving an implacable state more than state-political functionaries serving a local community. Kampung members have become "accomplices in their own oppression. Believing the rukun warga, its offices and officials are theirs, they readily assist the state to cramp their movements, to limit their employment opportunities, to constrain their incomes" (Sullivan, 1992: 170), a misrecognition in Sullivan's view. It is a case of what Bernat (1999) referred to as cultural violence, the terrorization of society into conformity.

The question raised here is whether this expression of community cohesion does indeed constitute a militaristic culture, the violent imposition of state strategies on the civilian population, thereby under-mining kampung residents' capacity to achieve their own interests. The issue raised by Sullivan is whether acts of group celebration are "spontaneous" and thus of the residents' real choosing or state-imposed and against their best interests. Sullivan asserts the latter, while acknowledging that such forms of cooperation have been taken over in neighbourhood discourse to the point where the residents "own" them. That makes the argument particularly difficult to sustain and leads him to declare that kampung members "misrecognise" what they are doing:

> The state contributes original formulations and representation to the project ... the communities are active in the construction and reconstruction of the discourse. This state-communal ideology now defines neighbourly practice and sanctions it, sets the ground rules for what may and may not be acknowledged as communal activi-ties and relations and thereby underwrites the benefits entailed in community membership (Sullivan, 1992: 177).

Even though the concepts and perceptions may have derived from communities, the state has made them its own, has enforced them, and Sullivan now interprets such communal practices as state impositions.

Sullivan examines the nature of work projects identified as com-munal projects by such terms as gotong royong (cooperative work) or kerja bakti (working bee). He cites a number of rural observers in Java who described villagers' reluctance to labour on public works on a scale larger than the hamlet community. In the urban context, Sullivan notes that people usually are called to labour on projects close to home such as a pathway, stairway, washing or toilet block or wall. However:

> ... to the extent the goods they produce are public goods which the government seeks to supply to other publics besides the par-ticipating communities, one can identify a corvee element even though the labour is not forced as it was at other times and other levels. But there is the rub. The perception and reality of benefits from kerja bakti action at the RW level generally nourishes the ideology of co-operation which can defuse or confuse reactions to demands made under the same seal for non-beneficial work at non-communal levels (Sullivan, 1992: 183).

There appear to be two issues in Sullivan's interpretation. Firstly, if at one level, gotong royong or kerja bakti is state coercion, should it be seen as such at all levels? Secondly, should the construction of pathways and washrooms and the like in kampung neighbourhoods by residents necessarily be seen as state coercion because other urban citizens on streetside do not have to expend their labour on similar projects? It makes no difference whether people willingly, even enthusiastically, contribute the labour because they are misrecognising what it actually is. Under this interpretation, it seems that the only practices that would not be seen as state coercion would be those that are not communal but individualistic. This is a point very similar to the arguments about militarism made earlier, where all forms of community practice in Indonesia today are seen as the product of militarisation. It is a view that renders Indonesian citizens as objects rather than active agents in their social construction. This is as extreme a view as that which regards all forms of cooperation as completely spontaneous and unaffected by state ideology.

CONTROLLED VIOLENCE AS THE CULTURE OF COMMUNITY

To counter this interpretation it becomes important to identify those aspects of local society that have remained free of the hegemony of violence and militarism and that form a basis on which a continuing culture of community has been built. Although these local forms have been encouraged since the fall of the New Order, they are by no means confined to this recent period.

In Ledok, proximity carries expectations of neighbourly relations, whose neglect can engender violent reprisals. People vary in the extent to which they meet neighbourly obligations such as attending a neighbour's life crisis ritual, the RT arisan or the RW working bee, or observing the rules for polite acknowledgement of neighbours, but it is possible for the 'community' of neighbours to bring such rules to the attention of the individual if need be. Over the years I have recorded various ways in which residents communicate their disapproval of another's actions. Stones were thrown on the roof of a miscreant's house, youths were beaten up, individuals were shunned in their time of need, persons were spoken to or counselled by community leaders, and the like. These indicate that physical proximity within these kampung borders does come with social obligations, that is physical proximity does entail social relations. Ignoring a neighbour is interpreted as the neglect of a social relationship and its attendant obligations. I now turn to an analysis of the role of violence in such relations.

In Ledok, the spirit in which kerja bakti labour is offered and the way it is organised does not support a conclusion that it is state-imposed or against residents' best interests. An extreme example will make the point. In the RW which I call Tanah Sosial (Guinness, 1986: 13), much of the land is state-owned and palace-owned land has been set aside for the most disadvantaged. Adjacent to this the Department of Labour made land available for porters (*kuli*) at the station to rebuild their homes. These homes were later replaced by three blocks of two-storey flats, constructed by the government and rented to needy households at Rp5,000 a month, around a tenth of the going rate. Later the Department of Labour administrators requested that two residents leave the flats because they were too well-off, one being a public servant while the other had established a grocery store in her flat. In 1996 the Department ordered residents to cut down trees they had planted and to demolish poultry yards, on the reasoning that open land had to be retained for community use. A dormitory was also maintained on the location for shorter-term residents, who needed to register with a resident appointed by the Department to manage the facility. Of all the RW in Ledok, this one was most obviously subject to state coercion and control. However, in October 2000 the men of the RW quite voluntarily and cheerfully gathered on a Sunday for cooperative work to clean out the public toilet and washroom block, landscape the surrounding common land, repair walls and trim and remove plants. The participants also extracted sand from the river and transported that to the site. About 30 men of all ages were involved in the work and refreshments were supplied by a number of women and older men. The whole task was organised by the *Paguyuban Rumah Susun* (Flat-dwellers' Association), consisting of 70 households in two RT, that is larger than the RT but smaller than the RW, a level of cooperation that did not comply with formal government structure of administration. This Paguyuban had been meeting for nine years and conducted both arisan and simpan pinjam. Household representatives met monthly, bringing with them Rp1,000 each, which was divided into four parts: refreshments for those attending the meeting, an arisan distribution to members in rotation, installation and maintenance of neon lights along the floodwall walkway, and the kerja bakti. At the same time, members contributed Rp1,500 towards the simpan pinjam, which made available to members loans to a maximum of Rp40,000. These regular meetings allowed people to discuss any aspect of community

Figure 8.5   The Tanah Sosial RW.

life and to plan improvements. There seemed to be no state cooption or exploitation in such an arrangement.

Sullivan's point may be that these residents perform a task that should be the responsibility of the state, that is the upkeep of common land and facilities. This is an idea which residents would strongly resist as implying that they have lost control over their lives and surroundings. Gledhill (2000: 152) suggests that analyses which emphasise Foucauldian programmes of power rob subaltern groups of their ability to define their own identities. In Ledok I observed some labour programs contributing to rather than detracting from the definition of local identity. I recall many gatherings of RT and even RW labour marked by comradeship and good spirits, in which presumably community 'identity' was being forged. It may well be that such an identity resembled state models and such labour contributed to state-approved projects, but neither of these points justifies an interpretation that such labour is coerced or that such cooperation is 'misrecognised' by members. Kampung members frequently see such projects as fulfilling their own plans and desires, whether or not they are approved by state authorities. Foucauldian analyses ignore the question of how anyone determines whether communal identity, or people's ability to define themselves, is actually of their own making or thrust upon them (Foucault, 1977, 1983). It appears to be in some sense a nonsensical question, given that people and communities are forever changing and forever absorbing influences from without. When they absorb such influences are they always under pressure or coercion to do so, and have they therefore "lost control over their communal identity (or more precisely, their ability to define themselves)" (Gledhill, 2000: 150)? Since Foucault sees power present in all social relationships, is it also possible to see individual and community agency also present in all social relationships? Foucault recognises the inevitable emergence of strategies of resistance to power, but is all action to be seen only in terms of conformity or resistance to state power? (Gledhill, 2000: 149–52).

Gledhill warns against the premature dismissal of organised popular political action stemming from depictions of subaltern behaviour as self-regulation or "misrecognition" of domination, as in the works of Foucault and Bourdieu. Gledhill depicts Bourdieu's approach in this way: "Symbolic power is based on 'social taxonomies' which subaltern groups 'misrecognize' as legitimate by failing to see them as arbitrary constructions serving dominant class interests." Gledhill suggests that "Bourdieu has little positive to say about the role of the lower classes and their political culture ... not only has Bourdieu increasingly focused on the study of elites, but his own perspective seems an elitist one, offering little scope for understanding how power relations are also shaped 'from below'"(Gledhill, 2000: 144). It seems to me that when kampung members take part in kerja bakti or RT/RW rituals, all of which may be state-sanctioned, they may place a different importance or adopt a different perspective on them. Their view or use of community may be different from that espoused by the state. Community cooperation focused on RW/ RT units represents the core of community and is considered essential to the well-being of residents. This cooperation is not a reflection of state coercion leading to popular "misrecognitions" but in direct opposition to the violence of militarism operated through the state.

The weakness of an analysis founded on a 'culture of terror' is that terror and fear are seen to be made cultural, to "saturate a social group's vision and distort its capacities to act" (Margold, 1999: 64). Margold suggests such an approach conceals not only questions of agency but also the cultural resources which the terrorised draw upon to respond to atrocities in what is often effective resistance. Citizens are not merely controlled by the state but in quite unique ways respond to pressures from the state according to their perceptions of the fluctuating power of the state. Sometimes that response may be violent.

This violence, as well as expressions of community, may indicate and characterise both state control and people's response to that control. People respond to the state's militarist regime by mimicking the violence of the state, both through militarist practices, sometimes of a communal form, and through violent resistance to state and capitalist discipline. However, it is not clear that all such organisational practices should be labelled as militarist and therefore violent, or that all social violence or community expression be attributed to the impact of the state. Certainly in Ledok, neighbourhood community involved ronda patrols and cooperative work patterns, mutual assistance, micro-finance associations, ritual performance and the like, of people's own choosing rather than a morality enforced through the violence of the state.

9

Empowerment in Development Practice

Development practice around the world in the 1990s turned towards participation and people's empowerment as the crucial and often missing ingredient in making a success of development planning and implementation. Participation had been part of the development jargon since the late 1950s and was a central component of community development approaches advocated by the United Nations and its affiliated organisations in the 1960s (Campfens, 1997: 20). Social activists and fieldworkers at the time suggested that the lack of participation by the populations targeted in development was the main reason for development failures (Rahnema, 1992: 117). Despite these views, much development practice was based on assumptions that local 'communities' were not yet sufficiently knowledgeable to participate in decision-making and that their participation should be confined to lending support through labour and resources for state-conceived development programs. Similarly, state development practitioners resented the time required to consult and involve local participants. However, in 1973 even the President of the World Bank was forced to admit that growth was not reaching the poor and that this was partly due to the poor being left out of projects. Leading international aid organisations acknowledged that the lack of popular participation was hampering development (Rahnema, 1992: 117). Majid Rahnema suggests that the renewed institutional enthusiasm in the 1990s for the rhetoric of participation was because it was no longer perceived as a threat to government. 'Target' populations with their increasing need for public services and consumer goods posed less resistance to the economic growth models of development agencies, while in developed countries appeal to participation had become publicly acceptable, allowing the raising of significant funds for these purposes through NGOs and the involvement of the private sector in the development business.

The rhetoric of participation implies some notion of the empowerment of people, particularly of people previously marginalised by development. However, Rahnema concludes that "there is little evidence to indicate that the participatory approach, as it evolved, did, as a rule, succeed in bringing about new forms of people's power" (Rahnema, 1992: 123). White (1996) points out that participation can simply mean a nominal inclusion of local people to legitimate a project or, for locals, to contribute resources and labour as a cost-saving measure for the project. Rahnema's argument is that these approaches tended to co-opt local beneficiaries into an elite system of power in which they are taught new ways of planning, thinking and doing, so that even the most sensitive of agents of change end up exceeding their role as catalyst and adopting a more authoritarian role. "Few were actors genuinely seeking to learn from the people how they defined and perceived change, and how they thought to bring it about" (Rahnema, 1992: 124). He and his fellow authors of *The Development Dictionary* deconstructed the discourse of development, suggesting that new approaches such as participation or empowerment did not "reverse or modify development's hegemony so much as provide more effective instruments with which to extend technocratic control or advance external interests and agendas while further concealing the agency of outsiders, or the manipulations of more local elites" (Mosse, 2005: 4–5).

Nevertheless David Mosse, whose book about a participatory development project in India derives from his own involvement as a practitioner, faults the way critics like Sachs identify "the relentless Foucauldian micro-physics of power (that) occur beyond the intelligence of the actors". Mosse opts instead for an ethnography of development that describes "the complex agency of actors in development at every level" (Mosse, 2005: 5–6). He declares his dissatisfaction with those who would see in development a "rationalising technical discourse concealing hidden purposes of bureaucratic power or dominance" (Mosse, 2005: 2). He wants to "reinstate the complex agency of actors in development at every level, and to move on from the image of duped perpetrators and victims" (Mosse, 2005: 6). He does not deny the interests and strategies of the state in managing its population but questions the monolithic explanation of such models. He stresses the capacity of local agents to translate government or other directives into action relevant to their own interests. "Subordinate actors ... create everyday spheres of action autonomous from the organising policy models ... but at the same time work actively to sustain those same models — the dominant interpretations — because it is in their own interest to do so" (Mosse, 2005: 10). Sarah White (1996) gives credence to forms of participation where locals add their voice to deliberations or where, in the only truly empowering form of participatory development, the poor transform themselves into a collectivity to fight injustice. This last she calls transformative participatory development. Her approach challenges the naïve assumption that participatory development necessarily empowers the marginalised.

Mosse identifies the contradiction inherent in participatory development. His critical analysis of the Participatory Planning Process (PPP) in the project with which he was associated in India asserted that the outside agents' self-representation as passive facilitators of PPP obscured the fact that they "retained the power to direct and shape" (Mosse, 2005: 91) "Hardly surprising, then, that development choices and legitimising 'local knowledge' derived from PRAs (Participatory Rural Appraisal) or village meetings reflected and endorsed an external analysis of problems and solutions." Although the villagers "increasingly anticipated and complied with outsiders' points of view in their self-presentation" (Mosse, 2005: 93), at the same time there was always potential for them to press their idiosyncratic local interests by forging alliances with benevolent members of the dominant class (Mosse, 2005: 98).

Despite their different viewpoints, for Mosse and Rahnema the ethnographic challenge is to focus not on the grand narratives of development, such as the hegemony of the dominant discourse or the success of economic growth, but to tease out the strategies and negotiations of everyday social action that make development work. The interpretation of development at the local level focuses on how the power of the development discourse is transmitted and how the interpreting communities respond. Mosse draws on the earlier work of James Scott (1985) on "weapons of the weak" to suggest that local participants in development negotiate their involvement in even the most hegemonic of projects. Local actors and local communities cannot be dismissed easily as the pawns of government programs or counterfeit constructions of state discourse. The ethnographic approach identifies the way local actors act within the frameworks ordained by wider society and state structures, yet within their own independent frameworks of action. Such an ethnography examines the local dynamics of communities in challenging assumptions of homogeneity and deciphering relations between rich and poor, formal and informal workers, men and women within the community, and their separate and collective relations with outside agents.

Paul Sillitoe (2007: 158) acknowledges the contribution of applied anthropologists such as Mosse who have sought to play a part in pursuing change. He suggests that anthropologists "need to advance methods that allow people to engage meaningfully in any intervention and that facilitate self-representations .... Participatory issues are central here, ensuring that people fully take part in any decision-making processes, facilitating use of their knowledge as they judge fit". Anthropology's contributions can include ensuring representation of different views, managing conflict when these clash, and reducing outsider manipulation.

For any anthropologist participating in the life of poor urban populations, it would be difficult to ignore opportunities and responsibilities to contribute to improvements in people's ways of life. During my stay in Ledok I became involved in community work projects improving the neighbourhood's physical infrastructure (paths, washing rooms and toilets, the bridge, the river wall) and social infrastructure (English-language classes, debt relief, music group, political campaigns). I turn now to examine a non-government organisation that sought in its development practice to replicate best anthropological practice by placing ethnographic enquiry and local participation as the defining modes of action. In doing so, it investigated the integrity of kampung communities and the dynamics of their relations with wider city institutions. I worked with this NGO from 1998 and engaged their leaders in many stimulating and fruitful discussions. By examining their practice, I seek to examine the nature of kampung communities with whom they worked and the contradictions inherent in participatory development practice. Their constant goal was both to draw attention to the strength of kampung communities and to seek a way to further empower these communities without undermining their independence by their assistance, addressing therefore the very contradiction identified by Mosse, or by Green who suggested that people's agency can only be accomplished through importing structures for participation (Green, 2000: 70). It was a conundrum that this group of young and dedicated enthusiasts constantly debated.

ROMO MANGUN'S PARTICIPATORY APPROACH

In 1981 a Jesuit priest, Romo (Father) Mangun (Y.B. Mangunwijaya), who had just resigned from his position as lecturer in architecture at the prestigious state Gadjah Mada University, took up residence with a group of rubbish recyclers and pedicab drivers on a riverbank below a bridge in the centre of Yogyakarta. His vision and mission was to reach the poorest and most disadvantaged of the city's population, not with the Catholic religion but with dignity and empowerment. He sought to demonstrate to the wider society his defence of the poor, to strengthen their bargaining power within the existing political system, and to improve their living standards. He lived there for five years and attracted a zealous group of students and intellectuals who shared his vision for such people. It was always for him an experiment built on the unfolding of everyday relations with these squatters and the wider city. When he had established the principles of action, he moved on to another social crisis point, that of villagers ousted from the Kedung Ombo dam site in Central Java. His vision was carried forward by his student followers who called themselves Yayasan Pondok Rakyat (People's Shelter Foundation).

Romo Mangun's story is well documented (Khudori, 2002a; 2002b). A prize-winning architect, government adviser, writer, novelist and social activist, he arrived in Ledok Code in 1981. The riverbank where he joined the rubbish recyclers was geographically part of Kota Baru, an elite housing area in Dutch times and still a fashionable residential and business area. The riverbank was officially unoccupied and had been used for some years as a rubbish dump. The dump had attracted rubbish recyclers, who were more popularly called gelandangan (homeless, vagrants), many of whom had originated from villagers where they could no longer earn a living. They settled among the bushes, trees, and banana and bamboo clumps along the riverbank in shacks made of cardboard and plastic sheeting drawn over wooden or bamboo frames. They slept on the bare earth, cooked outside on wooden fires, and washed themselves and their clothes in the river. They had little semblance of social organisation and gained for their site a reputation in the city as *daerah hitam* ('black district') of criminals and ne'er-do-wells. The municipal government through the army or police repeatedly demolished their shacks and moved on these gelandangan, but invariably they returned to continue their exploitation of the rubbish dump (Guinness, 1983). Paper, cardboard, wood, tin, and plastics were separated out from the other household rubbish and sold to urban middlemen, who then transported the materials to recycling plants elsewhere in Java. Others scoured the streets and house rubbish sites for food and cigarette butts.

> Scavengers of this sort were considered the dregs of city society, often abused by kampung and streetside children, snarled at by dogs, and accused of setting poisonous baits by kampung residents. The *gelandangan* acknowledged their social inferiority by avoiding eye contact with other citizens while they scavenged, seemingly oblivious to people and activities around them (Guinness, 1983: 75).

Gelandangan are urban residents without the formal residence rights held by most kampung people. Like many of those kampung residents, the majority of gelandangan had migrated from surrounding villages to seek a living in the city and had found a niche for themselves in the informal sector of the urban economy. Romo Mangun and the YPR activists recognised their basic rights as urban residents and acknowledged their potential to fit in with urban norms of governance and behaviour.

Darwis Khudori (2002b), who accompanied Romo Mangun in his activities at Ledok Code and had access to data collected by social work students under Romo Mangun's supervision, reported that 33 of 37 households in the Ledok Code settlement had debts with moneylenders, who charged up to 30 per cent per month in interest. Khudori identified an elite group who were either jago ('tough guys') or better schooled. This elite liked to live comfortably and spend their time gambling or demonstrating their fighting prowess. According to Khudori, they plotted together to exploit their weaker and unschooled neighbours, such as threatening that their homes would be demolished if they did not pay the elite protection money. The elite made the most of their greater urban experience to dominate the newer village migrants and force them to accept their strong-arm tactics and look to them for protection from outside criminals. They were also prone to domestic violence.

The social behaviour of the gelandangan reflected their marginality and their social dislocation (Suparlan, 1974). My own contact with them over the period 1975–1980 indicated that the jago were highly regarded among them (Guinness, 1983, 1986). Among themselves, the gelandangan emphasised equality, not hierarchy, and the sharing of equipment, resources and food. Their lifestyles were seen by some in the adjoining kampung as defiantly amoral, a rejection of the moral standards set by the wider urban society, particularly the court culture. For example, they often dressed skimpily, not just due to poverty but because they did not value the moral standards of the wider society, which in consequence saw them as sexually promiscuous. In keeping with their counter-image, they gambled, kept fighting cocks for illicit fights along the riverflat, stole and ate dogs, and drank alcohol.

Romo Mangun's approach was based on his conviction that the people of Ledok Code were poor for structural reasons. They had been forced to leave the village because government policies and capital investment privileged the urban sector and allowed it to live off the rural sector. When they came to town, the urban economy did not provide for them. They were marginalised not only economically but also socially and politically. Socially they were regarded as the dregs of society (*sampah masyarakat*). Politically they were not provided with Residents' Cards (Tanda Kartu Penduduk, TKP) because they were squatting on government or palace land and were not members of any official urban neighbourhood. Romo Mangun set out first to identify with the group by living among them, then to identify approaches that would improve their condition and empower them. He attracted a number of student activists who visited the settlement regularly and also arranged for students at a local Social Work High School to do their practical studies there. As a result, there was a constant presence of high school students documenting the social characteristics and changes in the settlement over several years.

However, Romo Mangun also identified what he termed a 'culture of poverty' that worked against these riverbank people improving their lives. In using this term Romo Mangun adopted a concept first put forward by Oscar Lewis (1959) to explain the persistence of poverty among Mexico City's slum-dwellers. These families, according to Lewis, in dealing with systemic poverty, cultivated an autonomous subculture and socialised their children into behaviors and attitudes that perpetuated their inability to escape the underclass. Since its formulation by Lewis, the concept of 'culture of poverty' to explain the poverty of the urban poor has proved popular among urban authorities and elites but has been roundly criticised by anthropologists and other social scientists (Valentine, 1968; Goode and Eames, 1996). Valentine, for example, points out that the behavioral patterns, values and attitudes identified by Lewis as constituting this culture of poverty are "situational adaptations with little or no specific subcultural rationale" (Valentine, 1968: 118).

This critique re-focuses attention on the structures of the wider society that keep people poor rather than the poor's socialisation practices.

Nevertheless, Romo Mangun clearly recognised that there were cultural traits particular to the Javanese that contributed to their poverty. The feudal Javanese culture that had arisen over the period of colonial rule was reinforced by the New Order government, which stressed the right of the elite to demand unquestioned allegiance from the people. Romo Mangun identified within this squatter population the attitude of accepting without question their inferiority in the wider society. He saw this cultural encumbrance as aggravated by their lack of social cohesion. Squatters worked against each other as they competed for materials on the dump and for space in the settlement. Because he saw this as a cultural trait deeply ingrained through upbringing, Romo Mangun believed that outsiders could be important in helping locals to recognise this attitude of subordination and to work with them to counter the outside forces that produced this subordination. In the spirit of *Pedagogy of the Oppressed* (Freire, 1972) and *Small is Beautiful* (Schumacher, 1974), he worked to instil a sense of equality among the settlers and dignity within the outside society.

Romo Mangun recognised, however, that no program driven by outside interests was likely to be successful. He thus challenged his group of enthusiastic followers with the contradictions raised by their participatory practices, where people's agency can be both enabled and undermined through the same participatory planning approach. As a solution, he stressed the importance of planning and implementing all ideas in discussion and cooperation among all residents. He sought what Sarah White (1996) calls a "transformative construction of participatory development". Nevertheless, it was an approach that included a strong role for the outside agency of people like himself.

On his arrival, Romo Mangun recognised that settler empowerment must start with their official registration as urban residents of Yogyakarta. He approached the government-appointed head of the adjacent kelurahan, a man with whom he had already cooperated in another settlement on the Code river, and gained their admission into his kelurahan of Terban, on the condition that the riverbank squatters agreed to "improve themselves" and raise their standard of living under the guidance of the Kelurahan Council (Khudori, 2002b: 44). Romo Mangun and his friends then began to work in the community of 37 households, proceeding by trial and error. They planned and built three public buildings and three homes for the squatters, using land the settlers had thought unusable because of the steep slope and the waste water canal that bisected it. They helped improve other houses and cleared a public space by the river for recreation. He and his friends helped with lessons for the children, beginning with English language and Koranic study and skills for the women. They set up a library with donations of books from contacts round the city. They helped establish a simpan pinjam and an arisan, installed a handpump and arranged for the installation of electricity. As the community developed, the residents formed an RT committee comprising a head and deputy head, secretary, treasurer and an informal group called *Paguyuban Manunggaling Tekad Agawe Santosa* (Strength-in-Unity Association) for discussions and poetry recitals.[10]

In 1983 Romo Mangun made headlines when he publicly op-posed city plans to demolish all houses along the river to a distance of 25 metres from the river centre in favour of a 'green corridor of trees, bushes and grass'. At first he wrote to the local papers and to the relevant authorities, then went on a hunger strike that attracted huge interest among the city elite and eventually forced the city government to back down. He continued to agitate for settlers to be guaranteed continued settlement, although he did not advocate land rights because that would have allowed them to sell their land to outsiders. He empha-sised the importance of community cooperation and for that purpose encouraged the formation of four cooperative workgroups (*Usaha Bersama*, UB). Members of these groups met every ten days to run a simpan pinjam, manage the housing, run economic self-surveys and discuss their problems and aspirations. Each group reported its activities to the RT Committee every 35 days.

A big challenge faced by Romo Mangun and those he worked with was the preservation of residents' power when they were absorbed into formal government administration. Becoming an RT meant that they became beholden to higher levels of the government administration, even though their formation into a recognised formal organisation promoted a sense of identity and power among them. The issue is raised by John Sullivan (1992: 170), who decided in the context of formal kampung structures that people were merely fooled into believing that such structures gave them any autonomy. Romo Mangun, however, persisted in pursuing that incorporation, while remaining aware of the dangers that it might undermine local autonomy. His approach was to respect residents' capacity to solve their own problems and not to encourage them in activities that made them dependent. Rather he sought to open up opportunities for them to reach a better and more just life. He admitted that the first stage in this progression required a large say from outsiders, but in a second stage he anticipated that residents would run their own arisan and simpan pinjam and come up with their own ideas for trading opportunities in the wider economy. This is reminiscent of the remark by Mosse that local participants can create spheres of action autonomous from the organising policy models, whether of government or non-government agencies, while at the same time working actively to sustain those dominant interpretations, because it is in their interest to do so (Mosse, 2005: 10)

Dharoko (1988), quoted at length by Khudori (2002b: 154–8), outlined the ambiguity of this kind of development in Semarang, Central Java, where he did his research. When development concentrates on empowerment through local organisation and participation, the poor take part in meetings, take on a role in the development, increase their incomes, improve their opportunities in the informal sector, set their own priorities and gain access to education, employment, and social services. On the other hand, the government is still providing the crucial information, taking the initiative in encouraging participation, convening meetings and introducing NGOs who play a large part in providing education, housing and health services. Khudori (2002b: 206) concludes that the formal neighbourhood units of the government, such as RT, RW and kelurahan, plus the informal associations such as paguyuban, can all play a role in empowering residents, as long as they are not used as mouthpieces or arms of government or tools for its propaganda. Their goal must be not just community harmony but also "conscientisation" about the issues of social organisation, law, justice, citizenship, nationality and globalisation (Freire, 1972: 15). They should also not be confined to a single neighbourhood but link neighbourhoods together with regular discussions and their own publications. He suggests that this provides a new role for those intellectuals, artists and students who wish to help.

YPR'S PARTICIPATORY APPROACH

Yayasan Pondok Rakyat (YPR) was formed in 1985 by a group of architects keen to continue Romo Mangun's initiatives in the urban kampung. Its membership currently includes architects, social workers, scholars, religious leaders, writers, artists and students. Their official statement says that they have joined together with one common interest — to participate in building a more just social order. Their four missions are: to open and increase the access of people to information on urban development; to actively participate in the process of public policy making; to build and enhance the bargaining position of urban poor communities; and to learn together with the urban communities to critically analyse and solve the social and environmental problems of urban development (Khudori, 2002b: 24).

One early activity was thrust on them in 1988, when on Romo Mangun's departure, the city government again tried to push through the green corridor demolition of riverside settlements. YPR realised that without Romo Mangun's charisma they could not use the same approach as he did in 1983. Instead they arranged weekly public discussions and a photo exhibition of the riverbank settlement, inviting prominent intellectuals and artists in the city to lead the discussions. As a result of the media coverage of these discussions, the city government again shelved its plans to demolish the settlement.

For a decade after that there was little to report on YPR activities. In 1999, with a new generation of student activists emerging in the post-New Order period, YPR kampung activities were revived. One of their first tasks was the establishment of a library of writings on urban society, which by 2007 totalled over 2,000 titles. This became a resource not only for YPR staff but also for the wider reading public, including a kampung readership where parts of the collection were circulated. YPR activists, many of them students or recent graduates, have since 1999 sought to establish strong relationships on an individual basis with residents in several kampung of Yogyakarta. They adopt the view that they need to live in a settlement and learn from residents what are the main issues faced by those kampung populations. Hence this period of familiarisation must precede any attempt to discuss 'development'. YPR see themselves as providing a service to kampung people, including training and educational courses, architectural and administrative advice, and financial support for kampung initiatives. In addition, they see a role for themselves in providing information to the wider society about kampung settlements based upon their long-term and in-depth familiarity with kampung residents. They have been able to market these research skills as a consultancy group and to raise funds to channel into kampung activities. One YPR researcher and director recently wrote to me about Badran, a kampung where he worked, a neighbourhood with a reputation for harbouring criminals, youth gangs, sex workers and other 'unsavoury' characters:

> The research I am undertaking does not only focus on the failures of these people, but on their successes. It is clear that state control of this kampung only reaches as far as the formal institutions of the kampung. Beyond that kampung residents act prudently within an informal arena, where they give keen attention in their discussions to how to negotiate with the outside society from within their social, political and economic circumstances. This enthusiasm for negotiation may well be their contribution towards the moulding of urban life in Indonesia (in translation, personal communication).

On their website (http://www.ypr.or.id) in November 2007, YPR espoused their approach by using three English-language words: 'celebrate', 'campaign' and 'continuing'. By 'celebrate' they seek to understand and extol the cooperative work and strength found among kampung people. By 'campaign' they refer to publicising within the larger city the diverse capacities and delights of kampung members, allowing kampung people themselves to have a voice in the wider city. By 'continuing' they seek the empowering of kampung people to maintain kampung diversity as an integral part of urban life.

This chapter will examine the activities of YPR from two perspectives: their copious publications and their kampung activities. Their publications provide evidence of their commitment to understanding in depth the nature of kampung life and illustrate YPR's conviction that kampung people both suffer from the structural inequalities of city and national societies and demonstrate considerable strengths in their response to these wider contexts by their economic diversity, political autonomy, cultural richness and social cohesion. These publications provide important ethnographic material and intellectual argument about the diversity of kampung in Yogyakarta, but they also comprise part of the strategy of action that YPR endorses in the kampung. Some publications have been produced in cooperation with kampung residents, others are aimed at convincing the wider urban society of the worth of kampung life. They thereby constitute part of YPR's kampung activities. An examination of these will allow us to ascertain how YPR have implemented a participatory development approach in the kampung where they work.

YPR PUBLICATIONS

Providing Information on Kampung

YPR's most visible activity has been its publications designed to high-light the lives of kampung people and urban informal-sector workers and to spotlight sources of disadvantage or aborted opportunity. In this regard they adopt an advocacy role, presenting the kampung to the wider middle-class audience. In working in the kampung, YPR activists have recognised and sought to challenge the views of the urban middle class towards the urban poor. A former staff worker in YPR put it like this (in translation):

> Kampung haunt the urban upper middle class and elite. By distancing themselves and protecting themselves from the kampung and those who live there, they construct an identity and place for themselves. They build real estate in areas that are cool, peaceful, luxurious, far from the city centre and the dirtiness and density of the kampung, and provide themselves with spacious parking, recreational areas, health clinics, shopping centres, banks and, of course, strict security. If they are in close proximity to kampung their streetside properties are enclosed within stone walls topped with barbed wire or broken glass, guard dogs, and menacing and physically intimidating security guards. With kampung located at the margins of the 'modern gaze' ... hidden or excluded because of their dirtiness, poverty and disorganisation, the 'ideal' image of the city and the nation can come to the fore. (Fauzannafi, 2004: 57)

These YPR publications target the disgust, derision and fear held by the wider middle-class, 'streetside' society of kampung residents. YPR activists portray the rich complexity and diversity of kampung life in order to convince urban managers of the importance of recog-nising, respecting and preserving these diverse societies and cultures. They highlight informal economic activities that remain hidden from the wider city population and draw attention to government policies that have undermined local initiative. Throughout these publications their aim is to depict kampung people in their humanity through human life stories.

The publications reveal the growth in YPR journalism of a critical advocacy. Their first journal, *Exploring Yogya*, begun in February 2000 and continuing monthly until its 24th issue in April 2002, was of a more descriptive nature. It highlighted interesting features of the city such as Kota Gede, the silversmiths' city, mosques, jamu 'herbal medicine' sellers, markets, the Slemania football team supporters, handicrafts, promotion salespeople and the like. Except for its last issue, the publication was bilingual in English and Indonesian and contained regular information on artistic performances, radio programs, seminars and tourist services such as taxis, as well as the monthly French-Indonesian Institute program. In closing the publication, YPR admitted that some had come to think of it as focused on tourist issues and tourists, although it was intended to be informative about all aspects of city society and environment. There were some fascinating details of history and people's lives and income sources but the publication took an uncritical view of the city, assuming that to describe and inform was to contribute to urban development. For that reason, the publication was of most interest to tourists, domestic or international.

YPR's second publication, *Warta Kampung* (Kampung News), proved more critical and more focused on kampung people and their issues and made a valuable contribution to the understanding of kampung society in Yogyakarta. *Warta Kampung* was first published in 2000 with three issues that year, four in 2001, two in 2002 and one in 2003, in all ten issues over four years. These fluctuations probably reflected the availability of the volunteer journalists and editorial staff. As with *Exploring Yogya*, this publication represented a high standard of journalism by a very small team of dedicated writers, most of whom had other commitments and relied on earning income elsewhere. It represented another feature of post-Suharto reform, with activists seeking to challenge conservative wisdom regarding the marginalised people of the city. A key contribution was the focus on particular kampung where YPR had become involved. Their writing thus reflected the days, weeks and months which they spent in the particular kampung, talking to residents and often working with them on community projects such as building a library, running classes for children, introducing credit schemes or facilitating kampung discussions. Each issue of the journal consisted of a number of features about that particular kampung, along with more general pieces. Their detailing of the history of the particular kampung and the views of kampung residents about developments in their settlement were designed not only to interest a wider public but to be read by the kampung residents themselves. They can thus be read partly as an experiment in raising self-awareness among kampung people, which was to be given much greater focus in later publications.

Each of the first seven issues featured a particular kampung within Yogyakarta, distinct in its own way and illustrating the diversity of kampung life to which YPR journalists sought to draw attention: Sosrokusuman (Issue 1) located adjacent to the city centre and threatened by commercial expansion; Papringan (Issue 2) on the edge of the city and still rural in part; Warungboto (4) on riverside and also partly rural; Kraton (5) within the palace walls and influenced by royal traditions; Gendeng (6) along the train line and home to students enrolled at nearby universities and colleges; and Gedongkiwo (7) on the border of the city with the district of Bantul to the south. Each of these issues presented its featured kampung through its history, the history of its name, the individuals who resided there, their livelihoods, and the changes in kampung activities and residents' livelihoods as the city expanded. This section was titled 'Inside the kampung' (*Liputan kampung*). For example, the fifth issue (2001) highlighted the success of people living in the shadow of the palace walls in Pinggiran, enjoying the patronage of palace officials. It examined the businesses of kampung women such as managing shops/stalls (warung) in the kampung and dyeing batik cloth. The sixth issue (2001) described how student boarders made an important contribution to family incomes of their landlords in Gendeng.

The issues also contained other short sections, 'Kampung to kampung' (*Kampung ke kampung*) with various news from around the city, 'Key figures from the kampung' (*Sosok wong kampung*) featuring prominent residents, 'Kampung symbols' (*Tengara kampung*) such as a former nobleman's house, a corner of the castle wall, a marketplace, an alleyway, and a former royal recreational park, which characterised that particular kampung, and 'Kampung slang' (*Kosa kampung*), a dictionary of the distinctive dialect of the kampung settlements. The impact of these issues was to alert readers to the rich diversity and humanity of Yogyakarta's kampung. Their targeted audience was primarily a middle-class readership who by habit dismissed kampung as uncivilised, poor, uneducated, backward, and lacking initiative. The YPR journalists faced a formidable challenge to transform the image of kampung on the middle-class conceptual map, even among the city's intellectuals.

Through residents' stories, *Warta Kampung* journalists revealed the wider city pressures on kampung life, while through residents' critical comments the relationship of the kampung with the wider city was explored. For example, the journal explored the threat to kampung life from the expansion of the commercial centre of the city. The first issue touched on the future of Sosrokusuman, wedged behind the main shopping street in Yogyakarta and threatened by the further expansion of commercial interests. YPR journalists reported that residents there declared they should not be forced to move out just because the government and commercial interests wanted to expand there. The journal also focused on the impact of outsiders renting rooms within the kampung and thus affecting kampung life. The journal's second issue described the steady transformation of Papringan as students and government workers came in to rent or buy space. The issue highlighted how kampung residents were influenced by wealthy incomers and increasingly sold land to finance their own aspirations for consumer items. The fourth issue focused on kampung Warungboto and the Muslim study groups that characterised the life of residents, particularly of its youth. Residents suggested that this semi-rural community had been strongly influenced by the schools run by the Muslim association Muhammadiyah in the nearby town of Kota Gede.

A More Critical Focus

Later issues had a sharper edge to them as YPR journalists became more comfortable with their role as advocates. From the eighth issue the descriptive *Kampung ke kampung* and *Sosok wong kampung* sections disappeared in favour of a new and textually dominant and more critical section called 'In the spotlight' (*Sorotan*). The change demonstrated two of the YPR goals, namely of critically examining the problems of urban development and of participating in the process of public policy-making. A third goal, that of informing people about urban developments, had been amply demonstrated in earlier publications. However, the fourth goal of YPR involvement, that of building and enhancing the bargaining position of urban poor communities and of learning with them to analyse critically and solve their social and environmental problems, was not to be achieved through publications alone.

One focus of this critique was the marginalisation of the kampung poor by the city's commercial expansion. The seventh issue (2001) featured an article on Gedongkiwo kampung, whose residents pointed to the negative impact wrought by the 1989 policy that divided the former RK into smaller RW. This administrative convenience focused on control rather than empowerment and led to community activities being undermined and community identities destroyed. The writer also drew attention to the tendency of palace officials to sell or lease land occupied by kampung populations for commercial development, thereby reversing the customary protection that the Kraton had afforded kampung settlements in allowing them to occupy palace land (Cucu, 2001).

In the new spirit of reform, the more critical edge in this seventh issue targeted the New Order regime. The eighth issue (2002) focused on development as a feature of the New Order government, suggesting that the government's emphasis on physical developments that were easily visible had produced a standardisation of development programs. These development projects taxed the people through demands for cooperation (gotong royong) and financial taxes (*iuran*) but did not reflect the aspirations of people. Drawn into this development mania and 'militarism', kampung people competed with each other to be the cleanest, best organised, neatest or most modernised kampung in a city that promoted itself as *Yogyakarta Berhati Nyaman*. Over the period of the New Order, kampung people were progressively marginalised, even by development targeting them and lauded by urban authorities as a generous gift to the disadvantaged who were otherwise dismissed as lacking in initiative and even interest in advancing themselves. This issue of *Warta Kampung* pointed out that kampung efforts in generating their own development still persisted, although rarely noticed by those outside (Kah, 2002). Throughout the financial crisis that beset post-1998 Indonesia, the 'little people' had demonstrated their strength and ability to continue without the state. Their neighbourhoods had been physically improved with donations from members who had migrated elsewhere, from residents themselves, or from nearby commercial businesses, and in the process residents' identification with the neighbourhood had been strengthened (Josh, 2002: 15).

The ninth issue (2002) featured four articles on Kampung Badran in the north of the city, to the west of Ledok. As with Ledok, Badran is situated on riverside land, which has encouraged a clear difference in social status between those living on higher riverbank ground, who work in government or private business and whose children attend university, and those living on lower riverflat ground, who are petty traders and home-producers of foodstuffs like tahu (soybean cake) and tempe (soybean biscuit), becak drivers and casual labourers. During the financial crisis, a new sense of community was created in Badran when upper and lower residents came together to provide food for destitute neighbours. This communal cooperation continued in 2002 in the form of a simpan pinjam association with 231 women members from both riverbank and riverflat. These articles particularly examined outsiders' negative image of Badran as a place frequented by prostitutes, thieves, drunks, gamblers and the like. It is an image frequently linked with riverside kampung because the maze of pathways and houses in these locales provide easy and safe refuge for criminals slipping back into the kampung after sorties into formal streetside premises of the city. Stories abound of how such criminals used Badran as a base in the past, but this stereotype has come to haunt present-day youth in Badran who are treated with suspicion and even hostility simply because of where they come from. This continues to scar Badran residents' relations with outside institutions, such as children attending schools where they are victimised. In responding to this stereotype, the *Warta Kampung* writers pointed out that religious observances, both Christian and Muslim, are a feature of Badran contemporary life. *Warta Kampung* critically examined the construction of a stereotype that dehumanises kampung residents and leads to residents being disadvantaged in the wider society. In response it put forward an alternative, more informed picture of these people that included their ability to work coopera-tively and independently of government in dealing with the conse-quences of the financial crisis.

The critical examination of Badran drew attention to the strength of communal cooperation in dealing with the financial crisis that brought down the New Order. An article in the tenth issue (2003) further examined the quality of community, drawing attention to the decline of collectivity within two kampung on the outskirts of the city. In conclusion, the writer asserted the need for empowerment through political organisation based on shared sentiment or shared need (Santosa, 2003). Santosa suggests that kampung collectivities, so strong in the past, had been challenged by the New Order policy which established RW administrative units, with the result, for example, that youth from adjoining RW within the former single RK began to be suspicious and even hostile towards each other instead of cooperating as they had in the past. This YPR writer sketched how kampung leaders attempted to reconcile the youth of adjacent RW through a concert and a cultural festival but with only limited success:

> The division of kampung into RW which was intended to facilitate social services should ultimately be seen as the creation of new authority patterns that conform to the new units. The tragedy is that each RW sees itself as powerful, with the authorisation to do whatever its residents like, without taking into consideration those in adjacent RW who still have emotional and existential links with the same territory (Santosa, 2003: 36).

A recurring observation in these later issues is the damage done to community life at the RK level by the 1989 policy of disbanding the RK and forming kampung residents instead into smaller RW units. With that initiative, many of the more successful community programs, such as among youth or in the provision of community facilities, were abolished.

These later issues documented how state and private capitalist initiatives within the kampung, rather than strengthening these communities, undermined them. They thus raised more general questions about the nature of development promoted by government. The tenth issue also focused on the promotion and beautification of Yogyakarta, condemning the commercialisation of the city as "up for sale until it is totally consumed". It began with an article highlighting a site near Gondolayu bridge, which for years had been identified as the site for a Holiday Inn, then suddenly and without any public consultation, became a McDonalds restaurant and a projected shopping plaza. This issue drew attention to the speculation in land by urban developers that ignored the kampung people who were most affected by this commoditisation of land. "City land is gobbled up by developers of universities, hotels or shopping plazas, land speculators, or a national elite of generals, company executives and top government officials, while its value for people's daily lives is swept aside. Even the cemeteries are reserved for the wealthy", the article concluded.

Although outsiders, the YPR writers were young people who engaged in wide discussions with kampung residents while they lived in the settlements. In their effort to live in these communities, they duplicated the experience of the many migrants who had drifted into the city in search of work, found accommodation in kampung and gradually been absorbed into kampung activities. In these later issues, *Warta Kampung* became more analytic and critical of the wider pressures on kampung residents. The writers tried to portray accurately the attitudes and experiences of kampung residents with whom they lived. In terms of their original goals of empowering kampung residents, *Warta Kampung* editors appeared to take more and more seriously their role of being advocates and social critics, not just reporters. However, as Romo Mangun had acknowledged before them, the YPR activists came to realise that being a voice for people was not always enough in bettering the residents' life situation. There were structural problems that loomed large over kampung life, inhibiting the free endeavours of residents and which kampung residents were powerless to address. It was on these that *Warga Kampung* increasingly focused.

As Romo Mangun acknowledged, this approach has its problems for, in the very act of dealing with structural obstacles lying beyond the purview of kampung residents, outside activists run the risk of undermining local empowerment.

Debating Participatory Development

In 2004 a new publication was produced in the journal — *Kampung: Kampung Menulis Kota* (Kampung: Kampung Portrays the City). By 2007 there were two issues of this journal, with further issues to be published electronically. The new journal's cover introduced it as a "popular scientific media that identifies and explores urban change in its widest sense. It introduces and problematises urban paradigms from diverse points of view and disciplines. It is a journal, focused on urban Indonesia, which is activist and visionary in scope". The contributors to the first issue all held academic qualifications: a lecturer in urban planning teaching and researching in France (Khudori), two lecturers in architecture at Duta Wacana University in Yogyakarta (Prawoto and Mahatmanto), a postgraduate student of anthropology in Manchester University (Fauzannafi) and a lecturer in anthropology at the Australian National University (Guinness). The second issue, entitled *Warga, Penduduk, Penghuni Kota* (Citizens, Residents and Occupiers of the City) continued the academic focus, this time on citizenship.

The first issue of *Kampung* included articles on two neighbourhoods where YPR members had spent much of their time. These two historical sketches indicated the direction in which YPR and other NGO activities were exerting their energies. In Tungkak, a kampung noted in the 1970s for its thieves and petty criminals and vagrants, former YPR staff member Fauzannafi (2004: 79) described how in the mid-1980s the government constructed a model administration and instituted programs to aid the garbage recyclers. The logic of government practice was to establish a relationship between the government as guide and donor and the people as poor, weak dependents in need of guidance and aid. In such a relationship, claims Fauzannafi, the state had the right to assert their authority through their directives and aid projects. An illustration of this was the insistence by government that only those with residency cards identifying them as Tungkak residents could benefit from this aid, even though many of the residents had arrived in Tungkak without the registration papers from their previous home that were necessary to obtain an identity card.

Fauzannafi's account focused on the way the state obstructs non-government activists within the kampung. He described the case of Darwin, a student activist in Tungkak, who was under suspicion because he did not carry a resident's identity card. Darwin kept busy organising savings and loans societies, making an income through busking and other informal work, organising mass weddings, circumcisions, and children's clubs among the most marginal in the kampung, but these were opposed by the RW administration. The activities of students such as Darwin came under criticism because they did not seek permission of kampung leaders for their initiatives and were accused by the administration of helping the kampung for their own private benefit. Nevertheless, Fauzannafi indicates that the activities of Darwin and other activists were achieving impressive results, despite the office-holders' suspicions. These student activists had linked with local youth organisations to achieve some important breakthroughs. One such youth organisation called *Semut* (Ant), formed by students from a private university, conducted community service in Tungkak, and was able to organise sporting events and national day celebrations and provide religious guidance at the local mosque. With Darwin, YPR and other activists, *Semut* conducted a 'people's organisation' by establishing discussions, fishponds, urban horticulture and the publication of a local bulletin.

One of the effects of their activities was to unite the youth of the two RW comprising Tungkak, overcoming what had been a widening break since the 1980s. Another was to discourage local youth from fighting over control of gang territory and instead direct their energies into activities either of a religious nature, targeting the 'sins' and 'diseases' of gambling, lotteries, theft and prostitution, or into social activism focusing on group discussions, income creation through urban farming or fishponds, or community bulletins. Such activism, in which YPR played a part, is portrayed by Fauzannafi as more positive and empowering of local youth than a Community Policing project in Tungkak. Organised with the police and government, the project required youth to spy and report on each other in order to prevent gang fights. The outcome of the student-inspired activities, by contrast, was to empower youth to help themselves and work together.

The other kampung featured in the first issue of *Kampung* was Badran (featured previously in *Warta Kampung* 9), whose residents were refused entry to hospitals and whose applications for formal employment were rejected solely because they listed their address as Badran.

In Badran the involvement of YPR activists focused on redressing this reputation. An exploration of its history was one way of doing this, by showing how the kampung's location off the street and out of the way had made it a convenient base within the area for those with criminal intentions. During the 1970s and early 1980s, Badran was recognised by city authorities as one of the riverside kampung where unemployed youth had formed gangs that terrorised city residents and businesses with brazen robberies, thuggery and killings. For that reason, Badran was frequently invaded by army and police personnel with loaded weapons seeking out these criminals. This reputation persisted long after these criminal elements were eliminated by the city authorities or reformed by kampung neighbours, and so worked against residents obtaining access to jobs, schooling or healthcare within the urban formal sector. The YPR director, Alipah Hadi Kusen, explained how such a reputation encouraged criminality as a mark of status and allowed outside organisations such as political parties to recruit thugs from the kampung (Kusen, 2004). His account documented YPR attempts to counter this reputation by exploring with kampung residents the historical causes and then identifying with them residents' potential to contribute to city life. YPR discovered that, because of their exclusion from formal employment, 75 per cent of residents had developed skills in music and almost half of the population had at one time or another earned an income from busking. Based on this discovery, YPR activists and locals together planned to develop these skills, through rehearsals, visits from outside experts, and performances. In this way YPR involvement in the community included joint participation in the planning and implementation of local action as well as advocacy by activists on behalf of the kampung communities (Kusen, 2004: 54). The YPR newsletter of 5 July 2004 terms such engagement by outside activists as an "urban advocacy movement".

The YPR focus on empowerment took another turn in 2003 when YPR supported the production of the news-sheet *Lorong Tungkak* (Tungkak Lane) by youth from Kampung Tungkak itself. The youth editors of *Lorong Tungkak* wrote (in translation):

> Lorong is designed to be a medium to see, reflect and understand the condition of Tungkak. It is intended as a meeting of minds between the younger and older generations of Tungkak, and between the various groups who live in Tungkak. Thus we hope that Tungkak will become a place where people get together, but not under the

control of an elite, to create a spirit of community between all
residents (*Media Kampung Lorong Tungkak* 2003: 2)

This was a radical step by YPR but entirely consistent with their aim
of empowering kampung communities. The 12-page news-sheet presented a history of Tungkak and a number of pieces by kampung
youth describing and reflecting on aspects of their lives, including their
livelihoods, aspirations and frustrations. As the first direct expression of
kampung views produced through YPR, this news-sheet is worthy of
further scrutiny. Included among the poetry and prose contributions
is a history of Tungkak derived from interviews with kampung elders.
Another prose piece by a Tungkak youth recalls the dictatorial manner
of the writer's father, from whom he ran away and sought independence
in Tungkak. His freedom is symbolised by the *lorong* (lane) that he
calls his "kingdom", but which is scarred by rubbish and darkness.
Another piece relates how kampung youth follow in the footsteps of
their kampung predecessors who had no time for school, dropped
out and then could not find work. The writer encourages youth to
persevere at school. Another piece describes how youth confine their
friendships to others in Tungkak because they rarely have the need to
go outside the neighbourhood. The news-sheet ends with two stories
of residents in jail and their relations with the jail police-guards. This
article shamelessly acknowledges the difficulties some residents have
had in living within the law.

Like Ledok, Tungkak is a riverside kampung and may for that
reason have more squatters and poor among its residents. Nevertheless,
the news-sheet reflects the attitudes of kampung youth more generally,
seeing themselves as struggling to make a mark in the wider city and
conscious of their disadvantaged position. In allowing the youth to
recognise and express their disappointments and disadvantages, the
news-sheet may well be enabling them to share some of their disappointments with each other and the wider community. *Lorong Tungkak*
featured their writing and their photos and, unlike the other YPR
publications such as *Exploring Yogya* and *Warta Kampung*, was intended
primarily for a kampung readership and produced by kampung writers.
In that sense, it represented an important advance in YPR's search
for kampung empowerment. A second issue of *Lorong Tungkak* was
published in June 2004. In the following years, three other neighbourhoods where YPR worked produced their own kampung media: *Bulletin
Kricak* (Kricak Bulletin), *Swara Badran* (Badran Voice) and *Kabar
Sidomulyo* (Sidomulyo News).

In 2007 YPR activists cooperated with two other NGOs, Anak Wayang Indonesia or AWI (Indonesian Shadow Puppet Children) and Perpustakaan Komunitas Golo (Golo Community Library) to bring together the kampung journalists involved in the four YPR media, more than four AWI media and one Golo publication. Three workshops were held over several weeks, focusing on critical writing skills, financing kampung media, and tools to map kampung. Their aims were to encourage these fledgling publications and to advance the writers' appreciation of other kampung, thereby linking kampung activists across the city. In general kampung residents had little experience of other kampung throughout the city and no incentive to make such contacts. YPR saw such contacts as essential to the raising of residents' consciousness of the common situations affecting all kampung.

From December 2005 to February 2006, YPR worked with the four kampung of Tungkak, Badran, Kricak and Sidomulyo to hold a festival called 'Kampung, the Future of the City' (*Kampung Masa Depan Kota*). The aim was to portray kampung in positive terms and to negate the stigma of kampung in the eyes of the wider city population. The festival included a transvestite karaoke competition, a solo buskers' competition, a busking group competition, a riverside cooking competition, an art workshop and a photo and art exhibition. The festival concluded with a seminar on the festival theme, at which the city mayor, academics and city dignitaries spoke. The YPR director, Kusen, was reported by the media as saying at this event that YPR had more recently directed its focus to fostering links between kampung and the outside society. The main problem, he said, was that kampung are sidelined by the wider urban population. The first stage in improving this situation is to open the eyes of the urban middle class to the wealth of kampung resources such as social solidarity, informal economic activities and love of life. Soon after this festival, the city mayor wrote in the local newspaper that kampung are the foundation of a city. A city, he wrote, that is alive and "stays on the rails" is built on kampung that are alive, clean, and orderly; moreover, he declared that the city government was investing resources to purchase space within the kampung for the creation of public space and meeting halls (*Bernas*, 4/2/2006). The creation of public recreational and meeting space recognised a dire need of residents. The loss of recreational space to housing and other structures as kampung space came under population and commercial pressures had become symptomatic of contemporary urban life in Java (Peters, 2007: 200–01) Such a recognition by government of the communal needs of kampung neighbourhoods was seen as a resounding success for the approach adopted by YPR.

YPR acknowledged this government recognition as qualitatively different from government approaches through the Kampung Improvement Program (KIP). From the mid-1970s, with World Bank funding, the New Order had undertaken the improvement of urban kampung throughout Indonesia, largely concentrating on improvement to paths, drainage, water supplies and sanitation (Dick, 2002: 244–7; Silas, 1992). In the eighth issue of *Warta Kampung*, Kah (2002) documents the history of the KIP in Yogyakarta. The KIP focused on upgrading roads, paths, and drains; the provision of rubbish disposal, toilets, washrooms and clean water; and the building of schools and health clinics for kampung residents. As the New Order gained in political and economic strength during the 1980s, these improvement programs were seen increasingly by government and kampung residents as a gift, undermining residents' own initiative and commitment to the improvements. At the same time, residents' own efforts towards improvements in their lives were ignored by government and mass media. A YPR discussion paper in 2007 (Yoshi and Himawati, 2007) suggested that kampung always become the object of control and development and ideally the "target" of projects. The state through its projects intended that kampung populations (often termed 'poor' populations) become cleaner and more orderly according to norms of behaviour advocated by urban elites. Yoshi and Himawati's discussion paper asserted that kampung have lost out when the needs of more important citizens or the city as a whole require it. Kampung, they write, were regularly swept aside in the urban developments of the 1980s and 1990s. Kampung residents were seen as useless, criminal and uncontrollable, and could thus be ignored in the context of city planning. YPR constantly aimed in their publications and their activities to counter that view.

For a week in July 2007, the second Festival Kampung was held, located in the neighbourhoods of Sidomulyo and Kricak. It included opportunities for kampung residents to work with architects and artists, including a visiting group of Melbourne University students. They worked together to redesign their homes and to depict their kampung life through drawings, photos, films and art. A nightly showing of films and slides of kampung life, a theatre performance and fashion show, and a travelling library with a range of children's activities all added to the festival. Once again the aim of the festival was to celebrate kampung life, to bring the diversity and richness of this life to the attention of both kampung and urban middle-class audiences and to empower kampung residents to maintain their ways of life.

COMMUNITY AT THE CORE OF KAMPUNG

In policy statements and explorations of YPR perspectives, there is strong and repeated assertion of the importance of community to kampung life. On the YPR website, Hersumpana, a YPR community worker states that the character of Indonesian cities is shaped by kampung communal pockets that support urban life and provide the basis for urban governance (Hersumpana, 2007). He identifies three key strengths of kampung community: first, the conduct of human relations in a tolerant and considerate way despite the heterogeneous and potentially conflictual mix of people found in the neighbourhood; second, the network of flexible and adaptive informal economic ties, enabling life to continue and providing support through credit institutions such as the arisan; and third, the dynamic 'cultural spirituality' that promotes understanding and tolerance among residents of diverse faiths.

In exploring the nature of kampung society, YPR activists have laid special stress on tracing the history of each kampung population in seeking a spatial and social identity within the pressures of the wider society. Yoshi, YPR's Coordinator of the Apprenticeship Kampung Division, states that spatial identity within the kampung neighbourhood collective provides a focus for individuals' daily life. "The household subsistence strategies, the networks of friendship and cooperation, and the experiences and emotions of living together in a kampung neighbourhood allow the formation of viable communities among the lower class" (Yoshi, 2007, in translation). He asserts that the history of the kampung as a community which over the years has formed and maintained groupings of neighbours to provide credit or enable infrastructural development or social activities can be seen in distinction to the official history of the kampung as an arena of government control.

YPR publications all emphasise the persistence of communal action and kampung cultural norms that engage community, even under pressure from wider social changes, because these activities and norms carry social importance for the local population. An article in *Warta Kampung* provides a graphic account of community action. In Yogyakarta kampung Mergangsan in the early 1990s, a group of youth had established a fishpond on riverflat. The Irrigation Service (Dinas

Pengairan) had ordered the return of the land for the construction of irrigation works but, in a move that angered kampung residents, the resumed land was handed by the Irrigation Service to a real estate developer for high-cost housing. Residents banded together to contest the case, supported by the local media, and finally received a financial and material settlement from the developer. However, residents could not forget the importance of the fishpond project for local youth. In 2001 several residents negotiated with a landowner to allow his vacant block to be converted by the youth into a fishpond on a harvest-share basis. Aided by several older residents, the youth dug the pond and stocked it with fish, using as their initial capital voluntary contributions from fellow residents. At the time of writing the pond had become a viable business, offering recreational fishing for a fee, providing continual work for the youth and an income of Rp50–70,000 per week into the kampung youth committee budget. This success had been achieved through the cooperation of diverse residents of the community (Cucu, 2002a).

The eighth and later issues of *Warta Kampung* also introduced a section on women. In the ninth issue, this section described how the financial crisis of 1998 had consolidated the sense of communal solidarity among the women of Badran. In this riverside kampung, women in the lower riverflat RT had cultivated solidarity and cooperative work, which was much more in evidence than among women above them in riverbank RT. However, as the financial crisis worsened, an outside women's NGO, Tjut Nyak Dien, introduced communal cooking to both RT neighbourhoods with the aim that through the cooperation of women from both upper and lower areas, the poorest residents could be served with a daily cooked meal of a plate of rice and vegetables for only Rp200. Following up on this initiative, the cooperation was continued among the women through a new community organisation called *Griya Rumpun* (Solidarity House), which numbered 231 women. Once every three months they gathered for a simpan pinjam activity, often accompanied by talks on such topics as reproductive health or violence against women. They invested seven million rupiah, takings from the first year of the communal cooking in kitchen and the revenue of household equipment rented out to residents organising ritual celebrations. The timely intervention of an outside NGO at a time when all were suffering hardship from the financial crisis created the impetus for the establishment of a strong community of women across the kampung.

Most YPR activities are built on the active participation of communities of neighbours. After the May 2006 earthquake which devastated the region, YPR joined with German-based GTZ (Deutsche Gesellschaft fur Technische Zusammenarbeit), an international cooperation enterprise for sustainable development, to institute a program of community action planning aimed at enabling communities affected by the earthquake to participate as communities in the rehabilitation of their kampung. Tungkak had been severely hit by the earthquake, with five persons killed and three-quarters of the houses damaged. YPR took responsibility for rehabilitating the homes of 14 poor rubbish-recycling families, who were being overlooked in state rehabilitation efforts. Because of its strategic location, the area these families had occupied for 15 years had long been coveted by private and state developers and the YPR action was partly aimed at protecting these families' occupation of the land. YPR enabled a reconciliation between these poor households and other kampung residents, who gave their support through kerja bakti and the services of kampung artisans to repair or replace the houses.

YPR through their writing and their social activities attest to the strength of community and the importance of acknowledging the community in development activities. In YPR assessments, community is not fundamentally driven by state management strategies but is a kampung response to protect the security and livelihood of every kampung household against the pressures of state and capital expansion. As expressed in institutions such as Rukun Tetangga, kerja bakti and arisan, community is the weft in the fabric of kampung life.

PARTICIPATORY DEVELOPMENT OUTCOMES

Another question is the extent to which the efforts of Romo Mangun and YPR have contributed to the empowerment of kampung people. A key distinction in this regard is whether the participatory development facilitated by YPR has remained just instrumental or actually become transformative. Has residents' participation in these development activities enabled an improvement in their lives that is both material and structural? This question addresses Romo Mangun's concern that the poverty of the poor is a structural poverty perpetuated by their marginalisation in the wider society and economy and thus largely out of their control. If that is the case, participation becomes transformative only when changes in the wider society allow it. Is it necessarily a failure of participatory development when wider urban society prevents full political, economic and social transformation from taking place? How much, therefore, should YPR and other agents focus on changing those wider structures as well as addressing kampung needs?

The Ledok Code settlement where Romo Mangun spent five years has indeed undergone a transformation. Residents there have achieved full citizenship rights; enjoy well-constructed homes, effective drains, recreational spaces, washrooms, and supplies of clean water; and have their own community organisations offering savings and loans, tutoring for their children, and outlets for artistic expression. Their settlement has even become admired by the wider urban population and tourists in the city take photos of its original architecture. More importantly, the residents in partnership with YPR have prevented all municipal attempts to clear them from the site in the name of beautifying the city. To this extent, the attitudes of the city elite have softened towards their settlement.

While Romo Mangun concentrated on a group of people who were 'stateless', without residency cards and thus beyond all municipal services, YPR focused subsequently on established kampung populations. Their involvement in these communities has been long-term, moulded as much by a desire to learn as to change. Their articles reflect a fascination with the unique histories of individual kampung, the diversity and inventiveness of people's livelihoods, and the richness of community life. Their research challenges a commonly held view of kampung people as boorish, ignorant, unorganised and lazy, or as a society who have only themselves to blame for their circumstances.

To the outside observer or development enthusiast, YPR's participatory development approach looks to be low-key — a mobile library, classes for children, arisan and simpan pinjam, support for the poorest in the repair of their homes. Kampung festivals, including displays, performances and workshops, local publications that allow residents to write about their own experiences, and small projects such as a fish pond for recreational fishing all strengthen community resources. None of these projects claims to transform the kampung economically or politically. Nor is it easy to assess their larger impact. However they may indeed be transformative in the long term, because they are in their essence building up kampung residents' self-perception as responsible and capable citizens of the city and equipping them to seek out partners within the wider society in realising their dreams. This is indeed empowering. It is important, however, to restate the point that

YPR repeatedly makes: that kampung people have always over the years demonstrated their own capacity to work within their communities and, with the limited resources at their disposal, to achieve a certain measure of security and recognition. What YPR has done is to recognise and foster that local capacity in new ways.

YPR staff write about both the constrictions imposed by capitalist development and about the impact of government policies and practices. However, the YPR activists are even more focused on the patterns of kampung life existing independent of both government and capitalist sectors. They portray kampung residents as creators of their own worlds, even within the structures imposed by government regulation and urban inequalities. They point out the strengths of kampung society, both in individuals' entrepreneurship and in community cooperation and highlight the positive efforts kampung people make to order their lives and deal with the structural inequalities they experience. The transformations they envisage, therefore, include not only residents gaining more recognition within government and business circles and having more say in changes that affect them, but also reforming their own communities to provide greater freedom, respect and opportunity for all residents.

Thus YPR, through their 'urban advocacy movement', have addressed issues of empowerment by publishing accounts that ennoble numerous aspects of residents' lives. They appeal to an outside readership in terms of the positive contributions made by residents. They have become advocates for the kampung by pointing out injustices and inequalities imposed by state or capitalist interests, while also becoming participants in change by articulating issues that they sense require change and encouraging kampung residents to reflect as a community on these issues. The fourth goal of the YPR movement — building and enhancing the bargaining position of urban poor communities and learning with them to critically analyse and solve their social and environmental problems — requires the long-term commitment to particular communities that has become the hallmark of YPR activities.

10

Conclusion

This book was inspired by living with and observing residents of a riverside kampung in Yogyakarta over a span of 30 years. I wanted to document the changes I had observed and, in doing so, to attest to the vitality and self-motivation of some of the poorest in the city. The book was also inspired by the efforts of student activists and their mentor Romo Mangun in the NGO Yayasan Pondok Rakyat to understand kampung society and to discover a way in which they could contribute to the well-being of kampung residents.

To this account I have brought my own subjectivity, one moulded by my own values and training. I was fortunate in my initial period in Yogyakarta to have worked at Gadjah Mada University in a team composed of a wide range of social scientists. This helped to set my anthropological insights in a wider urban framework. My own training predisposed me to look for structure and agency in human relations. Although I came to regard conflict and power relations as important ingredients of that structure, I was not dissuaded from recognising communal patterns of behaviour when they presented. My training and subsequent experience convinced me that any analysis must be founded on careful ethnography, that is the close observation of what people say and do on a daily basis.

In Indonesia I first carried out research in 1970 in a village of Betawi people on the outskirts of Jakarta (Guinness, 1972).[11] That was my first attempt to depict urban, or peri-urban life, at a time when anthropologists in Indonesia and elsewhere were focusing on village society and normative ethnic cultures. In 1975 I settled in the kampung of Ledok in Yogyakarta, not intended as a site of research, but simply as a place to live while I commuted daily to the nearby university faculty and research centre where I worked. I was attracted

241

to this kampung because of its riverside and wooded location, but was soon made aware of its marginalisation in the urban middle-class imagination by the amusement of my university colleagues at my insistence on living there. For them it was stifling in its poverty and lack of privacy. Living in the constant company and view of all one's neighbours was unavoidable in such a settlement. I was fortunate to live with a family who were familiar with foreigners, at least Dutch foreigners, and who openly and intelligently shared their insights into the local community. They espoused the importance of community and the morality of reciprocity and demonstrated to me on a daily basis how these were maintained. Had I lived with the sand-diggers on the riverflat, rather than just spending many hours with them, I might have stressed more of the inequalities that still frame kampung relations, both within the neighbourhoods and with the outside society. Nevertheless, riverflat neighbours stressed community just as strongly, even if they interpreted it somewhat differently.

The diachronic perspective of this research on urban kampung has added to an appreciation of what residents face in their daily lives and the development which has taken place over several decades, whether under official programs or as popular initiatives. The lives of kampung residents have changed radically over the years, reflecting not only changes in the wider Indonesian society, but also the initiatives of residents, both individually and communally. Most noticeably, the riverside settlement has been transformed from a mix of trees, shrubs and houses to a high-density neighbourhood where pot-plants are the only vegetation. Vacant land has been transformed into housing, increasingly multi-storeyed. Access to water and electricity, toilets and washrooms has become easier, title to land has been obtained, self-help financial organisations have multiplied, secondary education has become the norm with tertiary education a possibility, and the stigma of riverflat occupation has largely disappeared.

These changes have taken place during 30 years of the centralising and militaristic New Order government and the years of decentralisation and demilitarisation that have followed the crisis of 1998. Economic changes of globalisation and consumerism have brought other forces to bear on the expression of individual and group identity. Kampung people have responded not by rejecting change or ignoring the opportunities on offer but by accommodating the changes in the wider national and urban contexts to their own economic and social circumstances. They managed this partly through the informalisation of many of their encounters with the wider society and the consolidation of community as a guarantor of individual strategies of survival.

COMMUNITY

The social science literature on kampung and urban low-income neighbourhoods throughout the world proliferated in the late 20th century. That literature deals compellingly with the early images of low-income urban settlements and squatter areas as anarchic and lacking culture, identifying instead settlements of order, cultural coherence and economic ingenuity. In the eyes of state and non-state agents of planning and development, those new images of urban settlements too readily translated into assumptions of cultural and social homogeneity and political consensus behind elected leaders. As Chapter One indicates, more recently such notions of homogeneity and community autonomy have been questioned.

What I have presented in this book and in earlier writings is a detailed ethnographic account of how kampung residents engage in forming and reforming their communities amidst stark differences among residents in rank and social esteem. The complexity of kampung society lies in the weaving together of social diversity based on occupation, property ownership and origin, religious practices, age and gender differences, education, and cultural predispositions. This book addresses in detail how this works out in practice, such as in the ways youth construct their own spaces in the social order, the formalisation and the informalisation processes of economic, social, political and cultural dynamics, the community role of the individual leader and entrepreneur, the household life-cycle rituals and the elections. Each of these chapters indicates that 'community' is constantly being formed and reformed, under continual negotiation among residents as social and cultural agents and within the wider city and nation.

Caroline Moser concluded that social fragmentation is more likely among the urban poor than the rural poor. "Community and inter-household mechanisms of trust and collaboration can be weakened by greater social and economic heterogeneity, associated with wider distributional ranges of income, opportunities, and access to infrastructure, services and political influence in urban areas" (Moser, 1998: 4). She drew attention to the heterogeneity of urban neighbourhood populations, which would seem to threaten any expression of community or consensual cooperation. Ethnographic explorations of kampung societies reveal that community, cooperation and consensus accommodate the dynamics of social rank, formal structures of leadership and cultural norms of respect.

A case in which I was involved illustrates some of this complexity. In the early months of my stay in Ledok, the local RT leader, Sugi, with my encouragement, contacted a local NGO that was promoting biogas systems for the disposal of sewerage. He put to a meeting of the RT members the idea of connecting the local public toilet block to such a system, which would produce gas for lighting the alleyway and for household cooking for poorer neighbours, then dispose of clean liquid effluent into the adjacent river. Those present at the meeting agreed and the biogas system was duly installed on riverflat land adjacent to the public toilets, with resources and labour contributed by residents. Within months the system had been disconnected. Nearby riverflat residents complained of the odours, partly due to the system's failure to deal with the quantity of waste. More significantly, these residents complained that an RT meeting was not a suitable way to consult with them on a matter that so directly concerned them because they were reluctant in such a meeting forum to voice their misgivings and doubts, even though the project more immediately affected them. In such a forum, principles of harmony and consensus could easily overshadow those of equal participation. The enthusiasm of riverbank residents of superior social rank had suppressed the legitimate concerns of riverflat residents and had done so through ostensibly communal forms of decision-making.

Most dealings in the kampung comprised relations among people of differing social rank. However, the dynamics of community tended to minimise these social differences. Partly this was due to the vehemence with which those of lower rank stated their case through neighbourhood gossip rather than through the formal structures of RT or RW community. Partly it also reflected a morality that stressed mutual obligations of all residents, whatever their rank, to contribute labour and resources to community projects and to the concerns of the poorest individual households. Reciprocity was a dominant principle that leaders impressed on new arrivals and one which the lower rank demanded in their relations with their social superiors. The life of Sugi, the entrepreneur and kampung leader detailed in Chapter Two, demonstrates how service rather than privilege or power dominates the relations of the kampung elite with their neighbourhood community. Many kampung leaders pointed out to me that the state did not reward them for their services to the community and that they served out of dedication to the community rather than for personal gain.

Changes in the wider society brought about by development programs and modernisation introduced new elements into kampung society. That society has shown itself to be flexible in accommodating those changes while retaining a sense of the importance of community. In recent developments, Islamic reformism and the reform of election processes were both not only accommodated within Ledok society but, in turn, allowed a re-expression of the fundamentals of local community. In questioning slavish imitation of Western models of modernity, Partha Chatterjee suggests an alternative imagining drawing upon narratives of community that would mount a formidable challenge to narratives of capital (cited in Ong, 1996). Within such alternative imaginings, the community of kampung neighbourhoods has a place. The research in Ledok and the observations of the other researchers and activists such as YPR convinced me that an alternative imagining focused on informalisation processes and community expressions was a reality among kampung populations.

In Chapter One, I suggested that communities are seen as both facilitating individual freedom and curbing it. Zygmunt Bauman suggests that "there is a price for the privilege of 'being in a community', the price being in lost freedom to be oneself or the right to assert oneself" (Bauman, 2001: 4). The tension between the security of community and individual freedom is unlikely to ever be resolved. But for kampung residents, community allows them the security to assert themselves as individuals. Kampung residents contribute to community life partly because the neighbourhood provides them with the security to pursue their individual lives in the city. Hence they support communal activities such as community working bees, security patrols or credit programs because these enhance the quality of their individual lives. Community members look after each other and may even finance each other through savings and credit associations (Lont, 2005). The community thereby recognises people who would otherwise be marginalised, the extreme example being squatters and homeless. The neighbourhood provides them and all its members with association through youth or women's groups, religious associations, music, sport and the like. The RT and RW organisations protect their rights as urban residents. However, these neighbourhood communities also impose obligations on residents, obligations that could be perceived as imposed by a kampung leadership beholden to urban elite interests.

Indeed, these obligations may sometimes be interpreted as curbs on residents' behaviour. As residents contest and negotiate the freedoms and obligations of community, the sense of community is strengthened, at least in Ledok. It may be that in other neighbourhoods, the balance is lost and individuals withdraw their support of community, as happens in many streetside neighbourhoods. However, there is much evidence in this book of kampung residents in Yogyakarta and Jakarta continuing to attest to the value of community, even as they negotiate changes in the way it is expressed.

In a recent publication on the kampung of Yogyakarta, Hotze Lont (2005) documents the importance of community mechanisms for individual finances. Rotating credit (arisan) and savings and loans (simpan pinjam) allow individual residents to store up economic capital for times of necessity. He suggests that in such arrangements residents protect themselves against future demands by contributing to a variety of financial organisations, but that these self-help organisations only function through trust built up as social capital:

> Strong and dense social networks are an essential precondition for the continued existence of financial self-help organizations. No matter how great the need for lump sums may continue to be, they will cease to exist if those networks dissolve (Lont, 2005: 108).

Lont documents the survival of cooperation at the RK level almost two decades after the official RK administration was disbanded (Lont, 2005: 38–9, 128, 149). He also indicates the significance of constructing community relations between residents of *Ledok* (riverbank) and *Atas* (street level) in kampung Bujung, despite the social and economic differences that divide them, a result mirroring what I have described in kampung Ledok.

What has emerged in Ledok and other kampung communities is not a single form, unchanged through the waves of historical change. What people recognise as community, as documented in this ethnography, is a dynamic construction that reflects the transforming dynamics of state and kampung agents over years of state and capitalist expansions and contractions, reinvented through people's imaginative responses to those pressures.

STATE AND COMMUNITY

A central issue raised by this book is the relation between state and community. Peter Vandergeest in a study of rural Thailand raises the question of whether community self-help should always be seen in terms of the domination, exploitation and control that it hides, thus challenging some of the interpretations of state manipulation and popular misrepresentations that I discussed in Chapter One. Vandergeest (1991: 424) documents how local officials mobilised local labour "for the common good" on development projects as an act of power incurring obligation. Although he is careful to encourage a critical view of such practices, he argues that "such strategies can be aspects of processes of democratization and local empowerment which articulate local struggles with more general struggles for a new society". In this book, I have outlined a dissatisfaction with the way scholarly accounts of kampung residents largely deprive them of agency, an interpretation which views community practices as mere slavish adoption of government programs designed to control the 'masses'. Instead I have tried to present an alternative interpretation of at least one kampung I know well as relatively autonomous of state controls.

Intrinsic to the view of state control over kampung people has been the emphasis on the discourse constructed by the state elite and successfully spread through the population. Central to this discourse has been the concept that people in villages and urban settlements live in communities. This is a construct of a state discourse, say the critics, not an interpretation that reflects the reality 'on the ground'. Has community, even from colonial days, been simply the construct and instrument of a state that has discovered the efficiencies to be gained through people being drafted into a state program in which they appear to govern themselves, but realise the dictates of the state rather than their own priorities? Arun Agrawal, for example, agrees with such a view. In an article about the decentralisation of control over forest in India, he states that "state formation proceeds in part by coercion but in at least equal measure by local initiative, by the willing participation of those over whom new forms of state power come to hold sway" (Agrawal, 2001: 13). Over the colonial and post-colonial periods, communal management of forested land by village councils matched the objectives of state officials, such that Agrawal suggests that "decentralization of regulations makes villagers accomplices in their own control" (Agrawal, 2001: 25). This was facilitated by council members who came from upper castes and defined their interests as consonant with those of the government, becoming agents of state-facilitated protection, while ordinary villagers were marginalised by measures to control access to and "protect" those forests. In consequence, violations of forest regulations were frequent, particularly by untouchables (*harijan*), and by women seeking fodder and fuelwood, reflecting in part the poor's rejection of the state's discourse and practice.

Agrawal suggests that the advocacy of community as a building block of civil society in distinction to the state is a utopian vision characterised by dreams of "homogeneity, internal equality, stability and multiplexity of interactions among members" (Agrawal, 2001: 32). His refutation of this vision focuses on the "impress" of the state on "communal" institutions. As Fernando Coronil puts it, "As a 'magnanimous sorcerer', the state seizes its subjects by inducing a condition or state of being receptive to its illusions — a magical state" (Coronil, 1997: 5). The political legitimacy of the state is based on its seeming ability to meet local needs through local participation. In this Agrawal is in accord with the views of John Sullivan, who depicts kampung 'communities' as constructs of the state. Yet Sullivan clearly indicates the difficulty in drawing such categorical conclusions. He indicates that kampung residents have often adopted the notion of community in distinction — even opposition — to the state, emphasising the deftness of state constructions that have achieved such a popular mis-recognition. Sullivan asserted that anthropologists were too prone to take kampung residents' idealised versions at face value, while political scientists could more easily detect the machinations of the state. Clearly what is needed is an approach that can take both views into consideration.

In many situations the interests and strategies of state and people are difficult to distinguish, as when local peoples are enjoined by the state to manage their own affairs. Tania Li suggests that in Indonesia state formation and community formation have proceeded simultaneously as part of a single process. Rather than communities predating state formation, they have been "formed or at least reformed in interaction with the programs and initiatives of governing regimes" (Li, 2002: 277). In Ledok, the contributions of RT and RW/RK officers and their committees offer to the state a relatively ordered and quiescent civilian population that supports state programs of development at minimal cost to the state. The alternative of the chaotic masses rioting in the streets and destroying the symbols of modernisation means that the state values the role of kampung organisations in suppressing the potential violence of the common people (rakyat). As a result, the state offers kampung populations the development of infrastructure such as health centres, schools, women's groups, employment creation programs and credit schemes.

However, these are not magical tricks that hypnotise the kampung residents. Li (2002: 277) suggests that communities strengthen their own formation to engage with state institutions and possibly seek benefits from the state, even in opposition to the design of state projects. The developments I have outlined in Ledok over the last 30 years indicate the continuing vitality of local, communal solutions, despite marginality in the wider city. Kampung people are not slavish adherents of government edicts or controls. In their extremes of resistance, the violence of the 'masses' or the independence of youth demonstrate the autonomy of kampung residents, even as the order of community institutions provides more convincing evidence that residents live beyond the dictates of the state. The informalisation processes that characterise kampung social and economic relations indicate a multifaceted arena which derives its strength and flexibility from its relative autonomy from state controls.

Most kampung people remain very critical of state programs as doing very little to alter the structural disadvantages of their situation. Nonetheless, kampung people usually go along with most state programs, even when these involve them in considerable extra effort, such as the building of a river wall, because these state programs complement what residents are already doing. Community interests and pressures ensure that residents also initiate most of their programs independently of what the state ordains and according to needs identified by residents themselves. Chapter Two indicated the pressure under which RT and RW leaders operated to provide a service to their communities rather than to serve the state.

Chapter Seven showed that although kampung electoral officers, many of them RT and RW leaders, were under strict instructions to implement the national elections under the centralised control of the Indonesian Electoral Commission, their success at the local level protected community solidarity during one of the most serious threats to its harmony (rukun). They achieved this not by following state directives but by implementing their own program to ensure the smooth completion of the elections.

The discussion of formalisation and informalisation processes in Chapters Three and Four shows just how fluctuating and interwoven is the relationship between community and state. Building a bridge over the river was a community project that was not listed in any state development plans. Its successful completion was a triumph of community cooperation, yet the Subdistrict Head (Camat) was invited to open it as a means of giving it standing in municipal development plans. To take one more example, over the years kampung residents have made use of state and private corporate hospital and health services, as well as alternative healers, depending which is seen to provide the better service. In cases of severe illness, they may seek help from both. In the financial straits that most kampung residents found themselves in, particularly after the financial crisis (*Krismon*), informal processes that drew on mutual assistance made up for inadequate state programs for the poor. Indeed, at times these state programs even endangered the poor by undermining the strength of the mutual assistance and cooperation on which residents relied.

Arun Agrawal (2001) emphasised that the balance of influence between state and community shifts, at some times reflecting much stronger state controls, at other times more popular alternatives. This account has shown this to be case in Ledok. In 1988–89 the state increased its intrusion into kampung affairs by abolishing the RK units, which had become symbols of community power, and fracturing these into RW, thereby bringing in a new level of salaried administration in kelurahan to oversee these RW. For a while community power was undermined. However, these RW, some of them reflecting existing neighbourhood communities, soon acquired the sense of being local institutions fulfilling local needs. In addition, some kampung communities constructed informal organisations to continue the role that the RK had performed. In the kampung of Bujung as studied by Lont, kampung leaders established the Bujung Citizens' Association (Paguyuban Warga Bujung), which collected fees, organised funeral funds, initiated key celebrations and provided items for loan for all those neighbourhoods associated within the former RK (Lont, 2005: 38–9). Were people therefore tricked by a clever government into believing that state control over them was actually communal independence from the state? There are valid arguments and evidence to present for that interpretation, but it is clear that kampung people both support government programs where they stand to gain from them and act independently from and sometimes in opposition to government when necessary. Not all kampung people agree on the direction community action should take, just as Agrawal points out that richer villagers may decide it is in their own interests to appropriate government programs that are violently resisted by marginal villagers.

Parajuli and Kothari (1998: 25) make a strong argument for the autonomy of local communities from the state. They assert that neither the nation-state nor the non-government organisations of civil society provides a vibrant democratic space, while "local governance strengthens a process where power is built upward from the bottom, making it accountable and responsible to the ground and not to remote centralized authorities of power". They contend that "communities are redefining themselves and undergoing their own transformation as they reaffirm their own spaces.... These peasant and/or ecological movements critique existing inequities and injustices while regenerating their own communities and cultures" (Parajuli and Kothari, 1998: 28). Such an assertion mirrors the claims made for transformative participatory development, suggesting that local people and communities should be involved at every stage of development, from initial planning to final evaluations, with the goal of the empowerment of these communities. Such an approach assumes a community of people who have views to express that may — and probably do — differ from those of the state elite.

It is interesting that Parajuli and Kothari identify that grassroots governance is most meaningful and feasible where communities identify with a unique ecological space. Such ecological spaces exist also within the city, enhancing the feasibility of local urban governance. It may well be that kampung communities in Java are most vital when they perceive themselves to occupy a distinct ecological space. In the case of Ledok residents, their ecological space is clearly defined by the river valley, fringed on the other sides by city streets and street residences. It is a space that has provided important natural resources over the years, as well as privacy and protection from the wider city, and it is a space that it is easy for them to guard and maintain because of its discreteness. Accounts of other kampung occupying a distinct ecological space along the riverbank or beside a cemetery or railway indicate that Ledok is not unusual in this regard. Other kampung may be more permeable, less easy to define ecologically, and thus less amenable to the emergence of local community governance.

Since the demise of the authoritarian New Order, people all over Indonesia have been enthused by talk of more democratic governments. With the declining economic capacity of the central government, local people have focused on alternative solutions. In these circumstances, it is even less obvious that communities are simply the agents of state policy. What seems evident is that communities and individuals in those communities have their own interests and strategies which somehow accommodate those of the state in a relationship where neither is supremely dominant and the balance is constantly changing.

Notes

1. These include Clifford Geertz (1960), Hildred Geertz (1961), Robert Jay (1969) and Guinness (1986).
2. The *kendhuren* or *kenduri* is the formal ritual feast held at dusk. The term *slametan* is also used for this feast, although slametan may also refer to the larger combination of kendhuren with the *rewang*, the help which neighbours give before the kendhuren to prepare the food.
3. These figures are for the whole RK and thus include the streetside population of about 200 people.
4. Kampung people refer to streetside properties as *gedhong/loji* (large brick homes), referring to a distinction not only in location but also in class position and standard of living. See Mahasin (1990) and Guinness (1986).
5. Between January and September 1998 inflation was 75.5 per cent (Marianti, 1999).
6. See Note 2.
7. Newberry (2007) notes the increase in *sembahyang* in another Yogyakarta kampung, but chooses to regard these also as *selamatan*.
8. This jihadist organisation sent armed forces to Maluku and Sulawesi with the stated intention to defend Muslims against Christians. It was reputedly disbanded in 2002.
9. Up to 33 million votes nationally or 30 per cent of the national vote may have been affected in this way. See Lane, 2005; Castles, 2004.
10. *Manunggaling tekad agawe santosa* is a kind of common or popular saying or proverb meaning something like 'Strength comes from rock-solid unity of will' (literally: 'unity of determination makes for strength'). (Personal communication from George Quinn.)
11. These are seen as the original inhabitants of Batavia, the name for Jakarta in Dutch times, their culture a distinctive mix of Portuguese, Chinese, Arabic, Malay, Sundanese and other ethnic elements, which marked them off from the fast expanding migrant population of the capital.

Glossary

abangan	adherents of Javanese forms of Islam
adat	custom, tradition
anak jalanan	street children
apem	small round cakes given to neighbours in the month of Ruah
arisan	rotating credit scheme
banci	transvestite
Bapak	father or respected male elder
BAPPENAS	National Development Planning Agency
battra	healer
becak	pedicab
budi pekerti	natural ability, good deeds
buruh	labourer
camat	subdistrict head
campur sari	a mix of various styles of music
dagang	trader
Dewan Perwakilan Daerah	House of Regional Representatives
Dewan Perwakilan Rakyat	House of People's Representatives
Dewan Perwakilan Rakyat Daerah	House of People's Representatives at provincial or district levels
Dharma Wanita	Women's organisation
dukun	spirit medium, traditional healer
dukun perwangan	healer with spiritual power
dukun tiban	healer whose power is revealed in dreams
gali	criminal gangs
gedhong	large streetside brick homes
gelandangan	homeless person

gotong royong	mutual cooperation
halus	refined, sensitive
ibu jamu	herbalist
Ibu	mother or respected female elder
ICMI	Indonesian Association of Islamic Intellectuals
ilmu	(special) knowledge
jago	tough guy
jagongan	relaxed evening ritual of chatting and card-playing
jamu	traditional medicine
Jaring Pengamanan Sosial	Social Safety Net
jagongan	evening social celebration
kampung	off-street neighbourhood
kampungan	boorish, uncivilised
karyawan	employee in formal sector
kasar	unrefined, coarse
kaum	neighbourhood Islamic official
kecamatan	Subdistrict office
kerja bakti	communal work
kelurahan	administrative unit above the kampung
kendhuren/kenduri	formal neighbourhood ritual at nightfall
kerukunan	social harmony
kios	kiosk
Koperasi Unit Desa (KUD)	Village cooperative
Krismon	the financial crisis of 1998
kromo	high-level Javanese language
kroncong	Javanese music using ukulele and guitars
Kuliah Kerja Nyata (KKN)	applied studies, university community service
lesehan	pavement restaurant
loji	large brick streetside home
Majelis Permusyawaratan Rakyat	People's Consultative Assembly
massa	the masses
mesjid	mosque
Muhammadiyah	the largest reformist organisation in Indonesia

mussolah	prayer room
Nahdlatul Ulama	traditionalist Muslim organisation
ngamen	busker
ngelmu	knowledge
Normalisasi Kampus	government policy banning campus political activities
Olahraga Hidup Baru (Orhiba)	a movement blending exercise with spiritual powers
padat karya	government work program
paguyuban	community association
pegawai (negeri)	government employee
pembangunan	development
pemuda	youth
pengajian	community recitation of the Koran
pengindung	leasee of house land
perumahan	housing estate
PKK	Family Welfare Organisation
pos ronda	security patrol post
prihatin	diligent, careful to keep standards up
puskesmas	health clinic
rakyat, rakyat kecil	little people, masses
Reformasi	post-1998 reform era
remaja	youth, teenager
ronda	security patrol
Ruah	eighth month of the Muslim year
rukun	social harmony, solidarity
Rukun Kampung (RK)	local-level administrative unit incorporating a kampung
Rukun Tetangga (RT)	local-level administrative unit of about 30 households
Rukun Warga (RW)	local-level administrative unit of about five RT
santri	devout Muslims
satpam	security guard
seksi pemuda	youth organisation under RT/RW administration
sembahyang	community prayers
simpan pinjam	savings and credit association
siskamling	local security patrol
slametan	household ritual

sumbangan	gift or donation weddings or funerals
swasta	private entrepreneur
tabib	healer
tekyan	street children's sub-culture
tetangga	neighbour
warga	citizen
warung	foodstall
wedigengser	untitled, flood-prone riverflat land
wong cilik	little people, the masses
Yayasan Pondok Rakyat (YPR)	People's Shelter Foundation

Bibliography

Adnan, Zirdaus (1990). "Islamic Religion: Yes, Islamic (Political) Ideology: No! Islam and the State in Indonesia", in *State and Civil Society in Indonesia*, ed. A. Budiman. Clayton: Centre of Southeast Asian Studies, Monash University, 441–78.

Agrawal, Arun (2001). "State Formation in Community Spaces? Decentralization of Control over Forests in the Kumaon Himalaya, India", *Journal of Asian Studies* 60, 1: 9–40.

Alexander, J. (1987). *Trade, Traders and Trading in Rural Java.* Singapore: Oxford University Press.

Amit, Vered and Nigel Rapport (2002). *The Trouble with Community: Anthropological Reflections on Movement, Identity and Collectivity.* London: Pluto Press.

Anderson, B. (1972). *Java in the Time of Revolution.* Ithaca, New York: Cornell University Press.

———— (1988). *Revolusi Pemoeda.* Jakarta: Pustaka Sinar Harapan.

———— (2001). *Violence and the State in Suharto's New Order.* Ithaca, New York: Southeast Asia Program Publications, Cornell University.

Anon (1999). *Kucuran J P S Macet di Sana-Sini.* Jakarta, 7 December 1999.

Appadurai, Arjun (1996). *Modernity at Large: Cultural Dimensions of Globalization.* Minneapolis: University of Minnesota Press.

———— (1998). "Dead Certainty: Ethnic Violence in the Era of Globalization", *Development and Change* 29, 4: 905–25.

Arifin (2003). "Ledok Macanan", *Warta Kampung* 10.

Arifin, M. (2003). *Beberapa Perubahan Dalam Kehidupan Masyarakat Kampung Ledok Macanan.* Department of Anthropology, Gadjah Mada University, Yogyakarta.

Aspinall, E. (1999). "The Indonesian Student Uprising of 1998", in *Reformasi: Crisis and Change in Indonesia*, ed. Arief Budiman, B. Hatley and D. Kingsbury. Clayton, Melbourne: Monash Asia Institute, Monash University.

Azuma, Y. (2001). *Abang Beca: Sekejam-Kejamnya Ibu-Tiri Masih Lebih Kejam Ibukota.* Jakarta: Pustaka Sinar Harapan.

Bamba, J. (2000). "Jalan Buntu Menuju Sebayan", *Basis* 49: 9–10.

Barker, Joshua (1998). "State of Fear: Controlling the Criminal Contagion in Suharto's New Order", *Indonesia* 66.

———— (2001). "State of Fear: Controlling the Criminal Contagion in Suharto's New Order", in *Violence and the State in Suharto's Indonesia*, ed. B. Anderson. Ithaca, New York: Southeast Asia Program Publications, Cornell University.

Bauman, Zygmunt (2001). *Community: Seeking Safety in an Insecure World.* Cambridge: Polity.

Beard, R. (1998). *Capacity of Community Based Planning to Reduce Urban Poverty: A Case Study of Gondolayu Lor in Yogyakarta, Indonesia.* Vancouver: University of British Columbia.

Beazley, Hilary (2000). "Street Boys in Yogyakarta: Social and Spatial Exclusion in the Public Spaces of the City", in *A Companion to the City*, ed. G. Bridge and S. Watson. Oxford: Blackwell Publishers, 472–88.

Berman, L. and H. Beazley (1997). "The World's First Street University", *Inside Indonesia* 50: 11–2.

Bernat, J.C. (1999). "Children and the Politics of Violence in Haitian Context", *Critique of Anthropology* 19, 2: 121–38.

Berner, E. and R. Korff (1995). "Globalization and Local Resistance: The Creation of Localities in Manila and Bangkok", *International Journal of Urban and Regional Research* 19, 2: 208–22.

Bowen, J. (1986). "On the Political Construction of Tradition: Gotong Royong in Indonesia", *Journal of Asian Studies* XLV, 3: 545–61.

Bowen, John (1993). *Muslims through Discourse: Religion and Ritual in Gayo Society.* Princeton, NJ: Princeton University Press.

Breman, Jan and Gunawan Wiradi (2002). *Good Times and Bad Times in Rural Java.* Singapore: Institute of Southeast Asian Studies.

Bremm, H. (1988). "Nachbarschaftsbeziehungen in Einem Javanischen Kampung", in *Netzwerkanalyse: Ethnologische Perspektiven*, ed. T. Schweitzer. Berlin: Reimer, 47–62.

Bunnell, T. (2002). "Kampung Rules: Landscape and the Contested Government of Urban(e) Malayness", *Urban Studies* 39, 9: 1686–1701.

Campbell, Caroline and Linda Connor (2000). "Sorcery, Modernity and Social Transformation in Banyuwangi, East Java", *Review of Indonesian and Malayan Affairs* 34, 2.

Campfens, H. (1997). "International Review of Community Development", in *Community Development around the World: Practice, Theory, Research, Training*, ed. H. Campfens. Toronto: University of Toronto Press, 11–46.

Castells, M. and A. Portes (1989). "World Underneath: The Origins, Dynamics and Effects of the Informal Economy", in *The Informal Economy: Studies in Advanced and Less Developed Countries*, ed. A. Portes, M. Castells and L. Benton. Baltimore: John Hopkins University Press, 11–37.

Castles, L. (2004). *Pemilu 2004: Dalam Konteks Komparatif Dan Historis.* Yogyakarta: Pustaka Pelajar.

Cederroth, Sven (1995). *Survival and Profit in Rural Java: The Case of an East Javanese Village*. Richmond, Surrey: Nordic Institute of Asian Studies (Monograph 63).

Clarke, J., S. Hall, T. Jefferson and B. Roberts (1996). "Subcultures, Cultures and Class", in *Persistence through Rituals: Youth Subcultures in Post-War Britain*, ed. S. Hall and T. Jefferson. London: Routledge.

Cohen, A.P. (1985). *The Symbolic Construction of Community*. New York: Tavistock Publications.

─────── (1988). "The Crocodile that Lurks: The Relationship Between the Poor and Their Local Government in Jakarta", in *Urban Society in Southeast Asia*, ed. G.H. Krausse. Hong Kong: Asia Research Service, 81–102.

Cohen, P. (1997). *Rethinking the Youth Question: Education, Labour and Cultural Studies*. Basingstoke: Macmillan.

Cohen, S. (1972). *Folk Devils and Moral Panics*. London: MacGibbon & Kee.

Coronil, F. (1997). *The Magical State: Nature, Money and Modernity in Venezuela*. Chicago: University of Chicago Press.

Cribb, Robert, ed. (1990). *The Indonesian Killings of 1965–1966: Studies from Java and Bali*. Clayton: Centre of Southeast Asian Studies, Monash University.

Cucu, R. (2001). "Ndalem Condro Dalam Cerita Kampung Dan Pudarnya Kraton", *Warta Kampung* 7: 23–4.

─────── (2002a). "Gubug Aluamah: Kommunitas Kolam Dan Mancing", *Warta Kampung* 8: 30–3.

─────── (2002b). "Pemuda Dalam Perjalanan Masa", *Warta Kampung* 9: 6–9.

Dharoko, A. (1988). *Low Income Settlement Development: Study on Urban Kampung in Semarang, Indonesia*. Department of Architecture, University of Newcastle upon Tyne, Newcastle upon Tyne.

Dhewayani, Jeanny (2005). *In Pursuit of the Spirit: Student Prayer Groups in Yogyakarta, Indonesia*. PhD thesis, School of Archaeology and Anthropology, Australian National University, Canberra.

Dick, H.W. (1990). "Further Reflections on the Middle Class", in *The Politics of Middle Class Indonesia*, ed. R. Tanter and K. Young. Clayton: Centre of Southeast Asian Studies, Monash University, 63–70.

─────── (2002). *Surabaya, City of Work: A Socioeconomic History, 1900–2000*. Athens: Ohio University Press.

Dwiyanto, A. (1999). *The Economic Crisis, Social Security and the Government Program Failure: The Study of Three Villages in Java*. Paper, The Economic Crisis and Social Security in Indonesia workshop, Berg en Dal, the Netherlands, 7–9 January.

Earle, Timothy (1997). "State, State Systems", in *The Dictionary of Anthropology*, ed. T. Barfield. Oxford: Blackwell Publishers, 445–6.

Eipper, C. (1996). "Suburbia: The Threat and the Promise", in *Social Self, Global Culture*, ed. A. Kellehear. Melbourne: Oxford University Press, 81–90.

Eko, S. (2000a). *Masyarakat Pascamiliter.* Yogyakarta: IRE.
———— (2000b). "Ritual Tujuhbelasan yang Militeristik", *Flamma* 16–7.
Ertanto, B. (1994). *Tak Ada Ktp, Silahkan Pergi dari Kampung: Studi Mengenai Politik Identitas Anak Jalanan di Kampung.* Yogyakarta: Yayasan Humana.
Evers, H.-D. and R. Korff (2000). *Southeast Asian Urbanism: The Meaning and Power of Social Space.* Singapore: Institute of Southeast Asian Studies.
Fauzannafi, Muhammad Zamzam (2004). "Sejarah dan Institusionalisasi Kampung Tungkak", *Kampung* 1: 57–87.
Foucault, M. (1977). *Discipline and Punish: The Birth of the Prison.* London: Allen Lane.
———— (1983). "Afterword: The Subject and Power", in *Michel Foucault: Beyond Structuralism and Hermeneutics*, ed. H. Dreyfus and P. Rabinow. Chicago: Chicago University Press, 208–28.
Freire, P. (1972). *Pedagogy of the Oppressed.* Ringwood: Penguin Education.
Friedman, J. (1994). *Cultural Identity and Global Process.* London: Sage.
Frith, Simon (1981). *Sound Effects.* London: Constable.
Gaonkar, Dilip Parameshwar (2002). "Toward New Imaginaries: An Introduction", *Public Culture* 14, 1: 1–19.
Geertz, C. (1960). *The Religion of Java.* Glencoe, Illinois: The Free Press.
———— (1973). "Ritual and Social Change: A Javanese Example", in *The Interpretation of Culture*, ed. C. Geertz. New York: Basic Books.
Geertz, H. (1961). *The Javanese Family: A Study of Kinship and Socialization.* New York: Free Press of Glencoe.
Geschiere, Peter (1988). "Sorcery and the State: Popular Modes of Action among the Maka of Southeastern Cameroon", *Critique of Anthropology* 8, 1: 35–63.
Gibson-Graham, J.K. (1996). *The End of Capitalism (as We Knew It): A Feminist Critique of Political Economy.* Cambridge, Massachussetts: Blackwell Publishers.
Gledhill, J. (2000). *Power and Its Disguises: Anthropological Perspectives on Politics.* London: Pluto Press.
Goode, Judith and Edwin Eames (1996). "An Anthropological Critique of the Culture of Poverty", in *Urban Life*, ed. G. Gmelch and W. Zenner. Prospect Heights, Illinois: Waveland Press.
Grant, Emma (2001). "Social Capital and Community Strategies: Neighbourhood Development in Guatemala City", *Development and Change* 32: 975–97.
Green, Maia (2000). "Participatory Development and the Appropriation of Agency in Southern Tanzania", *Critique of Anthropology* 20, 1: 67–89.
Gugler, Josef (1992). "The Urban Labour-Market", in *Cities, Poverty and Development: Urbanization in the Third World*, ed. A. Gilbert and J. Gugler. Oxford: Oxford University Press, 87–113.
Guinness, Patrick (1972). "Attitudes and Values of Betawi Fringe-Dwellers in Jakarta", *Berita Antropologi* 2, 8: 78–159.
———— (1977). "Five Families of Sand Diggers", *Prisma* 6: 5–15.

————— (1983). "The Gelandangan of Yogyakarta", *Bulletin of Indonesian Economic Studies* 19, 1: 68–82.

————— (1986). *Harmony and Hierarchy in a Javanese Kampung.* Singapore: Oxford University Press.

————— (1988). "Suppression or Restraint: Ethnography and Translation in Javanese Cities", *Canberra Anthropology* 11, 2: 96–109.

————— (1990). "Forced into Opposition: Yogyakarta's Kampung People", *Inside Indonesia* 22: 13–5.

————— (1991). "Kampung and Streetside: Yogyakarta under the New Order", *Prisma* 51: 86–98.

————— (1994). "Local Society and Culture", in *Indonesia's New Order: The Dynamics of Socio-Economic Transformation,* ed. H. Hill. St. Leonards: Allen & Unwin, 267–304.

————— (1999). "Local Community and the State", *Canberra Anthropology* 22, 1: 88–110.

Hardjono, J. (2000). "The Effect of the Economic Crisis on Working Children in West Java", in *Transition in Indonesia: Social Aspects of Reformasi and Crisis,* ed. C. Manning and P. van Diermen. Singapore: Institute of Southeast Asian Studies, 163–83.

Hart, K. (1973). "Informal Income Opportunities and Urban Employment in Ghana", *Journal of Modern African Studies* 11, 1.

Hasbullah, M. (1999). *The Making of Hegemony: Cultural Presentations of the Muslim Middle Class in Indonesian New Order Period,* Faculty of Asian Studies, Australian National University, Canberra.

Hatley, B. (1982). "National Ritual, Neighbourhood Performance: Celebrating Tujuhbelasan in Indonesia", *Indonesia* 34: 55–67.

Hawkins, M. (1996). "Is Rukun Dead? Ethnographic Interpretations of Social Change and Javanese Culture", *TAJA* 7, 3: 218–34.

Healey, P. (2000). "Planning in Relational Space and Time", in *A Companion to the City,* ed. G. Bridge and S. Watson. Oxford: Blackwell Publishers, 517–30.

Hefner, R. (1985). *Hindu Javanese: Tengger Tradition and Islam.* New Jersey: Princeton University Press.

————— (1990). *The Political Economy of Mountain Java: An Interpretive History.* Berkeley, CA: University of California Press.

Hersumpana (2007). *Gerakan Kota (Kampung) Kita: Kampung Masa Depan Kota '(Ber)Budaya'.* Yayasan Pondok Rakyat, http://www.ypr.or.id [cited 1/12/2007].

Hilmy, Masdar (1998). "Cultural Acculturation of Javanese Islam", *Al-Jami'ah* 62, 12: 17–38.

ILO (1972). *Employment, Incomes and Equality: A Strategy for Increasing Productive Employment in Kenya.* Geneva: International Labour Office.

Jay, Robert (1969). *Javanese Villagers: Social Relations in Rural Modjokuto.* Cambridge: MIT Press.

Jellinek, L. (1991). *The Wheel of Fortune: The History of a Poor Community in Jakarta.* North Sydney: Allen and Unwin Australia.

Jocano, F.L. (1975). *Slum as a Way of Life: A Study of Coping Behavior in an Urban Environment.* Quezon City: New Day.

Johnstone, M. (1981). "The Evolution of Squatter Settlements in Peninsular Malaysian Cities", *Journal of Southeast Asian Studies* 12, 2: 364–80.

Josh (2002). "Hanya Mengingat, Bukan Membayangkan", *Warta Kampung* 8: 10–5.

Kah (2002). "Program Perbaikan Kampung: Sejarah Dan Perkembangnya", *Warta Kampung* 8: 6–9.

Kahn, Joel (1992). "Class, Ethnicity and Diversity: Some Remarks on Malay Culture in Malaysia", in *Fragmented Vision: Culture and Politics in Contemporary Malaysia*, ed. J. Kahn and F. Loh. North Sydney: ASAA in association with Allen and Unwin, 158–78.

Kapferer, Bruce (1988). *Legends of People, Myths of State.* Washington: Smithsonian Institution Press.

Khudori, D. (2002a). *The Altruism of Romo Mangun: The Seed, the Growth, the Fruits.* Yogyakarta: Yayasan Pondok Rakyat.

————— (2002b). *Munuju Kampung Pemerdekaan: Membangun Masyarakat Sipil dari Akar-Akarnya Belajar dari Romo Mangun di Pinggir Kali Code.* Yogyakarta: Yayasan Pondok Rakyat.

Koentjaraningrat (1961). *Some Social-Anthropological Observations on Gotong Royong Practices in Two Villages of Central Java.* Ithaca: Southeast Asia Program, Cornell University.

————— (1985). *Javanese Culture.* Singapore: Oxford University Press.

Koning, J. (1999). "Krismon and the Reformasi: Life Goes On", Paper, The Economic Crisis and Social Security in Indonesia workshop, Berg en Dal, the Netherlands, 7–9 January.

Korff, R. (1996). "Global and Local Spheres: The Diversity of Southeast Asian Urbanism", *Sojourn* 11, 2: 288–313.

Krausse, Gerald H. (1975). *The Kampungs of Jakarta, Indonesia: A Study of Spatial Patterns in Urban Poverty.* Department of Geography, University of Pittsburgh, Pittsburgh.

Kusen, Alipah Hadi (2004). "Upaya Menghadirkan "Citra Lain" Dari Ledok Badran", *Kampung* 1: 39–55.

Lane, M. (2005). "The Distraction Is Over", *Inside Indonesia* 81: 19–20.

Lee, Y-S. (1998). "Intermediary Institutions, Community Organizations and Urban Environmental Management: The Case of Three Bangkok Slums", *World Development* 26, 6: 993–101.

Lewis, Oscar (1959). *Five Families: Mexican Case Studies in the Culture of Poverty.* New York: Basic Books.

Li, Tania (1996). "Images of Community: Discourse and Strategy in Property Relations", *Development and Change* 27: 501–27.

———— (2002). "Engaging Simplifications: Community Based Resource Management, Local Processes and State Agendas in Upland Southeast Asia", *World Development* 30, 2: 265–83.

Lont, H. (1999). *Steady but Not Strong: Mutual Associations and the Monetary Crisis*. Paper, The Economic Crisis and Social Security in Indonesia workshop, Berg en Dal, the Netherlands, 7–9 January.

———— (2005). *Juggling Money: Financial Self-Help Organizations and Social Security in Yogyakarta*. Leiden: KITLV Press.

Mackie, J. (2000). "Opening Address", in *Indonesia in Transition: Social Aspects of Reformasi and Crisis*, ed. C. Manning and P. van Diermen. Singapore: Institute of Southeast Asian Studies, xxii–xxviii.

Mahasin, Aswab (1990). "The Santri Middle Class: An Insider's View", in *The Politics of Middle Class Indonesia*, ed. R. Tanter and K. Young. Clayton: Centre of Southeast Asian Studies, Monash University, 138–44.

Manning, C. and P. van Diermen (2000). "Recent Developments and Social Aspects of Reformasi and Crisis: An Overview", in *Indonesia in Transition: Social Aspects of Reformasi and Crisis*, ed. C. Manning and P. van Diermen. Singapore: Institute of Southeast Asian Studies, 1–11.

Margold, Jane (1999). "From 'Cultures of Fear and Terrror' to the Normalization of Violence", *Critique of Anthropology* 19, 1: 63–88.

Marianti, R. (1999). *Widows, Krismon and Some Lessons from the Past*. Paper, The Economic Crisis and Social Security in Indonesia workshop, Berg en Dal, the Netherlands, 7–9 January.

Mas'oed, M., S. Panggabean and M.N. Azca (2001). "Social Resources for Civility and Participation: The Case of Yogyakarta, Indonesia", in *The Politics of Multiculturalism: Pluralism and Citizenship in Malaysia, Singapore, and Indonesia*, ed. R. Hefner. Honolulu: University of Hawai'i Press.

McGregor, Katharine (2007). *History in Uniform: Military Ideology and the Construction of Indonesia's Past*. Singapore: NUS Press.

Meagher, K. (1995). "Crisis, Informalization and the Urban Informal Sector in Sub-Saharan Africa", *Development and Change* 26: 259–84.

Moser, Caroline (1998). "The Asset-Vulnerability Framework: Reassessing Urban Poverty Reduction Strategies", *World Development* 26, 1: 1–19.

Mosse, D. (2005). *Cultivating Development: An Ethnography of Aid Policy and Practice*. London: Pluto Press.

Mulder, N. (2000). *Indonesian Images: The Culture of the Public World*. Yogyakarta: Kanisius.

Murray, A. (1991). *No Money, No Honey*. Singapore: Oxford University Press.

Musiyam, M.F.W. and Farid Wajdi (2000). *Kerentanan dan Jaring Pengaman Sosial: Rumah Tangga Miskin Kampung Kota*. Surakarta: Muhammadiyah University Press.

Newberry, Jan (2007). "Rituals of Rule in the Administered Community: The Javanese Slametan Reconsidered", *Modern Asian Studies* 41: 1–35.

Ockey, J. (1997). "Weapons of the Urban Weak: Democracy and Resistance to Eviction in Bangkok Slum Communities", *Sojourn* 12, 1: 1–25.

Ong, Aihwa (1996). "Anthropology, China and Modernities: The Geopolitics of Cultural Knowledge", in *Future of Anthropological Knowledge*, ed. H. Moore. London: Routledge.

Parajuli, Pramod and Smitu Kothari (1998). "Struggling for Autonomy: Lessons from Local Governance", *Development* 41, 3: 18–29.

Peacock, J. (1968). *Rites of Modernization: Symbolic and Social Aspects of Indonesian Proletarian Drama.* Chicago: University of Chicago Press.

Pemberton, John (1994). *On the Subject Of "Java".* Ithaca: Cornell University Press.

Peters, Robbie (2007). From Revolution to Reformasi: The Kampung in Surabaya, PhD dissertation, Sociology/Anthropology, School of Social Sciences, La Trobe University, Bundoora.

Pinches, M. (1994). "Modernisation and the Quest for Modernity: Architectural Form, Squatter Settlements and the New Society in Manila", in *Cultural Identity and Urban Change in Southeast Asia: Interpretive Essays*, ed. M. Askew and W. Logan. Geelong: Deakin University Press, 13–42.

Pred, A. and M.J. Watts (1992). *Reworking Modernity: Capitalism and Symbolic Discontent.* New Brunswick, NJ: Rutgers University Press.

Rahnema, M. (1992). "Participation", in *The Development Dictionary*, ed. W. Sachs. London: Zed Books Ltd, 116–31.

Rapport, N. (1997). *Transcendent Individual.* London: Routledge.

Ricklefs, M.C. (1991). *A Modern History of Indonesia: c. 1300 to the Present.* London: MacMillan.

Rosyad, Rifki (1995). *A Quest for True Islam: A Study of the Resurgence Movement among the Youth in Bandung, Indonesia*, Archaeology and Anthropology, Faculty of Arts, Australian National University, Canberra.

Santosa, Iman Budhi (2003). "Mencairnya Kolektivitas Kampung Pinggiran", *Warta Kampung* 10: 34–7.

Santoso, Siti Supardiyah (1999–2000). "Profil Penderita Diabetes Melitus yang Berobat ke Pengobatan Tradisional", *Buletin Penelitian Kesehatan* 27, 2–3.

Scarry, Elaine (1985). *The Body in Pain: The Making and Unmaking of the World.* Oxford: Oxford University Press.

Schumacher, E.F. (1974). *Small Is Beautiful: A Study of Economics As If People Mattered.* London: Abacus.

Scott, James (1985). *Weapons of the Weak: Everyday Forms of Peasant Resistance.* New Haven: Yale University Press.

———— (1998). *Seeing Like a State. How Certain Schemes to Improve the Human Condition Have Failed.* New Haven: Yale University Press.

Sen, M.K. (1979). "Rehousing and Rehabilitation of Squatters and Slum Dwellers with Special Reference to Kuala Lumpur", in *Public and Private Housing in Malaysia*, ed. H. Sendut. Kuala Lumpur: Heinemann, 183–208.

Sidel, John (2006). *Riots, Pogroms, Jihad: Religious Violence in Indonesia.* Ithaca, NY: Cornell University Press.

Siegel, James (1986). *Solo in the New Order: Language and Hierarchy in an Indonesian City.* Princeton: Princeton University Press.

———— (1998). "Early Thoughts on the Violence of May 13 and 14, 1998", *Indonesia* 66.

———— (2001). "Suharto, Witches", *Indonesia* 71, April: 27–78.

Silas, Johan (1992). "Government-Community Partnerships in Kampung Improvement Programmes in Surabaya", *Environment and Urbanization* 4, 2: 33–41.

Sillitoe, Paul (2007). "Anthropologists Only Need Apply: Challenges of Applied Anthropology", *Journal of Royal Anthropological Institute* 13: 147–65.

Sjamsuddin, Nazaruddin (2005). Menyelenggarakan Pemilu yang Damai Demi Merah Putih (Court Address on 25 November 2005 in the Trial of Prof. Dr. Sjamsuddin as Chair of the Electoral Commisssion). Jakarta.

Sobary, M. (1997). *Fenomena Dukun Dalam Budaya Kita.* Jakarta: Pustaka Firdaus.

Solahudin, D. (1996). *The Workshop for Morality: The Islamic Creativity of Pesantren Daarut Tauhid in Bandung, Java.* Archaeology and Anthropology, Faculty of Arts, Australian National University, Canberra.

Somantri, G. (1995). *Migration within Cities: A Study of Social-Economic Processes, Intra-City Migration and Grassroots Politics in Jakarta.* Faculty of Sociology, University of Bielefeld, Bielefeld.

Sullivan, John (1980). "Back Alley Neighbourhood: Kampung as Urban Community in Yogyakarta", in *Working Paper,* No. 18. Clayton, Melbourne: Centre of Southeast Asian Studies, Monash University.

———— (1992). *Local Government and Community in Java: An Urban Case-Study.* Singapore: Oxford University Press.

Sullivan, Norma (1987). "Women, Work and Ritual in a Javanese Urban Community", in *Class, Ideology and Women in Asian Societies,* ed. G. Pearson and L. Manderson. Hong Kong: Asian Research Service.

———— (1989). "The Hidden Economy and Kampung Women", in *Creating Indonesian Cultures,* ed. P. Alexander. Sydney: Oceania Press.

Suparlan, Parsudi (1974). "The Gelandangan of Jakarta: Politics among the Poorest People in the Capital of Indonesia", *Indonesia* 18: 41–52.

Supraja, M. (2000). "Membangun Ruang Publik Penyongsong Demokrasi", *Flamma* 5: 1.

Susanto, B. (1992). *Peristiwa Yogya 1992: Siasat Politik Massa Rakyat Kota* Yogyakarta: Kanisius.

Tadie, Jerome (2002). "The Hidden Terrritories of Jakarta", in *The Indonesian Town Revisited,* ed. P.J.M. Nas. Singapore: Institute of Southeast Asian Studies.

Taussig, Michael (1987). *Shamanism, Colonialism and the Wild Man.* Chicago: University of Chicago Press.

Taylor, Charles (2002). "Modern Social Imaginaries", *Public Culture* 14, 1: 91–124.

Tonkiss, F. (2000). "Social Justice and the City", in *A Companion to the City*, ed. G. Bridge and S. Watson. Oxford: Blackwell Publishers, 591–8.

Troy, P. (2000). "Urban Planning in the Late Twentieth Century", in *A Companion to the City*, ed. G. Bridge and S. Watson. Oxford: Blackwell Publishers, 543–54.

Valentine, Charles (1968). *Culture and Poverty*. Chicago: University of Chicago Press.

Vandergeest, P. (1991). "Gifts and Rights: Cautionary Notes on Community Self-Help in Thailand", *Development and Change* 22: 421–43.

Vanhelden, F. (2001). "'Good Business' and the Collection of 'Wild Lives': Community, Conservation and Conflict in the Highlands of Papua New Guinea", *The Asia Pacific Journal of Anthropology* 2, 2: 21–42.

Walker, Andrew (2001). "Introduction: Simplification and the Ambivalence of Community", *The Asia Pacific Journal of Anthropology* 2, 2: 1–20.

Wearing, R. (1996). "Alternative Communities: Beyond the Fringe", in *Social Self, Global Culture*, ed. A. Kellehear. Melbourne: Oxford University Press, 129–39.

Welsh, Bridget (2006). "Local and Ordinary: Keroyokan Mobbings in Indonesia, 1995–2004", in *Annual meeting of the American Political Science Association*. Marriott, Loews Philadelphia and the Pennsylvania Convention Center, Philadelphia.

White, Sarah (1996). "Depoliticising Development: The Uses and Abuses of Participation", *Development in Practice* 6, 1: 6–15.

Winayanti, L. and H.C. Lang (2004). "Provision of Urban Services in an Informal Settlement: A Case Study of Kampung Penas Tanggul, Jakarta", *Habitat International* 28, 1: 41–65.

Wolf, E.R. (2001). *Pathways of Power: Building an Anthropology of the Modern World*. Berkeley: University of California Press.

Woodward, Mark (1989). *Islam in Java: Normative Piety and Mysticism in the Sultanate of Yogyakarta*. Tucson: University of Arizona Press.

Yoshi, F.K.M. (2000a). "Lain Lubuk Lain Belalang, Lho! Dari Dulu Hingga Sekarang", *Warta Kampung* 1: 1–2.

———— (2000b). "Dari Kotoran Manusia Hingga Tumbuhnya Sebuah Kesadaran", *Warta Kampung* 1: 16–7.

———— (2001). "Pos Ronda: Pos-Nya Keamanan yang Diadi-Adakan, Posnya Identitas (Orang Kampung) yang Direbut-Rebutkan", *Warta Kampung* 7: 3–12.

————. "Kampung Anak Kampungan". Yayasan Pondok Rakyat, http://www.ypr.or.id, 2007 [cited 1/12/2007].

———— and Ani Himawati. "Melihat Kota Secara Spasial: Kampung Masa Depan Kota". Yayasan Pondok Rakyat, http://www.ypr.or.id, 2007 [cited 1/12/2007].

Index